CRAIG WOOTON

authorHOUSE®

AuthorHouse™
1663 Liberty Drive
Bloomington, IN 47403
www.authorhouse.com
Phone: 1 (800) 839-8640

Published by AuthorHouse   06/23/2017

ISBN: 978-1-5049-6794-5 (sc)
ISBN: 978-1-5049-6795-2 (hc)
ISBN: 978-1-5049-6793-8 (e)

Library of Congress Control Number: 2015920950

Print information available on the last page.

Contents

1   My First Real Flying Job 1

2   My Beginnings 8

3   Mike the Monkey 13

4   Double Close Call Flight 22

5   Millington, Tennessee 33

6   Close Call of a Different Kind 37

7   Helicopter Firefighting 45

8   Off to Hawaii 52

9   Good Ol' Mom.. 61

10   The Draft Lottery 78

11   In the Jungles of Myanmar.. 82

12   Back to California... 106

13   Turtle Rider 111

14   Humphrey, the Almost Killer Whale!............................ 127

15   Boot Camp 133

16   Three Doomed Flights 145

17   Ed the Elephant... 154

18   Guam-Bound... 159

19   Tuna-Boat Bounce 164

20 United States Navy 168

21 A Simple Trap 191

22 Getting Blasted 195

23 Dubuque, Iowa 207

24 The Emerald Triangle 212

25 If It Bleeds, It Leads 223

26 Teaching Japanese Students to Fly 230

To my beautiful wife and wonderful son and daughter. I love you all so very much!

Introduction

When my children were born, we were living in Japan, and I had only three English storybooks to read to them each night for bedtime stories. Those got old pretty quickly, and all I had were my lifetime adventure stories to tell them instead. As a helicopter and airplane pilot flying around the world, I've done all types of flying yet have had so many other adventures as well. As all storytellers will say, "My stories get better every time I tell them!" But I assure you that 99 percent of everything you will read is true. I had been told a couple times before, "You have to write a book!" but wasn't sure enough in myself. However, just before my son went off to college, I told him a story he had never heard before. After I finished, he said, "Dad, you have to write a book!" I knew then it was time. Some of the stories tell of my childhood moves, and other stories are my children's favorites from the hundreds I've told them over the years. The stories are in no particular order.

1

My First Real Flying Job

How could it get any better than this? Here I was flying over the Eastern Pacific wearing only shorts, sandals, and a T-shirt. With the doors off the old Bell 47 helicopter and the wind blowing through the cabin, the warm air was just right up at about 1,500 feet. We had departed San Diego and were on our way to find fishing grounds between San Diego and the Galápagos Islands, just off the coast of Ecuador in South America. Beautiful dark-blue water from horizon to horizon meshed with the light-blue skies full of puffy, white cumulus clouds. Sharks occasionally cruised below while eagle rays and giant manta rays glided ever so slowly near the surface, sunning themselves.

I had just started this tuna-boat job a couple of months before. It was my first real flying job. Yes, I had flown people at air shows while giving rides, done photo flights, or ferried other types of airplanes, helicopters, and people, but those weren't real jobs.

We were looking for signs for tuna. Of course, our biggest sign was a dolphin school. In the Eastern Pacific, dolphins and tuna feed together, so more often than not if you spotted a school of dolphins you would find tuna running just below them. The dolphins and tuna would attack schools of baitfish, like sardines, together and devour them. All we had to do was circle over the dolphins as they ran. At a certain angle the sunlight would hit the tuna underneath the dolphins, and they would shine like emeralds. The fishermen called them "shiners" because the sunlight would flicker

1

and shine off of each tuna and you could estimate, almost to the ton, how much was down below the dolphins. That was the greatest advantage of the helicopter. We could circle over and check first to see that there actually were tuna there. The poor skipper of a boat with no helicopter might see good signs, like dolphins and birdlife, but the tuna might have been taken the day before or even hours before. Then there would be only dolphins with just a few tuna that had managed to escape another tuna boat's net. So the skipper could circle the dolphins, set his net, and pull it in with nothing or maybe just a couple of tuna.

The next best sign that would lead us to tuna was birdlife. Birds would always gather over schools of tuna and dolphins while they were feeding and would dive down to pick up scraps from the fish being ravaged by the tuna and dolphins. They would stay over the spot feeding on those scraps even after the dolphins and tuna had moved on. We could race over to a spot with a great number of birds, having seen the birds from a good distance or been called over by the boat—which is equipped with bird radar—and then not have one fish underneath them. That was always so frustrating for the crew on the boat who would see the birdlife and think there would surely be a great tonnage of fish underneath them. They would get pumped up and excited. "All right, we're on to something!" And then what a letdown when we would call back to tell them there were few or no fish at all.

Other signs, simple little things, could bring tons of fish, like wood or logs, almost any type of junk or garbage, and boats lost by fishermen. Once we saw a beautiful dugout outrigger canoe that must have taken hours and hours to build from a single tree, in beautiful condition, floating on the ocean all by itself. I can only imagine the story behind the probable islander who lost his cherished canoe—what might have happened to him while he was in that canoe out at sea! There could be barnacles attached to the various junk or crabs that had tagged along that would draw smaller surface fish to gather and feed. This, of course, would draw the birds, bigger fish to feed on the smaller fish, and bigger fish from deeper and deeper. And if you were lucky, under all the fish there might be tuna!

Almost all the bigger sets, or catches, we made were from things like this. We once caught eighty tons of fish from a single six-foot-long two-by-four.

On this particular trip, we had gotten to about the farthest point from the boat that we had flown since starting the trip. As I made a turn in one of the patterns we were flying, searching for fish, I heard this loud crack followed immediately by a loud *bang*! The skipper—who always flew with me to handle everything running the boat and making the sets entailed—looked at me as we said in unison, "What was that?" I had no idea! I immediately turned back toward the boat, which was now just a white spot on the blue-green horizon. The controls all felt okay, and the engine instruments seemed to be functioning. However, on the old 47, there was only one temperature gauge for both the engine and transmission. You had to flip a switch from one position to another—up for engine temperature and down for transmission temperature. The engine temperature was okay, but as soon as I flipped the switch down to check the transmission temperature, the temperature needle jumped to the top of the gauge at the end of the red arc. Before I could even finish mouthing, "Uh-oh," I flipped the switch back to the engine temperature again, and the needle remained in the same place! I pushed the nose over to get more speed and radioed the boat to turn toward us and haul ass. At this point they couldn't see us, even with their huge binoculars, as we were forty miles or more away. Anytime I keyed up the mic to call them on the radio, though, a light would come up on a compass rose on their receiver, showing them the direction to find us. They knew which way to head.

Was this going to be the end? Not the end as in dying, but was this going to be the end of my flying for this trip? It was two months to the day since we'd left San Diego, and I was just loving the flying and was more worried about not being able to fly any longer. We were getting close to filling up the boat. Even if the helicopter was damaged beyond repair from whatever had just happened and I couldn't fly again, they wouldn't stop fishing until the boat was full. Though it would be harder to find fish without the helicopter and it would take much longer, they still could fish. I would just be sitting around twiddling my thumbs for who knows how long until they did.

I knew we wouldn't make it back to the boat. We were just too far away. Plus with the fully inflated "whale dicks," which drastically limit how fast you can go, I couldn't get much speed. Whale dicks are hotdog-shaped floats attached to the skids to *hopefully* allow you to stay afloat in case of ditching. I had tested the floats out before putting the helicopter on the boat by landing on a lake—out by Gillespie Field where the helicopter was based—and in San Diego Bay near the boat. It had felt funny, like I wasn't really down and needed to go down lower. But I had been down, and the helicopter had floated fine. So I was pretty confident that the whale dicks would keep us afloat. We had minimal survival gear and always wore inflatable vests anytime we flew. But with all the sharks I had been seeing, I really didn't feel like bobbing around in the water for a couple of hours waiting for the boat to find us. And with us in the water, the crew wouldn't have the helicopter to see in the sky and possibly wouldn't be able to receive our radio signals, which meant they might not be able to find us even with our big white floats.

It wasn't more than a few moments later when the engine started to cough. I didn't want to push it much farther than I already had. I could just autorotate if the engine quit, but I didn't want to damage the engine or transmission if I could help it. We were only about halfway back to the boat when we started to lose power. It was time. I cut the throttle to idle, lowered the collective, and entered an autorotation. I didn't want to kill the engine completely, just in case I needed it at the end, and idle shouldn't cause any damage for a minute or more. I set the best glide speed and checked my heading for the boat. I wouldn't have to make any turns; I was heading right into the wind. As we headed down to the beautiful but solid blue water, my depth perception wasn't the best. I kept my eyes on the boat as long as I could.

I always set my altimeter to zero on the boat before I took off, where I sat at about twenty or thirty feet above the water, so I had a small margin of safety. However, I don't remember ever looking at the altimeter again after we passed below four hundred or five hundred feet. A few seconds after that, I lost sight of the boat over the horizon. Looking straight out, I could judge our height fairly well, but glancing out the left side also helped. One thing I do remember is that I didn't see one shark while we were coming down. Thank you, Neptune!

As I neared the water, the currents made it look as if we were flying sideways. I had good forward airspeed, though, and I knew I had a good heading. The waves weren't big; the water was actually fairly calm, and with the wind blowing small whitecaps over the waves, I could keep the helicopter into the wind. When I felt I was close enough to the water, I pulled back on the cyclic. When my forward airspeed seemed to have slowed enough, I pushed it back forward to level off. As we leveled and began to settle, I pulled up on the collective to ease down to the surface. Looking out forward again, I concentrated on keeping the aircraft level with the horizon. To my complete and utter astonishment, I made the sweetest autorotation and touchdown I had ever made! We hardly even felt the helicopter touch. Like before, it felt as if we were still hovering. As I'd thought they would, the floats were keeping us up. But for how long? The engine was still sputtering along, so I shut it down and slowly used the rotor brake to stop the blades from spinning. Fortunately the sea was fairly calm, and we just slowly floated and bobbed along. So there we sat. It was actually quite peaceful and amazingly beautiful with basically the same view as from the boat, nothing but blue sky and ocean. There was no boat or helicopter engine noise, just the lapping of the water gently against the rubber floats. There was nothing to do but sit and wait for the boat. The floats were doing their job. We were sitting there perfectly level.

I looked back through the glass bubble and saw what had happened. I could even step out onto the left float and look behind the cabin. The piston-powered Franklin engine in the old Bell stands upright, like taking your car engine out and standing it up on the radiator fan. The rotor transmission sits on top of the engine, the upright back part. Coming out of the transmission at a ninety-degree angle, toward the front, is a shaft with a pulley on its end. A long fan belt goes around the pulley and down to another pulley on a huge cooling fan on the forward-facing part of the engine, just behind the cockpit. The fan cools both the engine and transmission. The shaft had broken off at the transmission, and the pulley and belt had departed! The crack we'd heard had been the shaft breaking.

The bang had been the belt and pulley going up and striking one of the blades. You could see right where they had hit. Though there hadn't been any serious damage, you could see rubber marks from the belt and a small dent in the skin where the pulley had hit one of the blades. We were really lucky that big, long rubber belt hadn't wrapped around any of the control linkages for the rotor head or flown back and wrapped around the tail rotor or any of its control linkages. That would have been disastrous.

The skipper never said a word. I think he was just scared shitless. Even later, though, I got no thank you, good job, or anything. We just sat there for a little less than two hours until the boat came. It was sure nice to see that big white boat come over the horizon! Once the boat came up alongside and tied up to us, the captain got off. Everything had cooled down, both the engine and transmission. I checked and filled both engine and transmission oil levels, pushed off, and paddled away from the boat to start up and fly the helicopter back on the boat. It would only take a minute, and I would shut it down as soon as I touched down on the helipad. We would do all the repairs once I put it up on the boat. Luckily, I had learned years before about on-water start-ups! After the engine starts, the main rotor slowly begins to turn to the left. As it spins faster, it causes the body to begin to rotate in the opposite direction. On a hard surface this is not a problem, as the weight of the aircraft will hold the aircraft still. When you throttle up and add power to take off, you add pedal as necessary so the tail rotor can push the aircraft in the opposite direction to counteract the torque. But on a frictionless surface like ice or water, the body slowly starts to turn to the right as soon as the blades begin to turn. Even if you push full left pedal to stop the turn, nothing will happen until the tail rotor reaches high enough speed, or rpm, to become effective. I only went beyond about ninety degrees before it took effect, but if I hadn't known on-water start-ups, I'm sure the turning would've caused a bit of panic.

The funny thing is that I wasn't scared like I thought I might be. I just went through the motions and did what I had trained to do so many times before. Later, as I sat and pondered the day's events, I had thoughts and got a little spooked! It wasn't my first engine failure. I'd had one in an airplane a few months before, but I had been directly over Laredo, Texas, airport and had simply spiraled down to the runway.

But I acted exactly the same in both situations—no panic, just doing what I had to do. Nothing else you can do! *God, please let this be the last!* Little did I know.

The engineer on the boat, using his micrometer and his amazing talent on his lathe, made an exact duplicate of the shaft coming out of the transmission, complete with splines and all. After attaching a spare pulley and belt I had in the shop, reinstalling them back in the transmission, and hooking them up with the engine, I did a run up on the deck. It was absolutely perfect! It ran as smooth as could be. The engine and transmission hadn't been damaged, and we were flying again in two days. We flew every day for the next ten days, filled up, and headed home without a single problem.

Aboard the MV (motor vessel) *Nicole K*, my first tuna-boat job and my first real job flying, with the Bell 47. Great helicopter but a little underpowered for this type of flying with the reciprocating/piston engine.

2

My Beginnings

I was born in Council Bluffs, Iowa, on February 1, 1953. I have only a slight memory of Council Bluffs because we left just a year or two after I was born. My old man joined the navy after he dropped out of high school in 1947 at age seventeen. He was a rear gunner in a dive-bomber on board aircraft carriers but just hated it. He was only in for a couple of years and couldn't get out quick enough.

Of course I didn't know it at the time, but he was a carpenter and a damn good one too! He made cabinets, new rooms, breakfast nooks, and various other things for us through the years, and they were perfect. He never pushed carpentry on me and my two brothers, and we never made much effort to learn from him, but he taught me a few things. I wish I could have learned more from him. When he came back to Council Bluffs, Dad started a construction business with his brother-in-law. Everything was okay for a while, but suddenly one night his brother-in-law packed up his family, took all his and my father's tools and money, and headed to California. Dad couldn't follow. With three little boys and no work, he didn't have much choice, and he decided to go back into the navy. He would do very well and end up staying in for twenty-five years.

He reenlisted to be a flight engineer on EC-121 Super Connies (Super Constellations). Those were big, triple-vertical-tailed, four-piston-engine, propeller-driven aircraft made by Lockheed Company that had actually been the first really big airliners. The navy had put big radomes (radar) on top that looked like the conning towers on the top of a submarine. They were called Typhoon Trackers in the Pacific and Hurricane Hunters in the Atlantic. They were used for both those things quite often, but they were really reconnaissance and spy planes. From this time on we would live on naval air bases or very nearby until I was eighteen years old. Living right next to the base runways all those years, watching aircraft take off and land day in and day out, was absolutely what started me on my quest to fly and to become a pilot.

Our first couple years Dad's training took us to Rhode Island, Oklahoma, Tennessee, Hawaii, and then Guam. I have no memory of Rhode Island; my first real memories begin at his next training base, in Norman, Oklahoma. It was an old base with hundreds of abandoned, run-down three-story barracks. Many of the two-hundred- to three-hundred-foot-long buildings had been remodeled and turned into apartments or housing for the sailors' families, with two or three apartments on each floor. Each building also had huge basements that were used for storage, but their main purpose was as tornado shelters. We three boys couldn't have been more than two to five years old, but Mom, who was a secretary and would be all her working life, and Dad pretty much left us on our own to do just about whatever we wanted to do. We weren't bad boys, but being little boys, we were curious about everything, and, like on most bases, you find your own types of entertainment or fun. But a lot of things that we did that we thought were fun, great fun, got us into trouble at times.

With our twenty-two- or twenty-three-year-old parents both working and training every day, they were busy just trying to support us. Living on bases all those years, we kids couldn't really get too far. The bases were fenced and gated all the way around, and the base security was always cruising around in their trucks—we called them "suck trucks." There were all kinds of things to do and places to go for kids—teen clubs, pools, movies, playgrounds, and ball fields. Each base also had a ten o'clock curfew for all children under fifteen years old. As my brothers and I got older, we would often stay out well past curfew, hiding from the suck trucks. Our parents never questioned us when we came home about where we had been or what we had been doing. As I look back now, I can't imagine my kids wandering around free at the ages we were then.

My older brother, Rick, was in kindergarten, and I was so jealous. I was too young to go to school yet, so my younger brother, Tony, and I just roamed around each day. Mostly we would break into all the old buildings and just explore from the basements to the roofs. One day I discovered how to open the basement door in our building. Tony and I both went in and just rummaged around, opening lockers and checking inside. In one locker I found a toolbox with big wooden matches. I started striking them and throwing them into the locker, which had a bunch of old greasy overalls and rags inside. After a moment or two nothing was happening, and we were getting bored. So I closed the door, and we left. We just went back upstairs and out to the front of the building to play again. I had completely forgotten about what I had done and was sitting in the grass playing with Tony. I don't think it could have been more than fifteen or twenty minutes later when suddenly the woman who lived in the apartment just above the basement came running out her front door, smoke trailing behind her, and screamed that the building was on fire.

The funny thing is—at least now it seems sort of funny—that I remember feeling very disappointed that I had started the fire and didn't even get to see it! The fire department quickly showed up, which was really exciting for us, but somehow they knew that Tony and I had been in the basement. My father had been called home, and he called Tony and me into the house and had us sit in front of him and the fire chief. As soon as the chief began to question me, I turned and pointed to my little brother and said, "He did it!" And my father and the chief believed me! In unison they both turned and looked at Tony, looked at each other, rolled their eyes, and shook their heads. For as long as I live, I will never forget my father's exact words to Tony: "I should beat your ass, but you are just too young to know better!" That was it! I couldn't believe it. That was so cool. I was in the clear. I admitted to my father years later in my mid or late thirties that I had actually done it. He told me he'd honestly believed that it had been Tony. I would also learn, years later, how close that little incident damn near got my father kicked out of the military.

Every place we lived through the years that the old man was in the navy, we went through so many adventures and experiences. Oklahoma was probably the first place I remember doing something exciting and fun with my father. He had been telling us how he'd raised pigeons with his father when he was a kid. We had seen lots of them flying around the barracks since we'd been there. So one really dark night my father took me out with a flashlight and a gunnysack. The first abandoned building we walked into was filled with hundreds of pigeons everywhere on every ledge and in every rafter. My father handed me the flashlight and told me to point the light directly into the face of one of the birds right above us. The bird seemed to instantly freeze to ice. It didn't even flinch as my father reached up, grabbed it, and placed it in the gunnysack. It was amazing. I shined a paralyzing light at one bird after another, and my dad filled up our sack one by one. Dad would take one of us out with him each night, and in just a few nights we had hundreds of pigeons. It was a great hobby, and I really enjoyed collecting the birds in all their various colors.

I did one of the stupidest things in my life around this time. Just before we were to move I damn near lost my left index or pointer finger by doing something really silly on a bike. I don't remember whose bike it was; it wasn't mine. My dad and mom couldn't afford bikes for us. I just remember I was playing with a bicycle that was sitting upside down on its seat and handlebars. I was having so much fun spinning the pedals as fast as they could go and decided I would see how much grease I could get off of the spinning chain onto my finger. Once I got the wheel and chain spinning as fast as I could make them go, I placed my finger under the chain, and grease quickly started building up on my finger. Then something in the chain, a wire or a broken link maybe, hooked my pointer finger and, in the blink of an eye, pulled my finger at least twice around, through both front and rear gears turning the chain! It all happened so quickly. My finger just came free by itself, and it didn't even really hurt. I hadn't even registered yet what had happened. Again, as young as I was then, I remember so clearly looking down and seeing my finger, from the tip of the fingernail down to the first joint, swinging from just a piece of skin holding it to the rest of my finger. I instantly ran home as fast as I could, screaming all the way home and into the hospital. The funny thing was it never hurt. Just the sight of it had sent me into shock and made me scream. The doctors sewed it back on, and after about a week my whole finger was turning purple. The doctors were tempted to cut my finger off right then but decided to give it just a couple more days. Sure enough, two days later when we went back in and they unwrapped it, the color was coming back. To this day I still have full use of my finger. The tip just looks funny, the fingernail is a little strange, and a zigzag scar runs all the way around the finger. Next stop, Millington, Tennessee.

3

Mike the Monkey

Monkeys were everywhere in the Philippines. They were like mice. They were all sizes and shapes; some were about three feet tall or a little taller. On the base in Subic Bay I hadn't seen any up close, but I caught glimpses of them occasionally darting through the trees, and you always heard them squeaking and screeching all around the base. The *Kitty Hawk* had gone to Hong Kong for sixty days, and our squadron was leaving one helicopter on a beach detachment while it was gone. The CO of our squadron had asked for volunteers from each shop to stay and take care of it. I was really surprised not a single person from the jet shop wanted to stay except me. I didn't care where the ship was going. If I could keep off of it, great! I moved into a temporary barracks, kind of like apartments, up on a hill above the flight line. It was surrounded by jungle, shady and cool. I took a bus each morning from the top, right out in front of my building. The bus wound down from one side of the hill to the bottom on the other side and dropped me off right in front of the hangar where the helicopter was parked.

The first night I was sitting outside on the back porch of my building up on the hill and saw some guys walking down past my building into the jungle. I thought they were just hiking around. However, the next day I saw the same guys come out of the jungle right across the street from my hangar while I was outside waiting for the bus after work. They told me that there was a trail that led right up to the back of my building and that it was actually quicker than the bus. The bus didn't exactly have a schedule, so you might have to wait some time for it, and it also made a lot of stops. So I said thanks for the info and headed across the street for the trail. Just as I was about to enter into the trees, one of the guys stopped, turned back, and said, "Oh yeah, be careful of the monkeys!"

"Okay," I said, not really thinking much of it. From what I had seen, just brief glimpses of them, they didn't look very big, and they would probably be more afraid of me than I would be of them. With the way they darted around, I was sure they would just run away if I ran into any of them.

As always I could hear them all around, but about halfway up the hill they seemed to be getting louder and louder. I came up and over a small rise as the trail turned into a big open area where the base had placed three big Dumpsters for all the trash from the barracks. I hadn't even known those things were there, but I was even more surprised and completely amazed at all the monkeys that were there. My building was still a ways to go, and I couldn't even see it or any of the other buildings yet. There had to be forty or fifty monkeys there, and they weren't little! They started screeching a little louder as soon as I came around the corner. The trail ran along all three Dumpsters, and as I got closer, they started acting like a bunch of pissed-off dogs you were trying to take food away from. I had heard before how looking directly into a monkey's eyes can be a threat to them, especially if you raise your eyebrows, so I tried not to look directly at them as I made a big arc out and away from them as far as I could. I was getting a little worried because they had jumped down off of the Dumpsters and were screaming, showing their teeth, and lunging three or four feet out at me and then back, basically telling me to keep the fuck back. As I got past, they all slowly climbed back up to their spots without taking their eyes off of me. There were two or three of them that were easily three and a half feet tall with big bodies and huge teeth. Soon, I was at my building. The trail was much quicker than the bus, but I wasn't sure if it was a good idea to go back that way again or not. Maybe that's why those other guys were all together. That might have intimidated the monkeys a little more than I did by myself.

From the very first day on the flight line I had been buying bags of little bananas that were absolutely delicious from a little old lady who sold all kinds of fruit to the guys all along the flight line. I'd been carrying a bag of those when I walked up the trail; could that have been the reason they'd come out at me like they had? Later that very same evening, I was sitting on the back porch relaxing, drinking a beer, and eating the bananas when something moving up in a big tree to my right caught my eye. It was another good-size monkey. He watched me as he slowly climbed down. He knew I was eating something and came down acting as if he were being really stealthy and I didn't see him. When he got down to the ground, he was on the other side of the tree from me and sat down. I could just see the left side of his face. He was looking out into the jungle but would occasionally glance in my direction, turning just his eyes and not moving his head, as if he were thinking, *I'm cool; he doesn't see me here!* "Hey, Mike!" I said, trying to get his attention and not startle him. It just came out; I was thinking, *Mike, monkey, it rhymes.* I tossed a banana right next to him. It startled him a little, but he just sat there for a little bit. Still not moving his head, he looked at it, looked out straight ahead, looked toward me, then looked back at the banana again. It was almost as if he didn't want to seem too eager or maybe wanted make me think he really didn't want it. After a minute or two he leaned out and picked up the banana. Still being cool, like, *Oh yeah, it's just a banana,* he held it for a moment. He finally brought it up to his nose, sniffed it for a second, and then took a bite. I knew he liked it, as he got up and started off into the jungle with his prize. I wouldn't see him again for the rest of that night.

When I went out the next morning to go to work, I figured I'd give the trail another shot, going down this time to the flight line. As I got started walking, there was Mike sitting just inside the trees on the other side of the trail that led down the hill. I was holding my last banana. I'd been planning to eat it as I walked down the hill. He sat right up when he saw me. As I walked toward him, he began to back into the jungle. I thought, *What the hell!* and tossed the banana underhanded to him. He jumped back away from it, but after it landed, he instantly jumped back out, grabbed it, and disappeared back into the jungle. I figured that was probably the last time I would see him again. I walked down the hill, expecting to see the Dumpster gang of monkeys again, but there were none. *Too early for them,* I thought.

After work I came walking back up the trail, again with my bag of bananas. Only a few smaller monkeys were at the Dumpsters this time, and they all took off as I got close. After getting cleaned up, I grabbed the bananas and a beer and then went to sit on the back porch. Mike was just walking slowly by. I didn't know if he'd been waiting and was just leaving or was just passing by on his way to the Dumpsters. As soon as he saw me, he stopped and sat down. He looked at me, looked away, and looked back, again and again. I acted as if I didn't see him. I sat down on the steps with my bag of bananas next to me. I took a long drink of my beer and just looked around casually as I patted the bag lovingly. His eyebrows went up! Slowly opening and reaching into the bag, still not looking at him, I pulled out a banana, peeled it, and ate it in three quick bites. Out of the side of my eyes I saw his mouth make that "Oooh!" shape. I knew I was teasing the shit out of him. I took out another, slowly peeled it, and acted as if I was going to eat it but then stopped. He did a double take, and I turned and looked at him dead in the eyes. He didn't look away, giving me a look of anticipation, almost like a sad puppy. *Oh please!* he seemed to say. I threw the banana, and it landed about three feet in front of him. He jumped right up to it, grabbed it, sat down, and ate it in two bites as he kind of looked around. He nonchalantly looked at me, waiting to see what I was going to do next. I threw him another, this time closer to me. He hesitated for only a second as I looked off to my right, and then he darted up, grabbed it, and ran off into the jungle. He didn't come back again that night either.

That went on for two more nights. I got him closer each time I tossed a banana to him. I'm glad they were so cheap. On the third night, he was out there again as usual, but this time I didn't throw him one. I pretended to fumble with it and dropped it a little to my left in front of me. I pulled out another and started eating it very slowly. He was so funny! He kept looking at me and looking at the banana like, *Okay, when are you going to pick it up and throw it to me?* I, almost sensually, took little after little bite of mine, just driving him crazy. He started and stopped three times, inching closer to me until he reached it. I was looking away as if I didn't see him. He looked at it and me a couple of times before he sat down, picked it up, and started eating it. He wasn't more than two feet away from me, and when he finished, he just sat there looking around. I already had another in my hand and very slowly placed it on the porch just to my left side. Then I put my hands on the step next to my legs and leaned forward a bit, acting as if I was looking around. He didn't even hesitate a second. I couldn't believe it! He came right up the steps and sat down right next to me. I didn't want to spook him, so I kept looking out and not at him. He picked it up and ate it slowly, and when he finished, he just sat there. After just a moment or so I felt him touch my hand. I have large blood vessels in my hands and arms. The doctors and nurses all love it when I give blood. They have no problem hitting a gusher on their first try. He was touching my veins and pinching them, and then he started rubbing my arm hair, checking it almost as monkeys did to groom each other, looking for bugs with both hands.

I was bummed. I was out of bananas, and I knew he might not stick around much longer without one. I wanted to touch him, but I didn't want to make any sudden moves and scare him off. I slowly eased my left hand toward him, but he inched away each time I got close, just like a cat that doesn't want to be touched. He finally stepped off the porch and slowly started to walk off. He turned for a moment and looked at me and around the porch, checking if I had anything else. Then, not looking back again, he walked away slowly across the trail and into the jungle.

The next night, I was hoping he would come close again. I was out sitting on the porch before I even saw him and had a banana already out sitting next to me. Sure enough, here he came. "Hi, Mike!" I said. "Have a seat." He walked smoothly and steadily all the way up to me, looking back and forth at me and the banana, and sat right down next to me. I almost busted out laughing and had to catch myself as he sat and picked up the banana. He took a deep breath and let out a long sigh like, *Oh man, what a day!* as if he'd had such a hard day at work and was relaxing for the first time. He slowly ate his banana, scanning around but never looking at me. When he finished, he looked at me with that *Well?* look. I reached into the bag, pulled out another, and handed it to him. He casually took it, and I sat up looking forward again with my hands on the step right next to his leg. I stretched out my pinky finger and rubbed his leg. He moved just a little, as if he were reacting to a bug touching him. Slowly and gently I began to brush his fur. It was funny, a little stiff yet soft. He seemed to like it, so slowly I raised my hand up and touched his arm as he ate slower than I had seen him eat before. He flinched just a little but didn't pull away as I gently stroked his fur and scratched him a little. I rubbed up his arm to his neck, and just like a dog getting his neck scratched, he seemed to like it. When I tried to touch his head, though, he cocked it over and moved a little away from me. I thought that was enough for today. I handed him a third banana before he had finished the second. He took it, stood up, walked out a couple of feet, looked back at me as he took one last bite of his second banana, and walked away.

The next couple of nights were almost exactly the same, but the last night that I was to spend with him was a little different. After sitting together a few minutes, my hand on the porch next to his leg, him eating another banana, he reached down with his little hand and grabbed my left index finger and lifted my hand up. He just stared at it for a second and then felt around the fingernail and rubbed the hair on my fingers. He actually scared me at first. When he brought my finger up toward his face, for a moment I thought he was going to take a bite of it. After a moment, he lowered my hand to his side but didn't let go of it. He just sat holding my finger, as if we were holding hands. I looked down at him out of the side of my eyes as he looked straight out and occasionally side to side, just as casual and relaxed as could be! He was so cool. Cool Mike. Mike the monkey, my buddy!

I don't think he ever once looked at me during this time. I didn't want to reach over and get him another banana, because I knew he would let go and I didn't want him to. His soft little hand was so cute holding my finger, and I think he liked it as much as I did. After a few minutes, without even looking or reaching for another banana, he just let go, gazing at my hand as if he were trying to be careful as he did so. Then he got up and walked away. "Good night, Mike," I said, half-expecting him to turn and say good night back to me, but he didn't hesitate or even look back at me; he just disappeared into the jungle again.

At work the next morning we were told the ship was due back in soon and we would have to get all our stuff out of the barracks and move back aboard ship sometime in the afternoon. So I decided to skip lunch and go up and get all my gear and check out of the barracks at lunchtime. I only had my clothes and toiletries there, so I just had to load up my duffel bag and go. I'd bought my usual bag of bananas earlier that morning, and I just grabbed them and headed up the hill. I was really bummed out and sad that I wouldn't get to see Mike again, as he only came out in the early evening, but I kind of chuckled to myself that I would finally get to eat all the bananas by myself! I walked across the road to the trail up to the top of the hill. As I started up, I could hear the usual sounds—the birds, the monkeys—but didn't pay much attention to them. Then when I was about halfway up the hill, it dawned on me. "Man, the monkeys are pretty loud again today. I wonder if they're back at the Dumpsters again?" I said to myself out loud. I had seen what I thought was a bunch of them up there on my first trip on the trail, but this sounded like a lot more now. As I got closer, they got louder and louder. When I came up over the rise and rounded the trees, I couldn't believe how many monkeys were there. "There must be something really, really good in the trash today!" I laughed to myself.

As soon as they saw me, they went ballistic. They were so pissed off, and they immediately started edging out toward me. They truly scared me this time and really freaked me out. They fanned out into an arc as if they were trying to surround me. They quickly had both the trail up and trail down blocked. They didn't look like angry dogs this time; they looked like a bunch of little crazed killers that wanted a piece of me and were going to get it! I really didn't have anywhere to go. The jungle behind me was too thick, and even if I turned and ran away right that moment, they would've been on me in a heartbeat. I dropped the bananas, raised my hands, and growled as loud as I could, thinking that might scare them off. They didn't even flinch. They just kept coming, and that really scared the shit out of me! I instantly started looking around for something to fight them off with; I didn't know what else to do.

No sooner did that thought go through my mind than every single monkey seemed to just freeze in its tracks. It almost went quiet. They actually seemed to be backing up. *What the hell?* I thought. *My deodorant not working?* They were glancing a little to my right. Not wanting to take my eyes off these little would-be killers, I glanced really quickly over my right shoulder. My heart almost stopped instantly, and I thought, *Fuck me, they are behind me already!* But then I did a double take: it was Mike! He was hunched over walking up to my right on all fours. He wasn't making a sound, but he was showing those big ass, scary teeth, and the hair on the back of his head and neck was standing straight up. As he came alongside me, every one of the monkeys backed away from me toward the Dumpsters. I picked up my bag and was about to run toward the barracks when he stopped and sat down right next to me. All the monkeys continued backing away, looking back and forth at me and Mike but trying not to hold eye contact with him.

"Mike, buddy, who are you?" I asked him. I reached in my bag, pulled out a banana, and handed it to him. He took it in his left hand and just held it, never looking at me but staring at the other monkeys and still showing his teeth. I said, "Mike, you deserve another!" So I gave him one more. He took it with his right hand, and for a moment he looked so comical that I again had to keep myself from laughing out loud. He looked like a cowboy with two six-guns, one in each hand, aimed at the others, holding them off! He put the banana in his left hand into his mouth and, with his fur still bristling, took a few steps forward walking on three legs. Most of the monkeys bolted in all directions. That was my cue! With the trail now clear, I took off for the barracks. I got there, stuffed all my clothes in my bag, then headed out the back one more time, hoping Mike would be there, but he wasn't. There wasn't a sound from the direction of the Dumpsters, but I wasn't about to go back that way. I yelled out, "Bye, Mike, thanks!" I walked back through the building and out the front door to the bus stop just as the bus was coming up the hill. As I boarded the bus, my duffel bag over my shoulder, I was especially sad now. We would be heading back to the States very soon, and I would never see Mike again. But I could not believe what I had just seen and what a good friend I had made in the short time we had together! I would never forget him.

This story was my kids' favorite bedtime story.

4

Double Close Call Flight

My next close call, or should I say my next two close calls, were on a single flight. It was the beginning of December, and I had been a commercial helicopter pilot for the last seven months. I had been a private fixed-wing pilot for some time but had no real desire to fly airplanes commercially. I had been working for Western Helicopters in Rialto, California, for a while. One day the parts manager came up to me and asked if I would like to go to Harlingen, Texas, to pick up and fly a Cessna 182 back to El Monte airport. "Hell yeah," I told him, just as long as Western would give me a few days off to go get it. Western did, and the guy who wanted the airplane gave me enough money to pay for gas and my expenses and asked me to try to hurry and get it back as soon as possible. He bought me a one-way ticket from Ontario, California, to Harlingen, Texas.

I began my flight planning for the trip while still in California. Unfortunately, there was a huge winter system moving down from the Northwest that would be covering most if not all my flight route all the way back to El Monte airport. I called the buyer and let him know that of course. He was cool with it and just wanted me to keep him informed of my progress. I assured him I would.

I had flown lots of Cessna models before and had quite a few hours in a 182. However, it was always with company pilots, passengers, and cargo. I was really looking forward to flying this one on my own. It was supposed to be airworthy, in good flying condition and with a good engine. It had been confiscated by the government for running drugs from Mexico to Texas, and the new owner had bought it through a government auction. I was excited and really looking forward to my first long cross-country flight by myself. I was planning on flying northwest right up alongside the border of Texas and Mexico the first day and stopping off in El Paso, Texas, to visit my father. He was working on the Stinger missile program for the military out at White Sands and living in El Paso.

When I stepped off the airliner at Harlingen airport, I was amazed at the humidity that hit me. It instantly reminded me of living in Guam when I was younger. At the same time I also thought about how the humidity would affect the airplane's performance, but I instantly dismissed my concerns. I would be the only passenger, and even with full fuel I would have all the power and performance I would need. Or so I hoped!

It was late in the afternoon when I got there, but I went straight to where the airplane was located. It looked pretty nice! It was in fairly nice shape, the paint was good, the windows were all in good condition, and the interior was nice too. It was not at all what I was expecting for being a drug runner, but I suppose that was the previous owner's idea, to be as least conspicuous as possible. So I grabbed a taxi, checked into my hotel, and headed for the hotel restaurant for dinner. I would start flying back at first light.

Before sunup I had showered, shaved, and had breakfast. I called flight service for a weather briefing. As expected, the weather wasn't looking great. Harlingen weather was fine, but the forecaster told me that he honestly didn't think I would make El Paso before the weather came down and conditions worsened. *Hey, I don't care! I'll go just as far as I possibly can and then land whenever I have to!* I thought. I had plenty of alternate airports along my route where I could land if I had to in case of an emergency or bad weather.

I got to the airport, stowed all my stuff on board, and then began my preflight. Everything seemed fine—oil, fuel, everything checked out. All instruments and electronic gear seemed to be working well, but there was one thing. When I took fuel samples from each wing tank and engine fuel

23

sump, I was getting a lot of water. *That's understandable,* I thought. It had been raining a lot off and on before I came to Harlingen, and it was hot and humid. The engine sump drained of water pretty quickly, but I had to drain both the left- and right-wing tanks at their drain points a few times before I didn't see any more water in either tank coming out into the little fuel sampler. That was it. I buttoned everything up, hopped in, buckled up, and started her up.

It was early; there were no other aircraft in the traffic pattern or flying nearby and no one on UNICOM, the airport radio, so I really didn't know if the radio was transmitting. I did know it was receiving, though, because I had gotten airport terminal information service (ATIS), and I had wind direction and altimeter setting information. So in the blind, which means I was transmitting without knowing if anyone could hear me, I broadcast my intentions to taxi to the main runway. The engine was running fine; temperature and pressure were perfect, as were all lights and radios. With not a person in sight on the ground or an aircraft anywhere to be seen or heard in the air, I taxied out next to the main runway and ran the engine up before takeoff. All gauges checked out, and power was good. The plane just felt powerful and good. Clearing both ends of the runway for incoming traffic, I taxied onto the main runway, gently throttled up, and off I went. This thing really had some power, and not having three other big guys or cargo in the aircraft with me made a big difference. I was really amazed how quickly the plane jumped off the ground and climbed away into the first light of day. "This is going to be a blast!" I said to myself.

It was a perfect morning for flying. I climbed up to about two thousand feet and leveled off. The sky was a beautiful blue, and puffy, white, fair-weather cumulus clouds were scattered all about just above me. This type of cloud is a good indicator of nice flying weather with possible light turbulence below the clouds and smooth air above. After about fifteen or twenty minutes, I climbed above the clouds and headed to Laredo, Texas, my first stop, in smooth air with clear blue skies above me.

I was flying visual flight rules (VFR), which requires you to fly with certain cloud clearances and visibility. It would be no problem above the clouds. I was completely clear of all clouds and had over twenty miles of visibility. I hadn't planned on flying instrument flight rules (IFR), which requires an instrument rating and an aircraft equipped for instrument flight. Before I'd climbed up above the clouds, I had been flying IFR, old pilot joke: *I follow roads!* I had been following the main highway out of Harlingen, which would lead me all the way to Laredo. Above the clouds, even as scattered as they were, at times I couldn't see everything below me. No problem, I would just use my navigation radios and follow signals from the various navigation stations all the way to Laredo. This Cessna was equipped with a nice radio set up. The old navigation system was still in use but being supplemented by newer GPS systems. Two VHF Omni Directional Range (VOR) navigation radios and two communication radios, dual nav/comms, sent out signals in all directions from each station that you could use to track inbound or outbound on. You could be using one communication radio dialed in to the frequency of whomever you wanted to speak to now and have the second radio already preset to the frequency of the next station you wished to speak to, so you wouldn't have to waste time flipping through the frequencies while you were flying. You could just press one button and flip back and forth between the frequencies. You could do the same with the two navigation radios. I checked my chart, my flight map, for the first nav frequency I would need and dialed it in. As I tried to dial in a signal to track to my first station, I instantly realized that both nav radios were inoperative, not working at all. So much for flying up on top. Without radio navigation I might not be able to see well enough all the way to Laredo to stay on course.

The clouds were still broken and scattered enough for me to make a nice, smooth, straight descent below the clouds. It had been perfectly smooth on top, but there was really only mild to light turbulence below the cloud layer. While I'd been on top, I could see way off in the distance that some high clouds were beginning to form, but I didn't think it would affect me in any way before I reached Laredo. However, just thirty minutes or so after descending below the clouds, it began to get darker in the distance. The clouds got lower and lower, and my visibility began to decrease. As I got closer to Laredo, I dialed in the radio to listen to the airport ATIS and found that the weather was still VFR but had changed quite a bit. It was good enough to enter the airport traffic area and land, but I knew I had better hurry and get in there before it got much worse. I could tell now that I would not be making El Paso today.

I changed over to the airport tower frequency to get an idea of how busy they might be and how much traffic was in the area. I was still too far away to call them yet, but instantly I was surprised that I wasn't hearing anything! Laredo was a pretty good-size airport and had been, at one time, an Army Air Corps training airport during World War II. My nav radios were out; my comm radios couldn't have gone out as well, could they? I had received ATIS, but it was unusual to not hear any other aircraft radio traffic at all. Maybe the weather was really bad and no one was flying? Oh well, not a problem! The procedure for communication failure when entering an airport traffic area, especially a tower-controlled airport, was just to enter the airport traffic area, making all turns to the left, and watch for a green signal light from the tower clearing you to land or a red telling you not to land. They would see me circling, and whenever I was clear to land, they would give me the green light.

At about twenty miles out, I thought I would at least try to call the tower. No answer, and I didn't hear any other communications at all from any other aircraft.

The weather was definitely getting worse. Visibility was rapidly decreasing, and I had been forced to steadily decrease my altitude to stay out of the clouds. I called and called and called and didn't hear a thing. So I started setting myself up to enter from the south and a little bit to the east to start my left turns around the airport in hope for a green-light signal. Just before I turned, I heard another aircraft call. It was a Piper Aerostar, a beautiful, sleek, powerful, and fast twin-engine airplane. I heard him call a couple of times with no answer, so I thought I would try to see if he could hear me. I called him and said, "Piper calling Laredo, can you hear me?" He instantly called me right back and said he heard me loud and clear. I asked him if he knew why the airport controllers weren't answering, and he said they had gone on strike that morning. No wonder I wasn't hearing them or anyone else!

I asked him where he was and if he was landing at Laredo. He said he was northwest of the airport and yes, he would be landing in Laredo. I told him I was southeast and would be doing the same. I told him to go ahead and go on in and I would follow. We couldn't see each other because of the weather, but I knew that little rocket would be hauling ass and would easily beat me in for landing. Right at that moment I thought, *Well, he's northwest; I'm southeast. Just in case, I'd better turn off to the right here a little bit.* I rolled into a right bank to clear myself a little toward the east. I'd just begun to pull back on the yoke to tighten up my turn to the right when that Piper came screaming out of the clouds right in front of me with an enormous *vvoomm*! His left wing went underneath my raised left wing by just a foot or two, and his wingtip passed no more than three or four feet away from my left door! My heart damn near jumped right out of my chest, which made me pull back even harder on the yoke into the turn. If I had not turned, we would've hit directly head-on! And, to top it off, just as I leveled off, my engine began to sputter and then quit.

I was just below one thousand feet with the airport down below my left side of the aircraft. I knew I could just spiral down and land pretty easily on one of the several active runways or one of the inactive old training runways that Laredo had. I instantly set up my glide speed and trimmed the aircraft as needed to give me all the time and control I would need to get myself down safely. As I came around, I found I was going to be able to land right on the north–south runway I'd been hoping for, landing heading north into the wind. I had always been taught, and I've also taught my students, to keep up a little higher airspeed than normal in situations like this, to give yourself a little more control and handling at the bottom, and to not use your flaps too early to get yourself to slow. I used minimum flaps as I came around on final for landing and kept my speed up. I was so glad I did, because as I got closer, I realized the angle I was using was going to make me short of the end of the runway. I had been so concentrated on the runway itself that I hadn't noticed a chain-link fence and gate near the approach end of that runway. I was headed straight for that gate. I didn't want to yank back and take a chance of stalling, so I held that angle until I was close enough to just ease back. I rose up and just over the high gate, pushed the nose back over, and touched down on the very first part of the approach end of that runway. If I had been going any slower, I would have never made that runway.

I didn't even use my brakes as I coasted down the runway, hoping I could reach one of the exits for the taxiway back to the terminal. But with landing at the very beginning of the runway and not having any power, I slowed quickly and was going to be coming to a stop well short of the first exit off the runway. I didn't want to stop on the runway and basically close that runway down, so I turned right and rolled to a stop in the middle of the grassy area between the runways. I stepped out of the aircraft and immediately started looking for oil, which I was sure would probably be all over the engine area and the sides and the underside of the aircraft. Something must have broken or cracked. There hadn't been any smoke or smell of any kind before the engine quit. I was completely surprised to find no leaking oil, burning odors, or damage at all. I closed everything up, checked both directions to make sure nothing was coming or going, crossed the runway and walked toward the terminal area. I hadn't seen the Piper aircraft land but was sure he had been well in and parked before I'd even touched down.

No one except one of the line boys, an aircraft cleaner and fueler, even saw me or knew I was there. He came up to me and asked if I had a flat tire. I told him no, that my engine had quit. I asked if he could give me a tow into the ramp parking area. He looked at me and in a shocked voice said, "Really, are you okay?" I assured him that I was and that the aircraft was fine and just needed a tow in. He told me to wait and then ran to a hangar and brought out a little tow tractor with a tow bar hooked on it. He picked me up and drove us out to the plane. He then jumped out, quickly and easily hooked up the tow bar to the nose gear, and slowly and gently towed the Cessna over to a maintenance facility that could check out the aircraft. He helped me tie the aircraft down and directed me toward the mechanics' office. I thanked him very much and gave him a nice tip.

There was just one guy in the mechanics' office, the only mechanic on duty. I introduced myself and explained what had happened. He said he was just doing paperwork and not busy and could come out right now and check it out. He asked me a few questions as he gathered up his tools.

The questions continued as he drove us in his truck to the airplane. Had I had power problems? Was the engine missing or running rough? Any loud noises or bangs? I told him no, nothing at all, except for the unusually high amount of water I had drained from the fuel tanks before I'd headed out. He gave me a big "Hmmmm!" and then began checking exactly all the things I had checked after landing.

After finding nothing he returned to his truck, brought out a five-gallon bucket and his fuel-tank drainer with a long hose, and began draining the wing tanks. As he drained the fuel, bit by bit water began to spit out into the bucket. He did both wing tanks, getting a lot of water out of both tanks as well as a little from the engine fuel-sump drain. I told him where I had come from and what the plane had been doing before it had been confiscated, and the first thing he said was "How in the hell did you get this far with that much water in your tanks?" That was exactly my question! I had drained and drained the tanks before I'd left, and I'd been positive there hadn't been any more left in the tanks. He told me that the gas the previous owner was using in Mexico had probably been kept in jerricans on secret runways from who knows where and that the condensation in the tanks that had been sitting still for so long was probably pretty substantial. Sounded good to me! But with the amount of water I saw at the bottom of that can, I don't know how I could've taken off, let alone cruise for as long as I did without one little hiccup or cough from the engine! He said it could have been the extreme right bank I made over the airport that allowed the water to break free from wherever it had been stopped up and enter the engine fuel lines. He said he would completely drain and visually check each tank before filling the aircraft to the top to ensure I wouldn't have another problem.

With the aircraft in good hands, I headed for another hotel. The weather had deteriorated to below VFR minimums—ceilings were below three thousand feet, and visibility was less than a mile. Any more flying for the rest of the day was out of the question! I called flight service from the hotel before I went out for dinner to get a forecast for tomorrow; it wasn't good—very low ceilings, low visibility, freezing rain, and snow. Not good for a small airplane with no anti-icing equipment on any of the wings or vertical and horizontal stabilizers! The forecast was actually bad for the next few days. Even so, I would call again in the morning. In the meantime, it was time for a drink after all of that!

In the restaurant that night, I would damn near sell the airplane for the new owner. No sooner did I sit down and order a drink than two girls walked up to my table and asked what I was doing in Laredo. There was no one else in the restaurant but us. After I told them, they told me they were waiting for a guy friend of theirs who was also a pilot and asked if they could join me. They were both Mexican, or so I thought. I was of course dubious as to what they might really be up to, but I thought, *What the hell.* They were both beautiful. I stood up to let them sit, and the shorter of the two sat on my side of the booth. It turned out the taller one was not Mexican but Vietnamese! I'm six foot one, and she was damn near as tall as I was! She was gorgeous. Within about five or ten minutes their guy friend showed up. He was a nice, middle-aged, well-off-looking gentleman, and I thought he must be the Vietnamese girl's boyfriend. Wrong! No sooner had he sat down than one of her feet, minus a shoe, began sliding up between my legs and rubbing my crotch!

It turned out all three of them were genuinely honest, nice people, and they were all avid flyers. The man was in the market for a new plane, but he was really looking for a Cessna Cardinal. That's basically a sleeker version of the 182 but also has retractable landing gear. He was very interested and wanted to see the airplane, but I told him that before I could do or say anything about the aircraft, I would have to call the new owner first. He was cool with that, and while they waited, I made a phone call back to the owner in El Monte, California. The owner was really jazzed, surprised that he might not have to do anything to it and would still make money without even seeing it in person. He said he would give me a commission if I sold it, which was cool, but I really wanted to fly it back to California! I had only flown the aircraft for a couple of hours. Deep down I really hoped the man wouldn't want to buy it.

So after we ate, he drove us out to the airport, and I showed him the airplane. He really liked it and said he wanted to buy it. My heart sank. But at least I would make some money and could enjoy myself in Texas for the next day or two. I gave him the new owner's phone number after he took us back to the hotel. I told him to get back to me and let me know whether everything went okay or not, so I could make my own plans. He dropped us off and left to take care of business.

When I finally returned to my hotel, there was a message to call the owner in El Monte. When I finally got through to him, he told me that he and the man had been going back and forth with each other for a couple of hours negotiating the price. It turned out the guy here wanted quite a bit off of the owner's asking price, and the owner just wouldn't budge. The deal was off! Yes! I would be flying back home in the morning! Maybe!

I woke up before sunup, opened the door, stepped outside, and instantly knew I wasn't going anywhere. Freezing rain mixed with ice and light snow was falling, and it was really cold. I could see how low the clouds were and could hardly see down the street. I called flight service anyway, and the first thing the guy said to me was "How does freezing rain sound to you?" "Not good!" I said. He said I could call again anytime but should expect the same weather for the next two or three days. Sure enough, each day the same controller told me the same thing. I stayed in Laredo for three days until the system finally went through to the east late on my last night there.

Again up very early, I got to the airport and did a complete preflight. The fuel tanks were all topped off, the engine and oil were great, and I drained both wing tanks and engine fuel sump without seeing one drop of water! After starting the aircraft on the parking ramp, I let it run quite a bit longer than normal before taxing out to the runway. I actually did three, not one, preflight run-ups checking, looking, and listening for any kind of possible trouble whatsoever. Again the aircraft sounded strong, powerful, and very healthy. I cleared again, again no traffic, taxied out on the main runway, gently throttled to full power, and was off again, climbing like a bat out of hell.

I flew, finally, in beautiful weather to El Paso and spent one night with my father. Then I continued on with fuel stops in Tucson, Arizona, Yuma, Arizona, and finally into El Monte, where it was so hazy and smoggy that after finding the airport, seeing it down through the haze, and descending for landing, I wasn't able to line up with the runway soon enough on approach to land and had to make one go-around before landing on my next try.

It was actually such a great trip, in more ways than one. Yes, I had two very close calls, within just seconds of each other, but what an exciting experience, an adventure! I really hated shutting the engine off, tying the aircraft down, and handing the keys over to the new owner. I wondered if I would have any more experiences like that again. But I would do my best to ensure I would never have another engine failure again! However, I would find, a couple more times, that there are so many things that cannot be predicted or that are beyond your control. What fun!

5

Millington, Tennessee

Dad's next training base was in Millington, Tennessee. Dad didn't qualify for military housing at the time. He couldn't have been more than an E-3 or E-4, third from the lowest on the enlisted ranks. Because of that and the fact that he wouldn't be there very long for training, we had to find somewhere else to live. We moved into a little house a few miles away from the base on an old country road between Millington and Memphis. I would learn later that the only way we could afford a place was by Dad making a deal to repair this old place, in his free time, for rent. He redid walls, the front porch, and steps; finished a half-done garage; and completely redid a rundown old storage shed that sat out in the middle of the field behind the house. This was the first time I saw how really great his carpentry skills were.

The house was a little two-bedroom place and was in pretty bad shape. But it had a big green front yard with two gigantic elm trees, a nice little backyard, and probably four or five acres of completely weed-covered old farmland that went back to a tree line that ran along a small river. There had been corn grown there before, but of course it was all just brown cornstalk stumps everywhere now. I remember Dad walking my older brother and me out to the edge of the field and handing each of us a lit torch. I instantly thought, *I'm getting a chance to burn something again? And it's okay? Cool!* The three of us walked back and forth through the field, burning everything away. Dad planted rows and rows of corn, tomatoes, and lettuce. It was really amazing how it all grew so beautifully well! The old man really did have a green thumb. This would be the only time I'd see him grow anything other than tomatoes, but from this time on, every single place we ever lived until he died, he would grow tomatoes. His tomatoes were absolutely the best. Every time he grew them they were the same. They were always better than anything I ever had from any store, farmers' market, or supermarket. Even to this day, I've never had a tomato that tasted or smelled as wonderful as his.

The first thing he started repairs on was the old storage shed. With its rotting gray wood, the whole building looked as if it would topple over if you just touched it. He stripped all the old rotten wood off, strengthened the framing, put up all new siding, and repaired and retiled the roof. It looked like a pretty little house. I thought he would just use it as another storage shed. He put shelves and racks all along the walls on the inside and built a big table for the center of the room. He also put up a huge heat lamp just above the table. He had made a new chicken coop with nesting racks all around the room complete with an incubator and egg warmer in the center of the room. He bought a few hens and one big, mean rooster. I've heard of rabbits multiplying fast, but I couldn't believe how quickly we had hundreds of baby chicks and chickens as well as hundreds and hundreds of eggs. Mom made a little money selling some of the chicks and eggs, but she told me that the old mom-and-pop store down the road would trade her milk and bread for her eggs and she liked that even better.

I knew my father had some rifles, but I had only seen them briefly a couple of times. He kept them safely stashed away from us boys. One day when I was playing in the backyard, Dad walked out to me carrying a .22 rifle and told me to come with him. He sat down about ten or twenty yards from the edge of the tomato and lettuce patch and talked to me a little bit about safety and how to use this eighteen-shot rifle. It was light and easy to use, and in just a few minutes I was aiming and hitting every single can the old man set up for me. Then he told me about the rabbits and how they were destroying our lettuce and told me to sit still for a minute and watch the garden with him. Sure enough, in only about five minutes out popped a couple of rabbits. Dad aimed and fired two quick shots from a sitting position, and down went both rabbits. He walked over and picked them up, and we took them back to the house, where he skinned and cleaned them. That was our dinner that night. Almost every afternoon after school, I would race home from school, get that rifle, and sit out there by that garden. I shot quite a few before they stopped coming around; we didn't have any more problems with our lettuce after that. Occasionally, Mom might see a rabbit or two in the lettuce patch through our kitchen window while she was washing the dishes in the early evening. She would call to me, I would head out, and they would be in the freezer that evening.

I don't remember ever going to any kind of a store or supermarket until we eventually moved to Hawaii. We hunted and fished a lot, and we grew almost everything else, so there wasn't much that we needed. But we three boys were literally eating Mom and Dad out of house and home. I remember many, many times eating only beans for dinner, but I never gave it a second thought. I liked beans. I had no idea how very little money Mom and Dad had or how hard they worked and struggled just to clothe and feed all three of us. We didn't have a clue how really poor we were through all those years, but we had great fun and were perfectly happy.

Mom and Dad were both pretty cool. They had lots of friends, and all my friends liked them a lot. Dad had all his navy buddies and their families to our house every Sunday. We would kill some chickens, pluck them, clean them, and fry them up. It was wonderful, and we always had a blast. It was always a feast. Mom always gave the other wives chickens and eggs; we had more than we would ever use. I had gotten used to killing chickens by this time. I would chase a few into the corner of our fence, grab one by the legs, flop its head and neck up onto the fence post, and whack the head off with a small hatchet. Then I'd just toss the body on the ground and let it flop around until it stopped. The farmer next door had a giant hog on the other side of the fence. He always came over when he saw me, and I would toss the heads to him. He absolutely loved those! But I hated plucking and cleaning the feathers off. We would hold the chicken under the faucet with water running on it as we plucked the feathers. To this day I can't stand the smell of wet chicken feathers. Tony always wanted to get involved with the killing and the cleaning, but every time he came anywhere near any of the chickens, that big ol' rooster would come after him! Everybody would laugh and laugh, poor little guy, watching him run from that rooster. He was pretty good at dodging and evading the mean bird, though.

Dad did a great job on that house and property. Just after he finished the garage, we moved off to Hawaii. After that, every house that we lived in that wasn't on-base housing, Dad would make deals that let us live rent-free or get rent at least half off. It just depended on what he did. He could add on rooms to a house, build cabinets, do plumbing and wiring, anything! He made beautiful kitchen cabinets—some from the floor up and others that hung from the ceiling; some with just wooden doors and some with glass built into the doors and all beautifully detailed. Once, a wealthy old guy told Dad that he would rent us one of his beautiful homes with a pool for half rent if Dad would build a room onto his house before we moved into the rental. When Dad was about 80 percent through with the construction on the old guy's house and we were about to move off base, the guy changed his mind! Right after Dad finished work on base that night, he went over to that guy's house with a sledgehammer and knocked down everything he had built. We didn't get the pool.

6

Close Call of a Different Kind

When I got to the Philippines in 1975, it had been placed under martial law by President Ferdinand Marcos. I had arrived by a US naval P-3 Orion from Guam. The aircraft carrier *Kitty Hawk*, one of the last nonnuclear-powered carriers and the ship I had been aboard on my way to the Philippines, had blown a boiler just off Guam. Our helicopter squadron was flying parts and other supplies out from the island. We weren't stopped dead in the water but were moving slower because of that boiler. The ship was going to take much longer to reach the Philippines. I went to my division officer and asked him if I could fly in on one of the flights to say hi to some people I knew from when I'd lived there from '66 to '69 or maybe check out some places I'd lived before. He said, "We're not really going to be doing much of anything. Why don't you just take a week and stay?" Cool! I went straight down, grabbed my bag and my surfboard, and hopped on the next helicopter leaving for Guam.

The guy I was going to see and stay with was an East Coast surfer I'd met at Imperial Beach Naval Air Station in San Diego right on the border of Mexico. I'd met him, as I had another surfer there, after a day of surfing. He had seen me driving back to the barracks with my surfboard on top of my car and had followed me back. There had been only three guys, myself included, on that small base who surfed at that time. This guy, a dental technician, had just recently arrived and hadn't known where to go. I'd said, "The beach is that way! Just joking." I had been there for quite a while and knew all the best spots in Imperial Beach as well as the rest of San Diego and all the way up the coast to Ventura. There was also Mexico so easily assessable. He was a great guy, and we'd hit it off right away. We'd surfed and partied a lot together, but he'd left pretty soon. He had only been in San Diego for some training and then had gone to be stationed in Guam. Of course, having lived in Guam for three years myself, I'd told him all the cool places he should go see, surf, and play. I'd had no idea I would be there soon.

He was totally shocked when I showed up. I didn't know how to contact him; I only knew where he was based. It really wasn't hard. The naval station was on the southern part of the island, and their dental department was pretty small. I found him as soon as I walked in the door. He took a week's leave also, and we had an absolute blast together. He had an extra bunk in his barracks room, and his roommates were all cool as well. They all smoked, and we partied hard. We surfed at a bunch of places he hadn't even known about. He had a somewhat girlfriend, and she hooked me up with her friend, who was a doll. We surfed every day and partied every night. I took them to Talofofo Falls, Marble Caves, and more. We really had a lot of fun. I had one small problem when I lost my wallet and my military ID card that was in it. We searched everywhere, except the falls where I probably did drop it, but never found it. It only took a few hours out of our day, some paperwork, a few phone calls, and a check on my leave papers, and then, after all was verified, I was issued a new ID card. My biggest nightmare was waiting for me in the Philippines.

When my leave was up a week later, I said my good-byes and caught the first navy P-3 out of Naval Air Station Agana. A few hours later we landed at Subic Bay, which was a naval base for ships and the naval air station together. As soon as the door opened, the US military police / customs guy came on board. He knew I was the only passenger staying; the rest of the crew were just on patrol. He immediately grabbed my bag and headed down the stairs. I wasn't worried about anything. I didn't have a thing on me; we'd smoked only what they'd had in Guam, and I hadn't been about to bring anything with me. I just had a couple of changes of clothes and my shaving kit for a short trip. I grabbed my board and headed out the door. The customs guy walked down the stairway/ladder with my bag, instantly set it on the tarmac, pulled out one shirt, looked into the breast pocket, stuffed the shirt right back in the bag, picked the bag up, and said, "You're under arrest!"

"For what?" I asked.

"For trafficking illegal drugs!"

I couldn't believe it! How could I have been so stupid? What could I have left in there? I was sure I hadn't put anything in there. I instantly thought of all the times people had been caught with various amounts of weed, hash, cocaine, or whatever and sworn up and down that they hadn't put it in there and didn't know how it had gotten in there. You always knew they were full of shit and lying out their asses. Now here I was, in the exact same situation! But I *really* did not know! What the hell could be in there? They put my board and bag in the back of a base truck, stuck me in the backseat with a cop on either side of me, drove me into the terminal, and took me into a back room. The first thing they did was take off my board's cover and thoroughly feel every inch and stitch of it. They did the same with the board itself, visually checking every inch of it and tapping on it and listening for hollow spots. When they finally gave up, I breathed a huge sigh of relief because I thought that was the only place any sizable amount could have been. Then they took everything out of my bag, searching and feeling it all over, and again, nothing. Then the guy who had checked my shirt pocket on the ramp took that same shirt, cleared a spot on the counter, and laid a white sheet of paper down. He turned the pocket inside out again and scraped it with his pocketknife. A couple of pieces of dryer lint, tiny pieces of ash from a joint that we had been smoking, and a few very tiny pieces of marijuana, just dust really, fell out. Then he got really excited, his eyes lighting up, when something else came out. "Aha!" he said. All the other guys had to bend down to see what it was. There it was, an unsmoked piece of marijuana that looked like a big booger. You just about had to use a magnifying glass to see what it really was. That was it! They arrested me again for transportation of illegal drugs and took my military ID card away from me. I couldn't believe it. These guys were all patting each other on their backs and saying what a good job they had done. It was really ridiculous! But this was 1975 military thinking. I was more concerned about my ID card because without it I wouldn't be able to do anything or go anywhere.

They threw me and my stuff back into the truck and took me to the ship, which had come in a couple of days before I got there. They told my division officer what had happened, and I was confined to the ship. All the division heads and officers came in and asked me about it, and I told them where I had been but not what I had done. I told them that one of the guys I'd met in Guam had liked my Hawaiian-print shirts and asked to borrow one on one of the group dates we'd gone on and that he must've put something in the pocket. They were all really cool to me and told me not to worry, that it was nothing. I hoped so, but I knew that they knew that story was bullshit, like all the stories from the other guys who'd been caught.

So I was stuck on the ship for a couple of days and was told I would have to see the executive officer of the ship, the second in command of the *Kitty Hawk*. Everyone said it would stop there, that he would give me a warning and that would be it. I wouldn't have to go to captain's mast, which is the ultimate court in the navy. If the executive officer sent you to see the captain, you were screwed! The captain was dead set against drugs of any kind and any amount. The minimum time for any drug offense was thirty days in the brig, the ship's jail; loss of rank; and usually reduction of your pay to half.

Appearances in front of the executive officer (called executive screening) and the captain are both quite the ceremony. Wearing my summer-wear dress white uniform, I waited outside the executive officer's office, which was guarded by marines. One of the marines then escorted me in. When I entered, the executive officer was standing behind a podium with various officers and other enlisted men on either side of him. The marine marched me right up to the podium. "Halt!" he said, and I had to stop and come to attention. Next he said, "Uncover!" I reached up and grabbed hold of my hat/cover and paused a moment until he said, "To!" Then I snapped it off and brought it down to my side at attention. I thought I would be able to say something, but I didn't get to say a word—no lawyer either. The executive officer read my charges, trafficking in illegal drugs, specifically marijuana. I thought I was supposed to say guilty or not. Nope, this was just a screening to see whether I should go before the captain or not. The next thing he said just floored me: "Well, you know how the captain feels about drugs. You'll have to go see him. That is all." His exact words! Man, my heart just sank. I was literally in shock. I really wasn't expecting that. I thought I was just going to get a strong lecture from him and that would be it. Instantly the marine ordered, "Cover!" I snapped my cover squarely on my head, my right hand still holding on until he ordered, "To!" Then I snapped my arm back down again at attention, "About-face! Forward march!" and out the door I went, escorted once more by the marine.

I went back to my squadron to talk with my division officer and see what he thought was going to happen. He couldn't tell me anything except that I had an appointment to meet with a guy from the criminal investigation division (CID). He was a civilian guy that lived at Subic who investigated all sorts of cases on a daily basis for the military. Then he reported to the captain all his findings and opinions. I thought, *Maybe he will help!* Another very, very wrong assumption.

The next day he met me in my division shop and had me follow him deep down into the ship to his temporary room/space. I had no idea where we were or what was about to happen. I was pretty nervous. When we got in and sat down, he seemed pleasant enough, and I began to relax. He just had me tell him about where I came from, what I liked to do—sports and so on—and where I had come from before being arrested. I told him about being a navy brat, having a girlfriend, and liking surfing and baseball and said that I'd been coming back from Guam. I didn't say one word about where I'd lived before, schools I'd been to, drugs or ever using any, or Guam. He typed away the whole time I talked. When he'd finished asking me questions, he said to hold on a second while he finished up his report. I was feeling pretty good. That had been simple and easy, and it had only taken about fifteen or twenty minutes.

When he finished, he handed me the report and a pen. He told me to read it, initial all the spots where he had made notations, and then sign it. When I started reading it, I felt as if it were something out of a bad dream.

41

He had listed dates and times I had smoked pot in high school and said that I had experimented with various drugs in college, that I smoked every time I surfed, and that I had been smoking the whole time I had been in the navy. He had made up the whole report! Yes, I had done a lot of things, but I hadn't said one word or admitted a thing to him that he'd written in his report. I said, "Are you out of your mind? I didn't say any of this!"

He said, "You know you did all of it." And then he yelled, "Sign it!" trying to scare me into signing.

I said, "You can stick this bullshit up your ass. You are fucked!" I threw it back at him and started out the door. All ship doors/hatches are raised about a foot off the floor, are big, steel, and oval-shaped, and are latched/dogged by a big long handle so they are kept watertight. I stepped over with my left leg, but before I could get my right leg over and out, he slammed that heavy hatch on my leg just above the ankle. I thought he was going to break my leg. He damned near did. He had his right shoulder against the door and was pushing hard. I yelled, "What the fuck are you doing?" He peeked his face around the door just as I started to push back. His mean, trying-to-be-intimidating face was gone now; he looked scared shitless, as if he thought I might come back in and kick his ass. I pushed hard with my shoulder once, then again harder, and out came my leg. He instantly slammed the hatch shut and locked it.

It took me a while to get out of there and find my way back up to my squadron office. I was so angry and upset I was almost in tears as I started to tell the officers in the room what had just happened. Our squadron executive officer walked in and asked what the hell was going on. I told him everything and showed him my leg. He wanted me to take them all back down there right now. We went back deep down into the ship, but I couldn't remember where the CID guy's office was, and we couldn't find it. The executive officer told me to calm down and get back to the shop and said he would look into it. I managed to calm down somewhat but had to go over the story time and again and show my leg cut and bruised so badly on both sides to everyone. They all knew about what was going on with me and having to go to captain's mast and were all surprised it was going so far. The whole situation had gotten way out of hand. They couldn't believe it. I really couldn't either, but I was still scheduled to go to captain's mast the very next day.

I really was a good sailor. I did what I was told, and I worked hard. Yes, I partied at times, but so did everyone else. I was polite and respectful to officers and got along well with all my squadron mates. My record was spotless. In boot camp, I had been chosen most outstanding recruit of the whole company and had been given a meritorious advancement. I'd been one of the top of my class in jet school and all the other training courses I'd taken before reporting to my squadron. I always had 4.0 markings, the best, on my quarterly reports, and I'd taken and passed the advancement exam to be promoted to E-4 on my first shot. My uniform was always immaculate, my shoes always polished and shined. Even my dungarees, my working uniform, always had perfectly creased pants and shirts ironed every day.

I had a pretty sleepless, restless night. I hadn't eaten much for dinner and felt like a condemned man eating my last meal at breakfast. I knew what was coming and still just couldn't really believe it. Knowing about the loss of rank and pay was bad enough, but being imprisoned by marine guards was a whole different ball game.

The marines were in charge of the ship's internal security and the brig. I had seen prisoners under their guard almost daily. They were brought up to the hangar deck each day to exercise, and I would see them occasionally here and there on their knees scrubbing and cleaning. They looked terrible, worn out, and scared! Their heads were shaved, and their dungarees looked as if they were worn to bed every night, worked in every day, and unwashed. The marines were merciless with the prisoners.

After I finished breakfast, I still had a little more time, so I went up on the flight deck. We were still docked in Subic Bay, and I wanted to get one last look around outside, enjoy the fresh air and sunshine, and just try to relax. I stood for a while on the forward edge of the flight deck as a warm wind blew across. I loved the smell of the heavy, moist jungle air. It somehow seemed much stronger this morning. I knew where I was going straight after my little visit with the skipper. I walked across the flight deck to the catwalk on the port/left side of the ship. I figured I would go down through the shop I worked out of when we were in flight operations and see if anyone was there. There wasn't. "Oh well!" I said to myself. It was time to go.

So I went out into the hall and literally ran right into one of the officers from administration. He said, "Where the hell have you been? We've been looking all over for you!" I thought, *Uh-oh, now what?* He said that the charges had all been dropped and that they weren't going to pursue it anymore. He then handed back my ID card. I stood there with my mouth open for some time. I didn't know what to think or even what to say. Had that really just happened? Was this a joke? Was I dreaming? I just said thank you to him. He smiled at me and shook my hand. That smile was the clincher. The fear, dread, and stress all went away almost instantly. One of those true euphoric moments!

I never found out why this happened. No one came up to me and said anything, and I didn't ask. I'm not sure if the small, miniscule amount of weed that they pulled out of my shirt pocket really made a difference at all. Under different circumstances I would have been gone. I was sure damn lucky it wasn't the Philippine police at a civil airport that had arrested me. Back then, under martial law, the death penalty was handed out for minimal amounts of drugs, and you could do a lot of time just for possessing paraphernalia. Just having rolling papers for marijuana could get you sent to prison! I know that what the civilian investigator did was probably the main reason I got off, but I have no doubt my record played a big role as well. Whatever it was, I wasn't about to question it. It was time to celebrate!

7

Helicopter Firefighting

In all the flying I have done, firefighting was and still is the best! Anyone can fly a helicopter, but to really work it, doing sling loads using various lengths of long line to lift or move things around or hooking on water buckets, also with different lengths of line, and go after a fire, that takes some skill. It is challenging, requiring all your flying skills, senses, and maybe just a little more. Not everyone can fly long line. It's very easy to overcontrol the helicopter, and before you know it, you can lose control of whatever it is you're trying to lift and move. And if the load begins swinging and you can see it out one of your side windows, that's not a good thing!

On fires you occasionally fly passengers, like taking fire crews to various fire locations or spotters to check and map fire lines, but mostly you're left on your own. A lot of the sling loads would be supplies for the firefighters. Tools, chain saws, food, clothing, fuel, generators, and just about anything else they needed would be loaded into nets, and I would sling them wherever needed. Most fires are in isolated areas in dense trees with no landing zones (LZs) and few roads. You might have to use a two-hundred-foot line to lower something down into tall trees; other times you might have openings you could fly into using shorter lines, but you rarely landed. We would be on the go constantly, and speed was essential. Often I would fly into a spot on a ridge or a mountainside and just hover with the forward end of my skids touching the side of the slope as the crew stepped out, walked on the skids, and jumped off. Other times I would hover above whatever obstructions were there, and they would simply jump out. The first crews would always quickly cut a clearing wherever I dropped them in, and I could turn right around and start bringing supplies or other crews back to that spot. If they cut it big enough, it could be an LZ.

We would pick up most loads from the firebase or from supply trucks on the nearest road. We would fly in with our long line and empty hook, and a ground crew would hook up whatever load we would be carrying out. We'd fly quickly back to the LZ and set the load on the ground. A crew member at that end would unhook it, and off we'd go again. For quicker turnarounds we often used a remote hook, an electrical hook we could release from the cockpit. A ground crew person would hook up our load to be delivered, but we wouldn't need anyone at the receiving end to unhook us. We could just drop it and jet back for another load.

Using water buckets to fight fires was absolutely the most fun. In time you learned techniques and tricks for how to drop water. Again, the location of the fire determined the length of line you would use with a bucket, like needing a longer line in areas of tall trees, for example. But more often than not we would use a short line that allowed us to carry the bucket at high speed. When you fly with a loaded, heavy water bucket, it tends to hang pretty much below you and doesn't swing back very far. But after you drop, you want to get back as quickly as possible to refill and come back. That empty, lightweight bucket on its own can swing up and hit your tail rotor, so depending on the length of the line, you have to be careful of your speed. I almost always used a short line that kept the bucket a foot or two ahead of the tail rotor even if it was swept all the way straight back. I could make much quicker turnarounds that way.

Very often there are lakes, ponds, rivers, or even small creeks nearby that you can hover down over and dip your bucket into to fill it up. After you push the electronic release button on your control stick and the water is released, it automatically recycles back up and closes. Then you simply have to drop in on any water source and set your bucket on the surface, and it quickly sinks and fills. Then steadily you come straight back up and out, and off you go back. Sometimes you might have to fight a fire in a flat land or very dry area without a water source nearby. In that case several fire trucks are strategically placed around fires with hoses at the ready. You simply zip in and hover next to the truck as the firefighters quickly fill your bucket with one, two, or three hoses. On two different occasions, I actually dipped my bucket into the pools of beautiful mountainside estate homes. Those were desperate situations, as flames were licking up the hills toward the homes. In both cases I saved the homes, and both times the owners were more than grateful and didn't mind losing all the money they had spent heating that water or the hundreds or maybe thousands of dollars' worth of their pool chemicals I had taken out to drop on the fire and stop it.

To be able to bring in any kind of load, keep it steady, and put it right in someone's hand or on a spot takes some skill. I always got a kick out of the guys at each new firebase or camp who would check out the new pilot's long-line skills. On every fire we almost always worked with crews we hadn't met before, and of course they were curious and wanted to see your skills and how good you really were, especially because their lives might end up depending on you. For example, I managed to impress a crew with my skills the first time I was to fly into a new firebase in Ramona, California. I had just departed Corona, California, with all my gear and a 150-foot sling when I received a call to fly into an LZ on a fire near Ramona on my way down there. I was to use the long line and pick up a load of tools and equipment and bring it into the firebase at Ramona. As I got close to the fire, I found an open field, went in to land, and put on the line. The crew soon saw me and steered me in by radio to their location on the top of a small mountain. They were working in tall, dense trees, and I couldn't see anyone until I got right on top of them. I lowered the hook and line down into a small opening in the trees and put the hook right in the stationary, outstretched hand of one of the crew. After I received the signal to pull up, I slowly increased the power, put some tension on the line, centered it straight up, and began to lift the load. It wasn't heavy at all, but I was surprised to see how full the net was with all the tools inside. I wasn't sure that huge net load was going to clear the trees I had to come up through. But I kept it nice and straight, lifted it up slowly and smoothly, and came right out without even touching a leaf! I actually heard one of the fire crew on the ground say that very thing over the radio back to the firebase. They didn't believe him.

I quickly got on the radio and made the appropriate calls to air traffic in the vicinity. This would be the first time I had ever been to Ramona Airport, but I had seen a map and diagram of the airport and the firebase on the airport and pretty much knew right where I needed to go. As I lined up with the taxiway for my long final into the firebase, I switched radios back over to them. I was expecting to set the load on one of the empty, marked, concrete helipads to be unloaded by some of the base crew. I could put it in the center of one of those easy enough.

Instead, as I slowed and headed toward the helipad I figured they would want me to set it on, I got a call from the fire boss saying they wanted the load placed somewhere else. The fire boss was on a handheld radio sitting in the grass in a chair about fifty feet beyond the last helipad. "Helicopter 947 Lima, do you have fire boss in sight?" he asked.

"That's affirmative," I said.

"I want that load right here on this spot!" he said as he stood up, walked forward, and placed something on the ground between where he was sitting and the helipad. "Do you have spot in sight?"

"Roger that," I said. I had no idea what he'd placed on the ground until I got closer. It was a roll of pink marking tape they used at times to mark LZs out in the field, about as big as a small roll of electrical tape. He then walked back over to his chair and sat down to watch. About that time I noticed all the other firefighters lined up off to the side to watch also, kind of snickering and smiling. It turned out, as I would find out later, most of the pilots they had been working with weren't worth a damn with long lines, and none had been able to nail the fire boss's little spot. I slowed and lowered as I got closer and got the load just above the tape before setting it on the ground. I put it dead center on top of that tape! One of the firefighters was right there when it touched and unhooked it. The fire boss never looked up and was stone-faced. I knew he was testing me. I'd had other guys doing that kind of thing to me for years. Now it was time to show off.

Holding the hook just inches off the ground, I slowly hovered forward over to his chair. I set the hook on the ground right next to the right front leg of his chair and then lowered slowly and moved the stick around just enough to coil the line into a pile right next to him. It looked just as it would if you did it by hand after disconnecting it from the helicopter. At about five feet above the ground I punched the remaining few feet of line off with a push of the release button on my control stick. It fell into a perfect coil. All a crew member had to do was simply walk over, pick it up, and stow it away. The fire boss never looked up at me the entire time. He just sat there looking straight ahead. I hovered back to the pad and landed. The other firefighters were laughing their asses off! When I shut the helicopter down and opened the door, the fire boss walked over to me, smiled, shook my hand, and said, "Welcome to Ramona, hotshot!"

That would be my final firefighting mission for the next twenty-five years. I absolutely loved all the people on that crew and had an absolute blast fighting all sorts of amazing, dangerous, but exciting fires! Just a few days later I was to be off to Japan for a second time teaching Japanese to fly. The firebase crew had a great going-away party for KN—my soon-to-be wife—and me on my last day there. They even had a huge wedding cake with little bride and groom statues on the top. I knew KN and I would soon be starting a family, and I wanted to be with them every day. I had done so much as a pilot and felt not flying would not be a problem for me. I haven't really missed flying in general, as I thought I might. I still fly occasionally, at least once almost every year. I have missed firefighting, though. It is truly wonderful and exciting. It's a bit like being a fighter or bomber pilot in battle; you actually see you're winning or accomplishing something. You're saving lives, homes, and property and know you are very much appreciated. It's a great feeling!

49

Me slinging supplies for fire crews near Ramona, California.

Mc doing a hover fill with no other water sources to dip into nearby.

Me looking for a safe spot to drop firefighters on a mountainside.

A firefighter hooking on food and water for crews up on
a mountain as I hover for a quicker turnaround.

8

Off to Hawaii

From Tennessee my parents, brothers, and I drove west to San Francisco, where we would board a US Navy transport ship for a five-day trip to Hawaii. It was pretty cool for us three boys—well, for two of us anyway. It was like an old cruise ship where we stayed on the upper levels of the ship. We couldn't go down to the large main deck area where the many sailors lived and worked. But we had a movie theater, a restaurant, a playground, and smaller open areas where we could step outside and look around whenever we wanted to. We didn't go out there very often. The weather outside was pretty cold and nasty almost all the way there. There was so much to do inside that I didn't mind at all. My little brother, Tony, and I had a blast playing with the toy cars in the playroom. I would sit at one end of the room and he at the other, and as the ship pitched up and down in the really rough seas, our cars would race back and forth. Other times we would sit side by side and see which of our cars would get to the other side first racing across the floor. We were never bored. We watched movies every day, and the food was great. Of course this wasn't the same for my older brother, Rick. He was seasick from the moment the ship set out. I don't remember him ever eating one meal with us—breakfast, lunch, or dinner—the whole trip to Hawaii. A steward would come down the halls playing chimes to call us to each meal. Rick couldn't even go in the restaurant without becoming ill. He would sit just outside the restaurant door in the small waiting area wearing a life preserver and holding a vomit bag or would stay in the room with Mom, still equipped with a vomit bag. She always brought something for him, but I know he didn't eat very much. In fact I never saw him eat anything. He didn't go to the movies or play in the playground at all either.

When we got to Hawaii, Mom and Dad moved us into an apartment in Waipahu, a little city west of Honolulu and the airport. We wouldn't be there long, but it was long enough to get into trouble right off the bat. One of Dad's squadron mates was living in the same apartment building, and my brothers and I met his son the second day there and went out to play. We didn't get far. There was a huge concrete building next to our apartment that was a pig slaughterhouse. There were no windows all the way around the building, which was pretty plain with only doors in the front. On the side between that building and our apartment building were two rows of trees, one row on either side of a small drainage ditch that ran parallel to the buildings. I didn't know what kind of trees they were; I just assumed they were coconut trees. As we were walking between the trees and the side of the building, one of us, I don't remember who, spotted a really big, long knife sitting on a small concrete wall. "Cool! It's a sword," we said. We had never seen a machete before, but it sure seemed like a sword to us four little guys.

Rick started swinging it around and took a big baseball swing at one of the trees. It surprised the shit out of all of us when the knife went through that tree like butter. Rick almost toppled into the ditch with his follow-through because he, as well as all of us, thought the knife would just stop and stick in the tree. Way cool! I wanted a shot, but our new friend grabbed it from Rick and started whacking down trees. *It must be so heavy and sharp,* I thought. Next, Tony got it. Being smaller, he needed two or three whacks to cut down one tree, but he started getting better and cut all but the last tree down before he finally gave me a chance. I was going to take my time. I slowly carved a square into the tree, then cut an *X* inside the square. "X marks the spot," I said as I started my backswing with the machete. Just as I started forward, someone clamped down hard on my wrist and yanked the machete out of my hand. It was an old Hawaiian guy, and I thought he was going to break my arm as he yanked me away and back toward our apartment building.

It was then that I saw all the trees lying across the ditch. I hadn't realized we had cut down that many. Dad and his crewmate were in our apartment and came running out when they heard the old guy dragging me back yelling all the way. I thought Dad was going to go to blows with the old guy after he saw the guy yanking me along and saw how red my wrist was once he'd pulled me away from the man. He made us kids go upstairs as the old guy told him what we had done. Dad could see it for himself. As it turned out, they were banana trees, and we had cut down all but that one. I don't know how much, but the old guy demanded a lot of money, and Dad and his friend had to pay everything they had on them. Then Dad came upstairs and got into one of our still-unpacked suitcases and pulled out three big piggy banks—one blue, one red, and one green. He placed them on the floor and smashed them open one at a time. We couldn't believe how much money was in each one, no pennies, just lots of nickels, dimes, quarters, and folded dollar bills in all three banks. Mom had been saving all her egg money for us, and we hadn't even known. Dad went down and paid the guy, and I guess it was enough.

That was it for him but not for us! Dad came back up and sent our new friend downstairs. He then whipped us one by one with his belt, way worse than just being spanked. Being the second or third to be whipped was the worst, as we could see what we were going to get next. This was the first of many ass beatings we would get for a long time to come. When he finished with us, his friend came up with his son and beat him too. After that we came down, and we all sat crying. Already black-and-blue belt marks were beginning to show from the bottoms of our backs to down behind our knees.

How the times have changed. Through the years, I remember my teachers seeing my welts and bruises and only saying something like "We have been a bad boy, haven't we?" And I would feel guilty and embarrassed. A parent today would be in big trouble, and rightly so, for beating a child as badly as we were so many times.

We soon moved over to the west side of Oahu to Nanakuli, Maili, and then Waianae.

Waianae was where I got into my first fight as the new guy! I went to school in an old white schoolhouse where we would gather outside every morning and say the Pledge of Allegiance and sing "America the Beautiful" as they raised the American flag. I remember that big old schoolhouse sitting back away from the ocean in a small valley nestled in beautiful green surroundings. Hawaii had just become the fiftieth state just after we got there, and everyone was very patriotic. That side of the island was, and still is, so quiet and serene. It is very different from much of the rest of Oahu.

The fight occurred only a day or two after we settled in at Waianae. I was outside playing marbles with some of the local neighbor kids. Back then, every kid had his or her own bag of marbles, and we all carried them with us everywhere we went. All you had to do was draw a circle in the dirt, put some marbles in the circle, and take turns shooting at them. If you knocked another person's marble or marbles out the circle, they were yours. I don't know how it started, but this big Hawaiian kid and I started fighting over a game. There were a bunch of kids around, and when this guy suddenly punched me in the face, he knocked me back into the kids surrounding us. They caught me and threw me right back at him. I was like a punching bag, and he was knocking the crap out of me! I didn't have a chance to do anything. He'd hit me, and instantly the kids hurled me right back into the blows of his fist. After the fourth or fifth blow, when they threw me back in at him again, I came at him with a hard overhand right, right to his nose. It was a lucky shot, and his nose seemed to explode like a tomato. Blood went everywhere as he fell backward screaming. He immediately jumped back up and took off for home crying as he fled.

As I turned for home, the crowd surrounding me parted, and I walked out. Mom was already walking toward me. She said she had seen it start and thought she would just let it play out, hoping I would learn a lesson from it. But when she saw I was getting the shit kicked out of me, she thought she'd better put a stop to it before I got killed. Mom had just gotten me cleaned up back at our house when there was a knock at the door. It was the big Hawaiian kid standing there with tears in his eyes, tape across his nose, and two big wads of cotton stuffed up each nostril. He had a small bag of marbles, which he handed to me as he said he was sorry. I said I was sorry too, and we went back out to play. Apparently, his mother had been watching also and had seen him picking on me and starting the fight, and she had sent him back to apologize. I'm glad she did; he would become my best friend. This type of new-guy fight would happen again and again; from here on out I would have to fight someone every time we moved to a new place.

We finally moved into military housing at Ewa Beach on the south side of the island right on the west side of the entryway into Pearl Harbor, and I started at my second elementary school on Oahu, third so far. I just loved living there. The housing area actually wrapped around from inside Pearl Harbor all the way around to the south side with beautiful white sand beaches. We spent most of our free time on those beaches. There was a lagoon that came in from Pearl Harbor into the center of the housing area, underground bunkers, and various other old military sites in the jungle that surrounded the housing area that we weren't supposed to be in, but we were constantly exploring them. This was also where I began playing baseball and fell in love with it, continuing to play almost all the way to the pros.

We all got more into guns and shooting and hunting after we moved into the housing area. Each family had a good-size storage shed behind their part of their duplex, and Dad turned ours into a loading room, an ammunition-loading room that is. He had a few more rifles and handguns by this time. He built racks and had them all mounted up on the wall. He made a loading bench with various hand-operated loading tools attached to it. One was for punching out spent primers from shell casings already fired and then pressing in new ones. Another was for measuring and loading powder into the shells, and another was for placing the bullet heads, which we would make, into the prepared shell casings. We would go to the shooting range or places around the island where people often went shooting and pick up old, spent shell casings that people had just left after reloading. We could find every kind of caliber shell that Dad's guns fired. We brought the good ones that hadn't been damaged home and cleaned them up. We would go to junkyards and take all the lead weights (used to balance wheels) we could find off the old cars and take them home. Dad had a big, thick, heavy black pot that he would heat up on the stove, and we would melt all the weights to molten lead. He also had little molds for every caliber bullet head. We would pour the molten lead into a hole in the mold, wait just a few seconds, then open the mold and tap out the perfectly shaped and grooved bullet head.

We made hundreds and hundreds of bullets, and all we had to pay for were the little primers and gunpowder! Dad had made friends with some of the pineapple growers, and they let us go out in their huge fields up near the mountains and shoot for target practice. That was really a blast, all the loading and then shooting. I didn't know any other kids that had that sort of hobby.

I also went on my first airplane ride when Dad started taking the three of us boys one at a time on two-day weekend hunting trips to Molokai. We would fly a little twin-engine Beechcraft from Oahu to Molokai on Friday afternoon, get up early Saturday morning, hunt all day, and then fly back on Sunday. The first time Dad had gone there, he'd gone deer hunting on his own for Japanese axis deer and gotten a real beauty. Of course he'd had the huge antlered head mounted, and we had that on the wall almost everyplace we ever lived. We'd also gotten a freezer full of venison that seemed to last forever. He took me pig hunting the first time and goat hunting the second time. Both times were just so cool, and I had the best show-and-tell stories of all the kids in elementary school.

The naval air base, Barbers Point, was located a short drive to the west. That was where my dad's squadron and all the single sailors' barracks were located. It was also where we would go to swim at the base's huge pool. We had a lot of fun at Ewa Beach and Barbers Point, but two things, one at each place, would affect me and my family for years to come. The pool would play a part in the first thing, and in the second I would see something here so amazing that it would stick vividly in my mind for the rest of my life.

The first: It was the summer of 1961 or 1962, and my brothers and I were out of school and being taken care of by a babysitter. Mom was working, and Dad was off flying at Midway Island. He would be gone for a couple of weeks. Our babysitter drove us over to Barbers Point pool for the day. She must've had a boyfriend or something, because after we got there, I don't remember ever seeing her again. The pool was gigantic, and there were hundreds of people there. The pool was built especially for high diving, and there were three different board heights, with the highest at least twenty-five or thirty feet high. So the pool was about thirty feet deep at the deep end. Rick had gotten a mask and snorkel from someone and was swimming around the shallow end. We still didn't know how to swim yet, so of course we stayed out of the deep end. But with a snorkel all you had to do was just keep your legs kicking and float along while looking down.

I was sitting on my towel in the grass area off to the side of the pool talking to a friend who could swim. I don't know why it was only me, but I just happened to look up and see Rick push off from the side of the deepest end of the pool and begin to slowly kick his way across the pool. I remember thinking, *Wow, he's making it across on his own!* At about two arm lengths from the edge of the pool, he looked down too deep, and water came into the snorkel. He stopped and started to panic. With all the people that were in the pool and all around sitting on the sides, no one saw him flailing away and splashing in panic. I told my friend, "Look, my brother's drowning! Please help him!" My friend actually laughed and said, "He's just playing!" By this time Rick had gone under. I ran around to the first lifeguard tower—there were four, one on each side. Not one lifeguard had seen him. The first lifeguard I told was just a young kid. He ran over and dove in but had to come back up twice because it was just too deep and he couldn't get down and get him. I had started to turn and yell for someone else when this huge guy blew right by me, dove in the water, and instantly came back up with my brother. I actually thought Rick was dead as soon as I saw him. He was all purple already. Back then no one knew of mouth-to-mouth resuscitation, so this big guy just laid him on his stomach and started pushing on his back. Water gushed out of Rick's mouth. I couldn't believe how almost black purple the inside of his mouth looked. Moments later an ambulance came and took him away.

I don't remember how Tony and I got home. I never saw the babysitter again, of course! Mom was at work in Barbers Point at the time. She was called and immediately went over to the dispensary. As I would find out a few hours later, when Mom brought Rick home, apparently he had not started breathing at all in the ambulance or the whole time the doctors were trying to resuscitate him. My mom was there watching when the doctor finally gave up and said, "Sorry, he's dead. There's nothing else we can do." And then he just left! Mom lost it I guess and was sobbing and crying her eyes out. Our next-door neighbor in the same duplex, a corpsman, just happened to be passing the room and saw my mom inside crying. To make her feel better, he put the oxygen mask back over Rick's face, and Rick immediately woke up! The doctor immediately ran back in and, after apologizing profusely to my mom, checked him out and said he could go home. What freaked Mom out a lot more was when Rick described seeing beautiful lights and feeling so warm and comfortable. From the time he went under to being transported to the hospital, which wasn't really far, to the time the doctor had spent on him, he'd easily gone thirty minutes, more or less, without oxygen. I would not realize until I was about sixteen or seventeen why he always embarrassed me anytime he came around me and my friends, why he dropped out of high school, why he was kicked out of the navy, and why he could never hold a job. All the things I would see in my older brother that made me dislike him so much—the fights and the strangeness yet bizarre brilliance—had to be due to that lack of oxygen.

The second: One night we all waited outside for what we thought would be a small light show in the distance. The United States was going to test a hydrogen bomb on Christmas Island south of Hawaii. Dad said Christmas Island was pretty far south so we might not see much. We had the radio on and were listening to the DJ broadcasting on that dark, moonless night. Everyone on the island knew about the test, and everyone in our neighborhood was outside looking south as the DJ counted down to showtime. There is no way to express in writing what I saw when he reached zero. It instantly became daylight but a more intense kind of white light, and it stayed like that for twenty or thirty seconds. As the light dimmed into different shades of red, you could see the clouds high and far away rolling and curling as if they were boiling. I was old enough then to understand things that were happening in the world, like the Cuban Missile Crisis, and knew about Hiroshima and Nagasaki and nuclear weapons in general. But this was a power I never could have imagined. It put a fear in me, a fear for our small world and what could happen if we were not careful. Mom actually broke into tears, crying and shaking really bad right after it exploded. It really scared her, and she had nightmares for months. I was just completely awestruck.

Next stop, Southern California.

The Wooton family in Ewa Beach, Oahu, Hawaii, around 1960 to 1962. I am on the left.

9

Good Ol' Mom

From about ten years old I knew I wanted to be a pilot. It was about that time we began living right next to, or always very near, the runways of the naval air stations where my dad was stationed. Also about that time the Vietnam War was beginning to pick up with a dramatic increase of aircraft operations. I would sit next to the runways, at the approach ends, at the departure ends, all around them, nearly every day with my binoculars and watch aircraft coming, going, and at times even crashing. I was seeing almost every kind of aircraft in the military's arsenal. I was hooked!

As my time in the military neared its end, I heard many stories about how difficult a time I might have trying to be a civilian pilot. The Vietnam War had really just ended a year earlier, and many pilots had gotten out of the military. Many had been forced out because they were no longer needed. The civilian market was being flooded with thousands of pilots, and not all of them were finding jobs. There were a lot of jobs, just too many pilots! So what were guys like me, with a license but very little flying time, to do? I kept hearing, "You have to have one thousand hours minimum to fly for any company." This was not entirely true but pretty standard as an insurance requirement for most companies. I could, kind of, understand the high requirement, but how was I going to get that much time without a job? I would find out much, much later what was actually required and not required. I was getting so sick of hearing the same bullshit stories and just the negative, mean things that everyone was saying. Everyone except my mom!

I was finally checking out of my squadron, Helicopter Antisubmarine Squadron Eight (HS-8), getting all my paperwork done and signed. I said good-bye and shook hands with the executive officer of the squadron, and he asked what I was going to do. I said, "I'm going to be a pilot and—"

This new young officer interrupted and yelled out, "You'll never fly commercially!"

I immediately shot right back, "What an ignorant, mean, stupid, fucking asshole thing to say!"

"Who do you think you're talking to—" he started to say.

I cut him off and said, "Obviously not the kind of officer who I would expect to say something like 'Good luck to you! You can do it! And thank you for your four years of service!'"

He stood up sputtering and stuttering, "Well … I'll … You'll …"

Again interrupting him, I said, "What are you going to do? Make me stay in for four more years?"

The executive officer said, "That's enough, Wooton." He told the officer to sit down and shut up and wished me good luck as he handed me my discharge papers and shook my hand one last time.

From that day on it was all negative from almost everyone else. I had trained and gone to school to be a jet engine mechanic in the navy, and I was pretty much guaranteed a job as a mechanic after getting my airframe and power plant (A&P) certificate or license. That would be easy. Maintenance jobs were abundant, and mechanics were needed desperately. But I didn't want to spin wrenches for a living. I wanted to fly! I knew a few mechanics who wanted to be pilots but were having a hard time because of companies telling them anything and everything to keep them where they were. Yes, they were hearing the same one-thousand-hours stories I was and being kept from pilot jobs. What were we to do? Yes, we had commercial licenses but only a few hundred hours of flying time, and there was no way we could afford to pay for hundreds more hours of flying time and survive. Yes, in time we could, but it would take years! I didn't want to get my A&P, because I didn't want to put myself in that position.

I had started aviation courses at Southwestern College in San Diego three months before I was honorably discharged from the United States Navy. You could request an early out from the navy up to three months before you were due to be discharged if you were registered and enrolled in school already. It was almost always guaranteed that you would be able to get out once you requested the early out and submitted the required paperwork. Two other guys from my squadron, one from the electrician shop and one from the hydraulic shop, had applied for early outs about the same time as me, and they were allowed to leave. But in the jet shop, one guy had recently retired, another had had a massive heart attack and died, and another had been in a bad car accident and would be in the hospital for some time. So "Sorry!" they said; they couldn't let me go. But they said I could go to school during the day and just work nights. Not a problem, I could do that! I was due to get out at the end of October and began classes the end of August.

It was almost like being out early. I was living near the beach, going to school during the day, working nights, and surfing whenever I could. It was great! My dad was retired from the navy and had been working for the military in civil service jobs for a while. He was going to be sent to Japan soon and would probably be there for a few years. He wouldn't be able to take my mom and little sister with him for some time, almost a year. He came down to San Diego well before he was due to leave and literally begged me to come up to the Riverside area, east of Los Angeles, and take care of them until they could go to Japan. I really didn't want to go to Riverside. I was in heaven in San Diego. I was really digging school and my classes. I was getting straight As and getting more and more excited about flying. I told him I couldn't move. I said I was sorry and explained that I was in school and had just started my first semester. But he didn't give up. As my first semester neared an end, he came down and again begged me to move up there. I gave in this time and said I would at the end of the semester.

So up I went. I was expecting to go to Riverside junior college but was disappointed to find that they didn't have an aeronautics program. I didn't know what I was going to do. Then, just by accident, while cruising around one foggy night in San Bernardino, the next big city north of Riverside, I came upon a huge lit sign for San Bernardino Valley College on the corner of an intersection. I came back the very next morning and found they had an excellent aeronautics program. I registered for full-time classes and was in just a few days later for the next semester. They also had a flying club with a flying team that competed in the Pacific Coast Intercollegiate Flying Association's Safety and Flight Evaluation Conference (SAFECON) each year. We would be competing against colleges from Washington, Oregon, California, Idaho, Nevada, Utah, and Arizona. How cool was that? My first year I participated in the meet at Cochise College in Douglas, Arizona, and the next year, at San Jose State University in California, I would win a gold medal in the power-off spot landing event.

I joined the club immediately and soon after started my flight training at Colton Airpark flying a Cessna 150. The hourly rate was seventeen dollars an hour, but club members got it for fourteen dollars an hour. That sounds ungodly cheap right now, but you have to remember that this was back in 1976–77 and I was a starving college student. That was a lot of money to me back then. There would be lots of time gaps in my logbook between flights before I would finally get my fixed-wing private pilot license.

During my years of college at San Bernardino and UCR I flew only rarely, but I knew I was a good pilot, and I still wanted to fly for a living. I was majoring in aeronautics and really took a liking to atmospheric sciences, the study of weather, when I was going to UCR. But I was beginning to wonder what was actually in store for my future. My first year in school I was living off my Veterans Administration (VA) school benefits for my service during the Vietnam conflict, but I needed more money.

I got a part-time night job in a shopping mall in San Bernardino at a men's clothing store specializing in European men's fashions. I worked in the back shipping and receiving orders, and each evening I drove half of the received goods in a van to the owners' second store in a Riverside shopping mall. That gave me a little more money for flying, but it was still slow.

My last year of school my younger brother, who had been in the navy also, was living in San Diego and selling life insurance. He was making a lot of money. He had a new home, a new Porsche, and a brand-new Harley Davidson. I was jealous and thought, *I could do that!* I studied and learned the requirements, regulations, and how and what his company sold. I took the required tests and got my insurance license. When I got out of school, I joined the San Bernardino office of the company he worked for and started out as an insurance agent. I absolutely hated it. I was not a salesman. I could not do what my brother was doing. I hated trying to talk to people who treated me as if I had the plague. I didn't last one week. I knew this job was a big mistake and that I needed to get out right away.

One day after walking around the downtown area all morning, going in and out of lots of businesses, and talking to lots of people, I knew I was through with this crap. It was around noon, and I was headed to lunch. I just happened to be standing on a corner next to a phone booth waiting for the light to change, and I thought I would call my mom and ask her if she wanted to have lunch with me. I told her what I had decided about my job, and she immediately said, almost shouting, "You have to go see Mary's husband!" I rolled my eyes back and groaned, "Mom, we talked about this before!" Mary was Mom's best friend in her office at work. Her husband, Ben, was the director of maintenance for Western Helicopters at Rialto airport. Mom had been trying to get me to go see him for months, way before I had gotten out of school. She was sure he would give me a job, but I knew what I would be doing there, and it wasn't flying. And without an A&P certificate I couldn't do much more than a little side maintenance.

However, Mom knew me, and she knew I had always done well at whatever I had tried. She always said, "If you just get your foot in the door ..." every time we talked about this, but I was worried. She begged me this time, telling me that Mary had just called her before I did. Apparently

Mary had just gotten off the phone with her husband, and he'd told her how badly they needed somebody at Western right now. Mom pleaded with me to go, and I finally said okay. She said she would call Mary back and tell them to expect me in about thirty minutes.

Less than thirty minutes later I was sitting in Ben's office wearing a three-piece suit. The very first thing he asked me, after our introductions, was "What do you really want to do?"

"I want to fly!" I said.

Just like everyone else, he said, "That will never happen! You're a helicopter mechanic with lots of experience, and you'll be able to do that and make a very good living."

I damn near got up and walked out, but where would I go then? It was Friday afternoon, and he asked if I could start Monday morning at six o'clock. I said yes. I would soon see how absolutely right Mom was. Good ol' Mom! My foot was definitely in the door!

When I got to Western around five thirty on Monday morning, Ben was already in his office waiting for me. I changed into my new uniform, dark-brown pants and khaki shirt with the company badge sewn on above the right front pocket and an American flag sewn on the left sleeve. They even had my name tag already made up for me. I looked like a sheriff! He walked me through all the things my new job entailed. By 6:00 a.m., I was cleaning toilets; vacuuming the front offices; and cleaning, washing, and fueling all the aircraft, both fixed wing (airplanes) and rotor wing (helicopters), as well as all vehicles. My official title was swamper. I also had to take care of all the buildings, the flight line (ramp), and all fuel systems. Every morning, after making sure everything in the offices was clean, inside and out, I would take care of all the aircraft and line equipment. I'd also check, test, and service the ramp's and trucks' fuel systems. My main job, which I did quite often, was driving the various-size fuel trucks to fuel and support the helicopters wherever they went. The helicopters couldn't always fill up because of the kind of work they did most of the time. I actually liked this job a lot. I got to get away from work, travel, and have a pretty good time doing it. The helicopters were mostly used for lift work, like lifting air-conditioning units onto the tops of tall buildings, building power lines, erecting towers on top of mountains, and hundreds of other things. It was amazing the places we would go and the things our helicopters would lift.

The company also did a lot of movie and TV work. I drove and sometimes got to fly to many of the jobs. We helped in or used our helicopters in many movies and TV shows. We also did many types of TV commercials. This was also a time before most police or fire departments had helicopters, so we were called to help with car accidents and aircraft accidents and to help fight fires. For a long time we would be the first to the site of an aircraft accident. I would see the aftermath of many accidents and witness many actually happen, including the tragedy on the set of *Twilight Zone: The Movie.*

But the coolest thing was that very often we would leave the helicopter and fuel truck on site, wherever we might be, for the night and fly back in one of the company's airplanes. Then we'd fly back again the next day. Other times, we would leave the fuel truck and just fly the helicopter back. On my third day with the company, after a full day of fueling a helicopter out in the high desert, I was told to park the truck, lock it up, and jump in the helicopter. We were leaving the truck up there.

As soon as we took off, the pilot asked, "Ya wanna fly?"

"You bet your ass!" I said. I flew it all the way home. That would happen a lot more in the future. In about six months with the company I actually had more time in helicopters than I did in airplanes. Thanks, Mom!

On many lift jobs the helicopter needed to be as light as possible. Often we would remove doors, seats, and extra flight controls to make the aircraft lighter. The mechanics would also take out the extra set of flight controls when we had to carry a lot of people around. The extra cyclic, collective, and pedals had to be taken out to make more room to put more people in the helicopter. The first time I went out on one of these operations, I wasn't driving a fuel truck and was just there to assist however I was needed. Just the pilot and I were flying out to the job, and at the end of the day just the two of us would fly back. The pilot already had the aircraft running when he signaled me to come and hop in. I jumped in, and off we went. Immediately I saw that the extra flight controls were all missing. I was so bummed out that I wouldn't be flying on this trip. I didn't say a thing, but in the future if the extra controls had to be removed, they would either be with me in my backpack if I was flying or safely stowed away in the fuel truck if I was driving. I built a lot of flight time going to and from various jobs—sometimes just a few tenths of an hour; other times two, three, or four hours.

By this time I had already received my private pilot license for single-engine land airplanes only. Once you had your private license, the VA would help you pay for your commercial license. They wanted to make sure that you were serious about flying before they shelled out the kind of money that might be required for your particular commercial certificate. If you went through the time and expense to get your private license, you were definitely serious. I was! Most everyone who wants to be a pilot usually thinks of working for the airlines. Before joining the navy, so did I. But after four years around helicopters in the navy and now a year at Western, I didn't want to be a commercial airplane pilot. I wanted to be a commercial helicopter pilot!

Western was also a flight school for both airplanes and helicopters, but it wasn't a VA-approved school and would cost me way too much to fly there. There was no way I could afford it. There wasn't anything nearby until a company at Riverside airport started a VA-approved school there. They had an old Bell 47 D-1 helicopter, and believe it or not, it was one of the main helicopters used on the TV show *M*A*S*H*! Many times during my training with that helicopter, I would go out to fly, and it would be gone for a day or two for the show. So I went down to the school and signed up. They were charging a hundred dollars per hour, wet (meaning with fuel), to fly with an instructor. It was about sixty to eighty dollars an hour to fly the helicopter solo. But the VA had a 90/10 program at that time, which meant they would pay 90 percent and I only had to pay 10 percent. So for just ten dollars I could get an hour of training with an instructor. That was just too cool. I couldn't believe it. However, about halfway through my flight training in the helicopter, good old president Reagan changed the VA flight benefits to 60/40. Oh man! It was almost like Nixon had done to me changing the draft rules in 1970–71. Well, even forty dollars per hour was better than a hundred dollars per hour, but it did slow me down a little. My flights were fewer and far between again.

Nonetheless, less than two years after starting at Western, I received my commercial helicopter certificate. The next day I went to work early to show people that I had my new license. Of course they knew I was going through the flight training over in Riverside, but I never really told them what was happening or how quickly my training was coming along. I hadn't even told them that my check ride had been coming up.

My first stop was to see the director of maintenance, Ben. He was sitting in his chair in his office and looked up as I held up my temporary certificate. The official one would come in the mail soon. I said, "What do you think?"

He said, "What's that?"

"My new commercial helicopter license."

He just sat there, a little wide-eyed with his mouth half open, and didn't say a fucking word.

I didn't say anything mean or nasty to him, just "See ya later!" in my happy-as-hell voice as I walked out.

Next I went to tell the director of operations, the chief pilot, and the boss. They were all busy, which I knew and understood, but both the chief pilot and the director of operations stood up, shook my hand, and said congratulations.

The boss just looked up from his desk and said, "That's great," and looked back down at his paperwork. Kind of what I expected from him.

I wanted to hit him up about flying possibly soon but knew it would probably be best to be cool for a while. Back to work.

In the two years I had been working there, they had hired and let go two guys who ran the auto shop and were my supervisors. The first guy had known everything about the company as well as the cars and trucks, but the second guy, who had been a fairly good mechanic, had had no aviation experience and hadn't cared or known hardly anything about the facilities or company in general. By this time I knew everything. I could tell you where every nut, bolt, and aircraft or automotive part was and knew almost every part number. I knew every pipe fitting for all water systems throughout the facilities and every wire electrical fitting and outlet—I knew where they were, what they were, and how to repair or change them. I knew all the outside fuel systems, lines, and filters and everything on the trucks as well. I knew when each vehicle or aircraft needed service or maintenance. I knew the exact hour on each aircraft Hobbs meter and each vehicle's mileage and next service date.

They were about to hire another guy to run the auto shop and be my boss. They called me in to talk about it with the director of maintenance, the chief pilot, the director of operations, and the boss. When they started going through the résumés submitted to the director of operations, I stopped them and said, "Why are you guys doing this?"

"What do you mean?" asked the chief pilot.

"Why don't you just hire a good mechanic, make me the facilities manager, and I'll run everything?"

They all looked at each other with a "Never thought of that!" look, shrugged, and nodded in unison. The director of operations flipped through the résumés and pulled out one from a guy he knew well. The guy had no aviation background at all, but he was a good mechanic, and that was just what we needed. The guy was perfect, and he would become one of my best lifelong friends. Done. I was the new boss; I was the new facilities manager.

It was funny because, just like when I'd first been hired, it was another Friday afternoon, and Monday morning I ceased being an hourly employee and became a salaried employee. They even had business cards made for me, and even though I wasn't really a company pilot yet, my cards identified me as facilities manager / pilot. It was happening! I had paid my dues, and it was time to act.

Just a few days after I got my license, I scheduled some flight time with an instructor to fly our little piston-powered Hughes 300 helicopter. I really couldn't afford it, but I wanted to show them that I was a good pilot and determined to fly. I had flown the Hughes 300, as well as every other aircraft in our company, many times before, but I had to get checked out in it and do some emergency procedures with one of Western's instructors before I would be able to fly it on my own. I only had to fly just under an hour with the instructor and was signed off to fly on my own. The next day I flew with my girlfriend and gave rides for a few of my other friends. Less than a week later I was told a nice twin-engine aircraft was coming in for fuel, which surprised me. Yes, we did sell fuel occasionally, both jet fuel and aviation gasoline, but we charged the highest prices for both of anyone at the airport. Mostly we just used all the fuel in our own aircraft.

After the aircraft parked and shut down and the doors opened, four or five men and women all dressed in suits stepped out and went straight into the boss's office. After topping off both tanks, I asked our chief pilot, "Who were the suits?" He said they were from our insurance company. Ding!

They were in a meeting with the boss for about two hours, and I kept a watch on their aircraft as I went about my work. When they finally came out, I was ready and waiting at the plane, doors open, paperwork ready for them to sign. As I helped them in, the guy I assumed was the boss came up to sign for the gas. After a few pleasantries—nice aircraft, nice day, etc.—I casually asked him, "Is it true the company's insurance requires a thousand hours to fly all these aircraft?"

He answered back very nicely, "Oh no. For the turbine jet engine aircraft, yes, but for all the other airplanes and helicopters—reciprocating/ piston engine aircraft—we just require the proper certificates or licenses with required category and class of aircraft." The categories were fixed wing or rotorcraft, and the classes were single-engine land or dual-engine land and helicopter or gyroplane. "And of course you have to be checked out by the company's chief pilot in each aircraft," he added.

"Oh, interesting." I said. "Thank you."

He climbed back in, their pilot started up the aircraft, and they slowly taxied back out toward the runway. I stood there with a huge smile on my face waving to them, and they waved back through their little windows.

I didn't want to show my hand too quickly, so I waited a couple of days before going in to see the boss and spring my little trap. I waited until just before noon, then went in and knocked on his door. "Are you busy right now?" I asked.

He didn't have a clue what I was up to and said, "No, come in. What's up?"

I flat out asked if he had found out anything more from our insurance company about me flying. "Is it really a thousand hours still?" I asked. The last time we'd talked he'd said he would talk to them, but he hadn't. He said he hadn't gotten a chance but would talk to them soon. *Horse shit!* I thought. He scooted his chair back from his desk and started gathering up his papers, as if to say, *Meeting over. Get out.*

I asked, "Well, how about if I call or go see them and check?"

He sat right up wide-eyed and said, "No, no. I'll do that. I'll talk to them tomorrow. Okay?"

"Okay, thank you!" I said and turned and walked out. What a lying fucker! He knew exactly what the insurance company's policy was; he had always known. Just as I had always thought, he was trying to hold me back.

Two days later, he called me into his office. He said that the insurance was okay for me to fly the piston aircraft but not the turbines. "Really? Cool!" I said. Wink, wink. Within two days I would start flying!

We did maintenance on other company's aircraft as well, and we had recently overhauled the engine and put new blades on a Bell 47 from a tuna boat. Their pilot had flown it up and dropped it off a couple of weeks before. None of the other pilots in our company had flown a 47 before, so the chief pilot asked if I wanted to give it a test flight with one of the mechanics. Gee, let me think. "I'd be glad to," I said nonchalantly. Here it was, finally, after all these years of dreaming, working, and hoping. I was walking out, with a mechanic, to fly officially as a real company pilot!

I flew that helicopter a few more times before their pilot came up to fly it back to San Diego. Next, I flew all day long for two days at the Rialto airport airshow giving rides around the airport for about five minutes each. Various passenger and photo flights came along, and then I worked a lot during the US Festival, a huge outdoor concert. For two days I flew back and forth all day long carrying people who didn't want to fight the traffic to and from that huge event. I flew a bunch of big-name rock stars, which was way cool, and even flew an MTV crew to make a video. After filming and flying around the concert area, they were very surprised and got really excited when I asked them if they knew about the nudist colony nearby. They definitely wanted to shoot that!

For the next eight to nine months I was flying often but not as long or as much as I would like. One day, while working out on the flight line, one of the secretaries called out over the loudspeaker that I had a phone call. I ran into my office. It was from one of the tuna-boat pilots I had been bugging for almost a year about a flying job on one of the boats. He asked me if I still wanted to fly on a boat, and I jumped right up out of my seat and said, "Yes!" He said it would be on a boat with a Bell 47 and asked if that was all right. I assured him that would be fine but said I had to check with my boss. I told him I would call him back in a few minutes, and he said he would wait.

I ran into the boss's office and asked him if he would let me take a two- or three-month leave of absence and then come back when I was through.

He said, "No, you'll have to quit!"

So I said, "Fine, I quit!" Of course I gave him the company's required two-week notice.

I raced back to my office and called the guy back. I would go down the following weekend to check out the aircraft and do whatever was necessary to get it ready for the upcoming trip. Of course they would need to meet me and have their mechanic fly with me to see if I was worth a damn or not. A couple of days later I was down at Gillespie Field in San Diego where the helicopter would be taken care of after each trip. It was immaculate. It had been completely rebuilt from top to bottom and looked like a new helicopter. I met everyone—the boat's owners, mechanics, and so on—and I liked them all very much. And thankfully, they liked me and thought that I was a fine pilot. I would no longer be a part-time pilot, a facilities manager / pilot. My career as a full-time pilot had begun! I love you always, Mom. Thank you, thank you, thank you!

Me taking Mom on her first flight in a helicopter.

Dad's first flight with me.

Me with "Superman" Christopher Reeve in Southern California.
He was a glider pilot and a very good one. We flew around
him while he was flying, filming him for a TV special.

Christopher just before takeoff.

The newspaper the morning after the *Twilight Zone: The Movie* accident.

Me with my helicopter and a beautiful chauffeur and her Rolls-Royce. Cover picture for a newspaper story on how to spend $10,000 in one day in the Inland Empire, San Bernardino, California.

As a member of the Valley College flying team in San Bernardino, California, I won a gold medal in the airplane power-off spot landing event. The SAFECON was attended by ten colleges, included fifty participants, and was held at San Jose State that year.

10

The Draft Lottery

As the Vietnam War grew larger and the need for more troops increased, the US government began to draft more and more men into service. They would draw balls from what looked like a bingo-game machine with Ping-Pong balls tumbling around inside. They picked one ball at a time from 365 balls numbered with all 365 dates of the year and assigned that ball a lottery number, starting at one. So for example, the first ball, November 17, was number 1; May 24 was number 2; and so on. I first became aware of the draft after we moved to Guam when I was thirteen years old. I wasn't eligible, but I watched just to see where I might be. They wouldn't draft all 365 dates picked. They were taking up to about 195 then. All the years before my eighteenth birthday I was really high in all the draws, 300 or better. The year I turned eighteen they changed the way they drew. They now had two machines. From one machine they would draw a ball with a date, and from the other machine they would draw a lottery number to be assigned to that date. For example, on the first draw they might pull the June 5 date ball from one machine and the 320 number ball from the other, and so June 5 birthdays would have a lottery number of 320 as opposed to 1.

The existing draft law was to expire at the end of June 1971, but in February that year it was extended for one year. By 1971, they were drafting up to about number 100. When my birthdate was drawn, February 1, they drew number 12! It kind of freaked me out a little, but my girlfriend instantly burst into tears. I wasn't really worried, though, because I knew I was going to college after high school and would have fifteen credits or more. Anyone in college with fifteen or more credits was deferred from the draft. This was really a big deal at the time. All the kids who could afford school wouldn't have to go, and the ones who couldn't did.

I had come back to Oxnard, California, again, from Iowa at the beginning of my senior year in high school. I would graduate from Port Hueneme High School, my third and final high school. After twelve years I had done well, gotten pretty good grades, and really wanted to go to college, but I couldn't afford a good college. Now that I was about to be free, I knew it might be hard to keep myself motivated. I registered at Ventura Community College and was doing okay. However, the partying had begun. It was a blast. I was an adult, and I was free even though I was living at home. And I dug it! I got a part-time job at Sunkist in Ventura, and for a few hours after school I would clean up and load trucks until the night watchman came in. It was cool. I moved into an apartment with my friend RM for a little while, and all we did was party. I went to classes, did my homework, worked a few hours, and then partied.

However, it wasn't long before President Nixon brought all of that to an end, pretty much. He ended all deferments and said everyone was going. Vietnam was slowing some but was still cooking. We watched battles still raging over there almost every night on TV while we ate dinner. I figured I would soon be on my way. My partying increased, and my class attendance slowed. I wasn't sure where I was going, what my future really was. My dad had been pushing me for a year to just join the military, saying, "Vietnam will be over soon, and you have a chance for VA benefits now if you join and come back!" That "and come back" made me a little nervous. He was right, though; there would be no or much-reduced VA benefits if the war ended. If I did go in, I would definitely want money for school and cheap loans for buying a home as well as much more when I got out.

I got by until the end of first semester and thought that was enough college for me. Sunkist had offered me a full-time job, and I thought I would give it a shot. I could have a little more fun before the draft came after me or I enlisted first. My girlfriend was a senior in high school, and we planned to marry when she finished. So I went to work full-time at Sunkist and just hated it. I spent all day cleaning, loading lemons into trucks, or stacking boxes of lemons to be cleaned, sorted, and shipped. I was working there with my best friends RM and JP. RM had been there first and had gotten me on part-time; JP had come later. All we did was work, get stoned every chance we could, and then party after work. In addition to drinking, we were smoking a lot then, something I'd said I would never do. But during a party in Iowa, of all places, a beautiful girl I'd been trying to get to know had smiled and passed me a pipe loaded with weed, and I'd taken it without hesitation. Later that night, while laughing my ass off and stomping around in ankle-deep water in a driving rainstorm, I'd wondered if it had been the beer, the pot, or both that had made me feel so great.

I really swore I would never do anything else, especially pills, until one of the nights I was cleaning rotten, purple, fuzzy lemons with a new guy at Sunkist. He was a Vietnam vet who had just come back, and this had been the only job he could get. That really made me worry! He walked up to me while I was sweeping up the rotten lemons underneath the conveyor belts and said, "Here, try these!"

"What are these?" I asked.

"White crosses!" he said, meaning meth. "They won't hurt you or freak you out or anything; they'll just help you work."

So I quickly popped down the two he gave me and went back to work. It wasn't long before I realized how much I really, really liked cleaning! I wanted to talk and share this with someone. I couldn't believe how good I felt. Before I left, he gave me a bunch more for later, and I shared some of them with my girlfriend. We had such a great night and the best sex! I gave some to JP and RM the next day, and they went straight to our new friend to get more. Those little pills were great at first, but I didn't like getting so wired up all the time, and after a short time I only did them occasionally.

My friends and I continued on working there and partying a lot. I still wondered if this was all I was going to have. Though the government and the draft hadn't come for me yet, the possibility still hung over me. One day a good friend of ours showed up driving a big, expensive, brand-new GMC van. He told us he had gotten a job at General Motors Company in Van Nuys, California. He was making eighteen dollars an hour while we were making a little bit above minimum wage. In 1972 minimum wage was $1.60. He was driving around in this beautiful, cool van, which was loaded, with a stereo and custom interior, and whenever we saw him, he always had beautiful girls with him. We were so jealous, but little did we know about assembly-line work. We begged him for an application. We would run into him often at parties or the beach and every time pleaded for an application from him, but he never gave us one.

Finally, I couldn't take Sunkist any longer and went to see the navy recruiter. I tested and scored really high and had my choice of whatever I wanted to do. I decided to go, and my girlfriend said she would stay by my side and wait for me no matter what happened or where I went. Boy, what a sucker I was! Two weeks before I was to enlist my GM friend showed up at Sunkist with an application for me. I was so bummed out and wasn't sure what to do, but I had had it with factory work. I was kind of excited about the training I would receive in the navy and what it could possibly mean for me in the future, but mostly I was excited about a new adventure. So I gave the application to RM, and two weeks later I was in the United States Navy. RM would go on to work at GM but really had some tough times. He did it, though, and retired after thirty years.

11

In the Jungles of Myanmar

I went to the local library and asked the librarian where I could find anything on Burma. He said, "You mean Myanmar."

I thought he said Miramar, as in Miramar, California, and said, "No, Burma near India and Thailand."

"It's called Myanmar now," he said.

I thought I was pretty up on world events, but I'd never heard that. I knew some of the country's history, mostly from World War II. I knew it had been a British colony for a long time, and of course I knew about Aung San Suu Kyi and her struggles for democracy and being under house arrest for so long. I was about to be sent there, courtesy of a foreign country's company.

The company I was flying for in Corona, California, had gotten in eight foreign guys (FGs) for flight training. They were going to be flying FAA N-registered aircraft in Myanmar and would need to be FAA licensed. They were all former army pilots, and we figured they would be great. Boy, were we in for a surprise. They were terrible and were the most arrogant, egotistical assholes I'd ever met. To be fair, they weren't all terrible, but most were. Many pilots, even Americans, have pretty big egos at times, but these guys were beyond that. The first one I flew with was the worst. As soon as I tried to tell him something, he said, "You don't have to tell me anything; I'm such and such nationality!" They didn't even want to look at the aircraft for preflight checks. They said that was the mechanic's job. They hadn't ever flown any of the aircraft we were going to be training them in, and we told them that the preflight was also a way to get to know the aircraft. They refused until we said they wouldn't be flying with us unless they did. Grudgingly they accepted. But every single time we pointed something out to them, they would say, "I know, I know!" That got really old, really fast!

I'd had bad student pilots occasionally that I would have loved to just strangle sometimes, but I couldn't, of course; I just had to talk them through things and maybe go over things a few times until they improved. I always told every student, from the first time I flew with him or her, that if I said I had the aircraft, he or she had to let go of the controls. I had never gotten to the point where I had to take the aircraft away from a student or let him or her have it verbally, until now! I put up with the FGs' attitudes and egos for a couple of days but finally lost it.

We were at Riverside airport, a tower-controlled airport, in the helicopter practice area on the north side of the field. We would take off toward the main runway but would turn right just before reaching it and remain on the north side in a right traffic pattern. We had always been warned to not overfly the active runway. Before the first takeoff, I warned this guy to stay clear of the runway. "I know!" he said.

He took off and flew right over the top of the runway as I said, "Runway, runway, *runway!*"

"I know, I know!" he said.

The tower called us and said, "Please do not overfly the active runway!"

I replied, "Roger. Sorry."

We came around, landed, and took off again, and I said, again, "Don't go near the runway!"

Again he said, "I know, I know." He then promptly went right over the runway again.

The tower called us again and said, "For the last time, please remain clear of the active runway."

After another apology from me, we came around, landed, and took off again. I said, one more time, "Don't go near the runway!"

"I know I know!" he said one more time. But he was headed right for the runway again!

I yelled at him, "I have the controls!" I took over and banked hard right, probably ten to twenty feet from the edge of the runway. I flew clear and landed in an open field. He looked at me big eyed, like, *What's going on?* I told him we were done for the day and that I did not want to hear one more "I know, I know." I said that unless he did exactly as I said, without any comment from then on out, I was done flying with him. He swallowed hard and nodded his head yes. I took off, cleared the airport traffic area, and gave him back the controls.

When we'd landed, I told him to shut the aircraft down and come inside when he was finished tying it down. I went straight into the office of the director of operations and told him what had happened. He informed me that, as I suspected, the other pilots were showing the same attitudes toward the other instructors. We called them all in, sat them down, and told them exactly what I'd told my last student: to stop talking back and do what they were told, or their training was over! And they did. They were still terrible pilots, though, and it took a lot of work to get them all up to speed to pass their check rides.

Army pilots are almost always flying off airport into rough or dangerous terrain. Many landings are made on sloped ground, and you must know certain techniques to be able to land safely. You have to know how it's done and how much of a slope you can land on without rolling the aircraft over, all the while being aware of your main-rotor and tail-rotor clearances. The first time I said we would be going out to do slope landings, they all said,

"What's that?" I couldn't believe it; they had never landed off airport! With all their flight time and years in the army, they had always landed and taken off from airport helipads. They were going to be flying in the jungles of Myanmar! Yes, the base camp had a hangar and concrete ramp with helipads, but the rig site, or well site, where they were building the huge drilling rig, did not. What if they had to make a precautionary or emergency landing out in the jungle somewhere?

These guys were going to be sent into the middle of nowhere to fly people and parts to build an oil drilling tower. Most of the flying would be long line and not passengers, and I'd assumed all these guys were experienced long-line pilots, but I was wrong. We soon found out the company wanted one of us to go with the FGs to fly. I thought that was cool. I was up for another adventure, but I knew all the other pilots would want to go also and wasn't sure if the company would want me or if my company would let me go. When it came close to the FGs finishing up and going, the boss called a meeting with all the pilots. When he asked us who wanted to go with them, we all raised our hands. There were really only two of us in the room that were qualified, though, as they were going to need long-line pilots. One other guy and I had a lot of long-line experience; the other guys didn't have any or had only minimal time flying external loads. The guy in charge of the FGs picked me. I thought he picked me because of my experience, but later he told me that while my experience was a big part of it, it was mostly because I didn't take any crap from his guys and he liked the way I set them straight in the beginning.

In the next few days I got checked out in the helicopter I'd be flying in the jungle, the Bell 214. What a workhorse that was going to be! I really liked it. It was big, fast, and maneuverable too. Soon after, I was on my way to Bangkok, Thailand. I had to go there and get a visa from Myanmar's embassy there first. It was actually just a little consulate building down some little side street. I spent three or four days there, then departed for Yangon (no longer called Rangoon), Myanmar. Yangon was hot and humid like Thailand, the Philippines, New Guinea, and other jungle areas I'd been to before and had that same dark, earthy, damp smell I really liked.

But I could see right off this country was quite different. Myanmar was really lacking. Even the airport in Bangkok, as well as the city, had been pretty modern and new, though surrounded by poverty everywhere. But Myanmar's airport was like something you might find in some very far-out-of-the-way spot in a third-world country. No hangars, just two terminal buildings and a small makeshift tower. And there were armed soldiers everywhere! I was the only white guy who got off the airplane. I was instantly taken to a side area to have everything I had completely searched, from my camera case and each film container to every pocket in all my shirts and shorts. They even unzipped and checked every single pocket of the two flight suits I'd brought.

I had seen the guy who was supposed to pick me up, but they held him back until they figured I was okay. Once I had everything all repacked, the driver and I were off to the company house outside of Yangon with the BBC playing over the radio. The drive was amazing. It looked like everyone was dirt-poor, far more so than I'd thought. Every house I saw was not much more than a shack until we got to the company's place. There were nice homes there but nothing lavish, kind of like North Shore beach homes in Hawaii tucked into trees and gardens. The area was really pretty. Everything was beautiful green jungle from the airport to this place.

What really amazed me, though, were the old homes left by the British—not really homes, that makes them sound small, but huge mansions from Britain's colonial heyday. All were tucked back off the road and semi-overgrown with vegetation. They all looked as if they'd been burned and looted—charred black, no windows or doors, only bare walls. However, you could see how really grand they must've been based on the overgrown gardens, fountains, walls, and gates. It looked as though each owner or builder had been trying to outdo his neighbor. The homes must have been really lavish in their time, and the owners must have lived the life of ease! I'm sure, to most people, they are reminders of colonization, but in a way it was almost sad to see these big, beautiful, grand artifacts gone forever, reduced to dilapidated skeletons among the lush, green floral surroundings.

We arrived at the company house just after dark. I was beat and just wanted to get something to eat and go to bed. There was really nothing around the neighborhood to do anyway. Early morning I discovered it was still a bit like colonial times. There were maids and a butler, gardeners working outside, and three of four cooks hard at work in the kitchen. I was served a great breakfast and afterward told the housekeepers I was going to go for a walk. They led me to the front door, opened it, and all lined up and bowed as I left, telling me to be careful and not get lost.

I headed down to the main road. I knew there wasn't anything to the left, because that was how the driver and I had come into the neighborhood, so I turned right. It was then I noticed the lake on the other side of the road through the trees. I hadn't seen that last night. The side I was walking on had a sidewalk lined with pretty little homes. There weren't any houses on the other side, so I crossed over. I looked for a place to get to the lake as I walked along, but there was a lot of underbrush in front of the trees and no way to get in. The first house I noticed coming up on my left had some railings and cones around the front, and I thought they must be doing some road construction ahead. I was still some way off but could see a guy standing out front. I had heard a lot of people speaking English at the airport yesterday and had been told many people around here spoke English very well, though with a British accent. *I'll bet he speaks a little English and can tell me how I can get into the lake,* I thought as I got closer. He looked an awful lot like he was wearing a uniform. Just as I thought that, he saw me. He turned toward me and put on his helmet, which had been on one of the cones next to him. It was then I also noticed the rifle slung across his chest. He turned and started walking toward me. I was sure he would think I was harmless, just wearing sandals, a T-shirt, and shorts, and would show me the way to the lake or to town.

He unslung his rifle as he walked toward me and brought it out in front of him. I instantly stopped just as my heart was about to as well. At that same moment I heard, "Craig!" over my right shoulder. It was the butler from the house. A little bit after I'd walked out, a couple of the staff had looked at each other and gone, "Uh-oh!" thinking exactly this might happen, so they'd sent someone after me. Turned out, this was the very house where Aung San Suu Kyi was being held under house arrest! No one was allowed on that side of the street near her place. Luckily the butler got me just in time and hurried me back to the other side of the street. The whole while the guard, joined by two more from the other side of the house, scowled at me as if he was disappointed that he wasn't going to get to shoot someone today. The butler showed me how to get to the lake. There really wasn't much to the lake and not much of a town or anything special to see, so we just headed back. I wish I would've had a chance to see Aung San!

The next day, I went back to the airport and got on board a twin turboprop for a long flight to Mandalay. After a quick refuel, we were off northwest along the Chindwin River up to a place near the border with India. We landed on a tiny asphalt strip in the center of a small village that was really pretty. The company's BK-117 helicopter was there waiting for me, and off we went to the base camp, about thirty to forty minutes' flight east over some small mountains. The base camp was right on the west side of the Chindwin River. There was a small maintenance hangar with a concrete ramp. The helicopters were parked out front because they were too big to fit inside. The housing units were prefab containers with bathroom, shower, and beds. There were about twenty of them with one big container that was the kitchen, cafeteria, and laundry all in one. The camp was fairly big. All the trees and brush had been cut back for it all the way up to the river's edge, and everything here had been brought up by boat.

Everything we would be flying out to the rig site—pipe of all sizes, drills, motors, generators, and so on—was stacked in neat order next to the river. The first thing that caught my eye, though, was the Fort Apache–style wood walls surrounding the camp on three sides. The rig was a drilling platform being erected over an oil deposit. On the first flight to the rig site I actually saw the oil literally bubbling out of the ground. Just like the early days of oil, tall towers had been built resembling giant Erector sets. The approach from the river side was open. A big gate had been built where a dirt road came in from a really small village about one hundred yards south of us. Just like the old cavalry forts, there were towers at each corner with heavily armed military guards in each. I mean *really* heavily armed guards, some with .50-caliber machine-gun bandoliers crossing over their chests and shoulders. Each had more hand grenades on him than I had ever seen any military person carry, and every guy was wearing a belt loaded with huge mortar rounds all the way around his waist. They were here to protect us from the guerrillas the military had been fighting for some time. None of this had been mentioned before I'd come here! In time these guys would scare me more than the so-called guerrilla threat would.

Two other American pilots had been hired besides me, but there would only be two of us at a time flying, as we would rotate on and off in country. There were eight FG pilots and three FG mechanics. There was also a British mechanic and one Singaporean mechanic as well. I had been told back in the States that all the flying would be dual pilot. I just assumed we would be flying American-American and FG-FG. I was in for a real surprise the first morning when I met the guy in charge of the operations here, Captain K. He flew with each new guy after we arrived, and once he gave his stamp of approval, I was Captain Craig.

I had a local kid from the village who was assigned to take care of me. He was a great little guy! He cleaned, made up the room, did my laundry every day, and ran errands for anything I needed. My first roommate was one of the other American pilots, who turned out to be a real asshole, and after two days I moved into an empty container room by myself. Everyone else was great and really nice to me. The food was good, and the kitchen staff would make anything I wanted every morning or evening. The local people were curious about us and were friendly whenever I met any of them. We weren't supposed to be wandering away from the base camp, but when I had free time, I would walk up or down the river and just say *menglaba* (hello) to everyone I met. *Jesutembare* (thank you) was the only other word I knew, but those two words were just about all I really needed. I drew a crowd whenever I went by the river or near the village. Way up here in the jungle most all these people had never seen a big white guy before. There was no electricity or TV, only small battery-operated radios that I would hear occasionally.

We had two big Bell 214s we would fly every day. The BK-117 was only used to go back and forth to that small airport. The first night Captain K called all the pilots into the hangar for a meeting and told us what we were to do. As mentioned before, though I knew the FGs weren't that great, I'd assumed they had long-line experience. We hadn't done any long-line practice with them back in California, because we were just getting them licensed. I should've known better! Captain K told us that we would be flying American-FG crews and that the American pilots were going to teach the FGs to fly long line. I was pissed! I immediately said so and told him that wasn't what I had been hired to do. I'd come there to work with those big boys; I didn't want to teach. He took me aside and apologized up and down. He told me what a good pilot I was and how much they needed me and, almost to tears, begged me to try. He was really just playing on my ego and emotions. I didn't have much choice. What was I going to do? Quit? I was in the middle of fucking nowhere! So I agreed. I'd figured I'd seen the worst from the FGs already. They couldn't get much worse, could they? What a sucker I was!

Every external load we would be carrying would push each helicopter to its redline, its power limit. Not only would we be carrying, almost every other load, giant eight-thousand-pound pipes but also more prefab buildings, loads of very heavy teak wood, and many other things that would be a challenge even for the American pilots who had pretty good experience.

The next morning I was up and had breakfast at five o'clock. Afterward I went out to preflight my helicopter. I was by myself at breakfast and for a good part of my preflight before the FG pilots showed up. This was the same every morning, and I would realize why sometime later. All the mechanics were already out there. The FG mechanics never talked to me unless they needed something, but the Singaporean and British guys were really cool and top-notch mechanics. When the FG pilots finally showed up, I told the guy who was to fly with me that I had already checked the aircraft out but that he was welcome to do his own preflight. He said no, that the FG mechanics had already checked. Now, yes, they had, but I couldn't believe he was putting his life into another person's hands. The FGs were right back to the way they'd been when they'd first come to California to train. I really thought I had instilled the importance of checking themselves, but oh well. That was why the FG mechanics wouldn't talk to me. They thought I didn't trust them. I didn't! I knew they were good mechanics, all licensed guys are or should be in taking care of aircraft, but you just can't take a chance in any aircraft you fly that some little thing might have been missed! A week later I would prove how important that was.

After breakfast I came out to my ship, and one of the FG mechanics was up doing some work on the rotor-head gearbox, the transmission. I said, "Morning!" He grunted as I started my preflight. I worked my way around the aircraft, untied the blades, and then climbed on top. Looking at the blades end to end, I began to turn them, checking rods, linkage, and swash plate. I'd just made one-half a turn scanning down from the top of the rotor mast to the transmission when I saw the mechanic's inspection mirror stuck in the swash plate next to one of the control arms. If I hadn't caught it, it could have caused major damage when starting up, or worse! Now, it happens; everyone makes mistakes sometimes, but all aircraft mechanics are supposed to inventory every tool in their box after doing anything on any aircraft. That's why all their toolboxes have slots and shelves for every single tool. If a mechanic looks in the box and a tool is not in its slot, that aircraft better not move or even start before that tool is found. I put the mirror in my flight suit and finished my preflight.

I went over to the mechanic, who was standing near the aircraft with his hands behind his back, watching me but trying to act as if he wasn't. I asked him if this mirror was his, and he said yes as he reached for it. I pulled it back and blocked him from getting it. I told him about the unwritten rule that nearly all pilots and mechanics know: if a pilot finds any tool, anything of the mechanic's on a preflight, it belongs to that pilot. The mechanic has to buy another of whatever it is. He had never heard of this rule and was getting pissed and talking louder. Captain K heard him and came over, and the mechanic started up and got very animated, probably saying in their language what an asshole I was and that I'd stolen his inspection mirror. When Captain K turned to me, I told him where I'd found the mirror and said that the mechanic wasn't getting it back and that I would snap it into pieces and shatter it on the ground before I gave it back to him.

Turned out Captain K knew the rule and started explaining it to the mechanic. The mechanic looked like he was going to cry but just looked down and walked away. The other FG pilots were standing there watching all of this, and when the mechanic walked away, I said, "See, guys, this is why I pushed you so much to do your own preflight!" They all nodded in agreement as they said, "Hmmmm." It didn't make a damn bit of difference; they still never did a preflight!

I never told anyone, but I took the inspection mirror back to the hangar office that night after dinner. I walked up to the mechanic, who was doing paperwork, pulled out his mirror, and started to hand it back to him. He brought up his hands and flinched. He thought I was going to punch him or something. He was in shock and took the mirror with his mouth wide open. I just said, "Be careful, okay?" He didn't say a word but nodded his head in a little half bow, saying yes. It was funny; after that the mechanics were finally nice to me every morning.

Quickly I felt more and more comfortable with the aircraft. I knew pretty much what it could and could not do as well as our route of flight to and from the rig site. After going over our first obstacle, a small village, there was nothing out there but jungle, and we could fly directly to the rig. That small village, our biggest concern, was directly across the river from our base camp. It was sort of split in two with about eight to ten buildings on the left and ten to fifteen buildings on the right, including a Buddhist temple. The two sides were separated by about fifty to one hundred feet. We had all decided from the beginning that we would never fly over the village or over the gap between the buildings. Even though we probably could fly over the gap, there were always people walking back and forth between the two sides. Outside our "fort," we were surrounded by tall teak trees cut back about one hundred feet on our north, south, and west sides. To our east, across the river and east of the village, the trees had also been cleared back, who knows how long ago, and from the village it was all rice fields for about a mile north, south, and east to where the hills began to rise up. So we would pick up whatever load we were to sling and head to the left, northeast, and then make just a slight right turn after the village to a heading of about ninety-five to one hundred degrees to the rig site.

I had already picked out a certain hill far in the distance that I would use each time that would line me up perfectly. However, just a week or so after starting my flying, an FG flying with the other American in the other helicopter panicked and pushed his hook-release button while carrying a big white prefab kitchen container. They were flying at a pretty good speed, and when it hit the teak trees below, it exploded into a million pieces. It left a long white line of debris that pointed directly toward the rig site. "Follow the white kitchen road!"

The very first loads I flew with each pilot, I would lift the load and have the other pilot just hold the controls and feel what I was doing. Doing long line is really about getting a feel for it, a seat-of-the-pants kind of thing where you know just what the line is doing. But we also had chin bubble mirrors outside below the nose in front of the window of the helicopter that would let you see the line. You could tell what it was doing and could control it accordingly with the mirrors, but I liked leaning out my side window and visually checking and steadying the load before I went anywhere with it. After lifting off and getting the line up and clear of everything, I would move the helicopter over, putting the hook into one of the loadmasters' hands. Then it was just a matter of centering the aircraft directly over the load while putting tension on the line. I'd say 80 percent of the loads we took ran transmission and engine torques right up to their redline limits. From the very first time I let one of the FGs take over, I immediately had to ensure they didn't pull the aircraft right up through those limits, which they tried to do every single time. I always had to hold my hand over the collective control, the power-up-or-down control, and keep tapping or pushing it down as they tried to pull harder and overtorque everything.

Those big birds were amazing! All you had to do was pull up and get tension on the line, then ease up to just below redline on the transmission torque gauge and wait. In that hot, humid, early-morning air the blades would start making these beautiful vapor trail circles around the aircraft. I called them my guardian angel halos. Then, after a second or two, without having to pull any harder, the load would begin to rise! You just had to hold it, let it come up and get clear, and then ever so gently ease the cyclic stick forward. The helicopter would begin to move, the blades would develop more lift, and then up and away you would go!

Once we were around the village and headed toward the site, most loads would settle down, but those huge pipes about thirty or forty feet long and three and a half to four feet in diameter would give us a ride. More often than not each load would usually weather-vane with the airflow of our forward motion and stay parallel to us all the way there. The pipes, however, would do one of two things. They would either catch wind going through one end and fly parallel with us, which I preferred, or they would turn until the wind stopped them perpendicular to us, pointing out each side. Talk about the tail wagging the dog! As you start out, your nose dips down forward and the load swings back a little, but it actually pulls back on you at the same time, and you begin to go nose up a little as the load tries to catch up to you again. So you have this teetering motion with a pretty violent shaking all the way out. Bump, bump, bump, bump … Then there's calm as the load comes a little forward. Then bump, bump, bump again. A little nerve-racking, but you get used to it. These FGs never did, though, and they would panic all the time.

As soon as we'd start out, I'd have to stay with them on the controls every time because they almost never got the aircraft centered over the load, and I would have to really push on the cyclic to center us. If you tried to pick up a load off center, it would swing out and could possibly hurt someone. As the load would come up, if it moved even the slightest bit, the FGs would panic and start overcorrecting back in the opposite direction. Soon they would be all over the place scaring the shit out of everyone on the ground. If the load moves left, you should ever so slightly move your cyclic control left and get over it, and it will stop. And if it moves right, you move right. Sometimes you can just pull a little more power, and as you start to get more lift moving forward, the load will center itself underneath you as you climb out. But the FGs could never even get going. Each time they would panic, stop their forward motion, and start overcontrolling, chasing the load all the time and yelling, in their exact words, "I cannot!

I cannot!" I would keep tapping the cyclic forward, trying to get them to just go, but would inevitably have to grab it, push forward, and get them out of a mess that would only get worse if I didn't. I actually let them go farther than I should have a couple of times in the hopes they would get the hang of it, but they never did. They had the loads swinging so wildly that twice if I hadn't stopped their swinging we would have been looking at our loads out the left or right side windows, and that would not be good!

After a couple of weeks I got probably one of the biggest scares of my life. I was flying army soldiers out to the rig site. They guarded that as well as the base camp. Suddenly there was a loud bang behind me. I snapped around to see what it was. I couldn't see anything wrong with the aircraft, but one of the soldiers was bent forward holding his stomach. I instantly thought he was getting airsick and was about to puke. At the same moment I began to smell smoke. It took a second to register that the smell wasn't from the aircraft; it was gunpowder I was smelling. A big pool of blood had started to form underneath the bent-over soldier. The soldier sitting next to him had his rifle sitting across his lap and had accidentally fired it into the poor guy's side. The shot soldier was already turning pale, and I knew he would need help quick. The blood pool was getting bigger, soaking into his shirt and pants. I was almost to the rig site, and both it and the base camp had small dispensaries with medical people, so I just headed for the rig. In minutes we landed. The other army guys got him out and carried him in. I kept the helicopter running and told them I'd wait to see if I would be needed to take him back. A couple of guys came out with a few buckets of water and washed the blood out. After about fifteen minutes, one of the medical people came out and told me to go back. The guy had died, and there was nothing I could do. Holy shit! Unbelievable. And what if that errant soldier had been pointing his rifle forward?

My FG partner and I flew back and continued working, flying loads back to the rig. On our third trip back to the site that day, I saw something new next to the area where we dropped our loads: a grave with a crude marker. I would see that every single time I flew in until I left. Poor guy! The soldiers really made me nervous after that, and they would give me even more reason to worry again later. Every night a local woman from the nearby village would set up a snack bar / beer joint next to our base camp. She only had warm Heineken beer; no electricity, so no fridge. She used gas lanterns for light. I would go out there each night after I'd finished flying and gotten cleaned up. I'd have my house boy take a plastic five-gallon bucket to the kitchen and fill it with ice every afternoon before I took off for my last flight of the day. He would take it to her, and she would put in a six-pack of Heineken for me. By the time I got back, they were nice and cold. She would cook little things for us if we wanted, but I didn't eat much except for peanuts that I brought with me. Mostly what she did was crush up what I thought the locals called beetle nut but was actually betel nut. She would roll the betel nut powder in betel leaves that you could chew to get high. Some of the FGs would chew it, but it was mostly the soldiers who chewed it, a lot! I never did. I had seen it in Papua New Guinea (PNG) the one time I'd flown in there. Those who chewed it would get high, but it would also stain their teeth a terrible red color. Here, as in PNG, everywhere you went people had these ugly stained red teeth.

I usually only stayed at the beer-and-snack hut for a little while. We had to be up at five, so I tried to be asleep by ten every night. The FGs stayed up late every single night. I saw the soldiers only occasionally, two or three at a time, in there at night. I guess lots would come in later after I'd gone to bed. One night my house boy came into the hut just after I'd sat down and opened a beer. Right behind him came a group of eight to ten soldiers all wearing ammunition belts around their chests and shoulders, with a couple carrying those huge mortar rounds. I thought that was pretty odd. It also seemed as if they had already been hitting the betel nut pretty heavy. They all looked really high, were loud, and seemed pissed off. I said, "Menglaba" ("Hi") as they walked in, but not one said a word to me. My house boy whispered to me that this was not a good time to be there just as more started coming in. They began to look at me not nicely, talking to each other as they did so. I could feel that something was wrong, very wrong. It was time to go. I left all my beer in the bucket and quickly but quietly ducked out the curtain door.

Turned out they all carried little medical pouches on their belts that contained small glass ampoules of morphine to be used in case they were wounded. Apparently they were using the morphine every day. After that night I always kept my eyes on them whenever they were near and stayed completely away from them if I could. I didn't have to fly them any more before I left, thank God!

The FGs never got any better at all. I began to see one reason why. They would stay up late every single night drinking. Sometimes they would wake me up late at night or early in the morning. One night, I heard them around three thirty in the morning and thought, *What the fuck? We've got to be up soon!* I got up every morning at five o'clock, ate quickly, and headed to the flight line. It was really foggy every single morning because of the temperature, high humidity, and being right next to a river. The fog would last until almost ten o'clock every morning. We got out a couple of times maybe around nine o'clock, but that was rare. It was really that bad; you couldn't or shouldn't be going anywhere in the conditions we had.

The FGs, looking like shit, normally rolled out about eight or nine in the morning. If we would've had to fly any earlier, they would have been screwed. But within just a few days I would have my first real thoughts of getting the fuck out of here before something bad happened! Even though we weren't flying until around ten every morning, the FGs insisted on lunch at noon every day and wanted to stop for two hours. I didn't want to stop; neither did the other American pilot. We were working, getting a lot done, and we just loved the shit out of what we were doing! So they would get out at noon each day, and we would keep picking up loads and flying them out. It was actually great because the aircraft was a little lighter with them gone, but mostly, we were happy we didn't have to fuck with them, babysit them, help them, and prod them on every single load. Depending on each load, we would do six to eight flights while they were out. I was smoking. It was a blast. Yes, we were supposed to fly dual pilots only, but even Captain K was happy with our progress.

After just a day or two, each of the FG pilots flying with me would get back in the aircraft after lunch reeking of alcohol! *Fuck me! How much worse is this going to get?* I thought. I would not let them lift or land one more external load after that. They seemed perfectly content to just sit back and relax as I told them each time, "I have the controls!"

One day we had a break. The other American and I never did that, but the rig workers called on the radio and asked us to please stop for an hour or more. *Cool, I could use lunch today,* I thought. I went into the cafeteria with the Brit and Singaporean mechanics. As we were just finishing lunch, we heard one of the 214s starting up. It was a little odd, but we thought that some FG mechanics must be running one up to check something. We finished up and headed out just as the 214 was lifting off with two FGs at the controls. All these people we had never seen before were watching from down by the river as the FG pilots lifted off and hovered over to pick up a giant load of teakwood. I had no idea who all those people were. They must have flown in while I was out flying.

I walked up to Captain K, who was standing in front of the hangar, and asked what was going on. He said the people were from all the companies involved in this project. The drilling company, the rig-construction company, the helicopter company, the oil company, and especially the Myanmar government people were all here to see exactly what we were doing and, of course, to make money. I told the captain that this was a really bad idea. He insisted that his guys would be fine and said their company wanted to see only them and how great they had become as pilots.

A lot of the people from each company had video cameras rolling, and there were four big news media crews with cameras rolling as well. The FGs hovered over to the load of wood with their long line and lowered it to the New Zealand loadmaster, who quickly hooked it up and ran for his life from underneath the helicopter. He looked back at me, and though we couldn't hear each other, I could see him mouth, "What the fuck is going on?" I just raised my hands and shrugged my shoulders. "I don't know!" I mouthed back to him. They started pulling up without first centering the line over the load, and instantly the load swung hard to the right. Whoever was flying tried to get going to stabilize the load, as I'd told them a hundred times before, but the load swung violently back to the left. He did exactly what he was supposed to do next and chased the load back as it swung right. Unfortunately he turned it too quickly to get going, and the load swung toward the village. They just made it to the other side of the river when he stopped and tried to stabilize the swing, which was getting out of control. But he just kept chasing it, and it got worse and worse and began to swing far beyond what the aircraft could handle. I actually thought we were all about to witness a deadly crash. I had already seen three others, and this looked like that was going to be the inevitable outcome.

The swinging had carried them over the village by this time, and just when I was sure the aircraft would break apart or be thrown to the ground by that massive load of teak, the pilot punched the load off. Amazingly it fell and landed right between the gap in the village in their rice field with an explosive force that sent water two hundred or three hundred feet into the air, all the way up to the helicopter. It was such a huge splash I thought that the water might even bring the aircraft down. Everybody turned and looked at us as the aircraft turned and came back to land. We all turned and walked away from Captain K. He was the one who would have to answer for his choice to fly only FGs! I thought we were done for sure, that the whole operation would probably be over, especially when about twenty monks dressed in their red robes and with their shaved heads came across the river in a boat. They got out of their boat and walked in a single file line right up to all the bigwigs standing by the river. They threw the twisted long line from that load on the ground in front of them and talked with the bigwigs. My houseboy told me later that the monks had told the bigwigs how close they'd come to killing so many people and had asked how were they going to compensate the village.

Not a day or two later I was flying with the pilot of that near disaster. We had flown out to the rig site and were to pick up ten workers going out on their time off and fly them back to the base camp. I was in the right seat, the pilot-in-command seat. I took off and then turned the controls over to the FG. The right seat had all the friction locks on the collective and cyclic controls; you can twist these locks to tighten or loosen the friction to hold the controls in place. I never tightened them down completely unless I was shutting the aircraft down and so could let go of the controls. In flight I would sometimes tighten the collective friction to keep it from creeping up or down, and I could then relax my left arm. About halfway back to base camp the FG asked me to loosen the friction on the collective.

No problem, I thought. *Sometimes it can be too tight.* All of a sudden he rolled the throttle off and slammed the collective all the way down! I had my seatbelt and shoulder harnesses on, not as tight as I should have, but I still went instantly weightless and came up out of my seat. Without the seatbelt and harness I would've surely slammed into the control panel above my head.

I instantly looked at the instruments, not knowing exactly what had happened, and saw the rotor rpm hit the redline and start to go over. The engine was running, and all was okay, but I had to pull hard on the collective to get him to ease up. "What the fuck are you doing?" I asked. He said he wanted to practice an autorotation, which is an emergency procedure you do if the engine quits. In an autorotation you lower the collective to conserve your rotor rpm and look for a place to land. But when you do that, you immediately get an upward flow of air into the rotor system that can actually increase your rotor rpm beyond its limits. If you don't watch it or control it, things can begin to leave the helicopter. I told him to look at the rpm, as I'd had to physically overpower him and pull up to bring it down to prevent an overspeed.

It was then that I looked back to check on the passengers. Thank God I always ensured each person was buckled in before we took off! They were fine, but they were all holding on for dear life, their eyes as big as saucers. I didn't say anything else; it was too late now. I asked him where he was going, and he said he was going for a clearing just beyond the tree line ahead and a little to our right. I got on the controls and stayed on them with him as he headed straight ahead, not toward the clearing. "You are getting too slow. Watch your airspeed!" I told him. "You need to come more right!" I added. He never would have made it. I finally pulled up a little on the collective and pushed the cyclic hard forward. I dove to get more speed right before the tree line, pulled up and over the trees, made a slight bank right, and brought the rpm back up with the throttle as we settled right into the clearing. He had a great big grin on his face as we stopped. He actually thought he'd done it. I told him again that I had the aircraft and took off.

We were just on the other side of the river from the base camp and soon landed on the ramp. I smiled and said good-bye as the passengers left. As soon as they were gone, before we even shut the aircraft down, I tore my headset off and screamed at him, "What in the fuck did you think you were doing back there?"

It startled him so bad he jumped up in his seat and looked at me with a stunned face. "What are you talking about?" he asked.

"Number one," I told him, "you never, ever do anything like that with passengers on board, and you never, ever, ever do anything like that again without telling me first!"

He just sort of nodded and got out.

I thought, *I'm done with this, with these dickheads!* The final nail in the coffin would come the very next day.

When you fly on tuna boats, in jungles, or really any faraway place, sometimes you might be a little more flexible and bend the rules when it comes to replacing parts or fixing problems you have. You would normally repair or replace a part as soon as it reached a timed tolerance or replacement point, but out in the middle of nowhere you might fudge a little. I had an engine mount on my aircraft that was moving beyond limits. I checked it during every preflight. On one of my flights vibrations began, and I landed next to a small river to check it out. I had let it go for a couple of days, but it was time. I had told the mechanics about it before, and I went back that night after I'd finished flying and told the head FG mechanic that it needed to be fixed. He said he would take care of it. They talked to the home company every night by radio (there was no phone) and could order anything we needed. An ordered part would almost always arrive the next day or two, flown out to us in the BK-117. I had shown him the parts manual and the exact part we would need, and he got on the radio and ordered it while I stood there. Cool, done. I left and headed for dinner but realized I'd forgotten to tell him that I thought all the hardware, the nuts and bolts, might be worn as well and that he should order them too. I went back, and just as I reached for the door to open it, I heard him talking to the home company canceling that order, saying that we would probably be fine for some time longer! I knew I was done right then.

I was only a couple of days from going out. We weren't really on a written contract, but we were supposed to fly for a month, go out for two weeks to wherever we wanted to go, and then come back again. A couple of days later I was on the BK-117 and promising to bring back all the things people wanted, knowing full well I was not coming back. I flew to Bangkok and then back to the United States. Before I left Bangkok, I called my company in Corona, told them all that had happened, and asked if I could still come back. They said, "Of course." I was gone.

The first thing I did when I got back to the United States was call the FG company in Los Angeles. They asked me how things were going in Myanmar. "I don't know. I'm in Southern California!" I said.

"What?" the company representative said.

After I finished telling him everything, the whole story, he said they would get back to me. The next day my company in Corona received a long letter from Captain K via fax. He said that those guys were all gone, that everything had changed, and that if I came back, I would be in charge and could train all the new guys as I saw fit. He must've been high! I didn't even answer back. I was home safe, and I was done!

The base camp in Myanmar on the Chindwind River. Everything was brought up the river by boat, and then we would fly it all out by helicopter to where the oil drilling rig was being constructed.

The rig site out in the middle of nowhere. It took about an hour round trip to reach the site, depending on the load we were carrying.

The reason we were flying out there. Right next to the rig, where we set many of the loads, oil was just naturally bubbling right out of the ground.

The woman who owned the little shack and kept my beer on ice for me just outside our compound. Here she is crushing up and rolling betel nut into betel nut leaves.

The two Bell 214s being serviced at base camp early morning.

One of the 214s slinging a huge part of a concrete mixer
almost as big as it is. There was nowhere to make an
emergency landing out there in all those hard teak trees.

12

Back to California

From Barbers Point, Hawaii, Dad's next duty station was Point Mugu, California. He was still assigned to C-121s. Point Mugu, the Pacific missile test range, was located just south of Port Hueneme and Oxnard and north of Malibu. We lived in a small house on C Street in Oxnard, and I started at my fourth elementary school there. Our time in this house was pretty uneventful except that we would begin to camp, fish, and hunt a whole lot more. We weren't at that house or elementary school for long, and soon housing opened up for us on the base at Mugu, where I transferred to my fifth and final elementary school, Ocean View Elementary.

The base was really cool, with its five-cent movie theater; a big pool, where I finally learned to swim; and nice beaches. We'd had fishing poles and guns for as long as I could remember, but the base also had all the camping gear and necessities we could possibly need—sleeping bags, tents, stoves, and so on, and even small camper trailers that you just had to sign for to check out. We were camping and fishing every chance we had, and we could hunt right on the base. We shot jack rabbits all the time. They tasted okay but not as good as the rabbits in Tennessee. The rabbits there were living high on all the vegetables around them, but here it was just low, dry grass and shrubs all the way to the beach.

My baseball playing took off also. I was good at it and just got better and better. I would play constantly from this time on. It kept me in pretty good shape, and it also kept me out of trouble. Rick and Tony played for a while but drifted away from it and began to get into trouble. Everyone did mischievous stuff on base—staying out past curfew, hiding from the suck trucks, TP-ing houses, throwing eggs on Halloween, and the usual, ringing a doorbell and running. Probably the worst thing we did was fill a paper bag full of dog shit, place it on someone's porch, light it on fire, ring the doorbell, and run. We would go a safe distance, hide, and watch whoever answered the door. They would immediately start stomping on the bag. We would laugh so hard we would give ourselves away, and more often than not we'd have to run for our lives from the super-pissed-off person with dog shit all over his or her shoes and a front porch to clean up. But that was about it.

Rick, though, just became more and more strange. He started picking fights with me all the time over absolutely nothing. I also had to protect Tony from him because he was always beating Tony up. Before we got to Hawaii, Rick used to knock me down, get on my back, and just pound on me. But soon after we'd gotten there, he'd knocked me down one time and had been about to do the same when somehow I'd knocked him off, gotten on top of him, and beaten the shit out of him. He hadn't bothered me since then until now. He seemed to completely move away from us. He had no friends and was always saying things to other people and pissing them off. I had to protect him from things he started. If I was around, I could usually defuse the situation; if not, he would get his ass kicked, which happened a lot. He was pretty fast, though, and could usually run away. He just didn't seem to know how to mind his own business or when to shut up.

Point Mugu was the last place where I, as the new guy, would have to really fight or hit someone. The first day at my new school, while playing softball on the playground ball field, all the guys were giving me that you-don't-belong-here attitude. I ran to second base after a base hit into right field. I beat the throw to the base by a mile, but of course they all said I was out. When I said, "You're kidding, right?" three guys walked over to me. One guy dropped his glove and reared back his right hand to punch me. I was already cocked halfway with my left side toward him, ready with a right. I was faster and unwound with a really fast straight shot right to his nose. Down he went! The others backpedaled away from me. I was safe!

As had happened in previous fights, later that day the guy I'd decked was my best friend. When I went home on the bus that day, everyone was so friendly and nice to me.

Rick continued to try to beat me up and start shit over and over, but I would get the best of him every time. Then he would always call Mom or Dad at work and say that I had beat him up. Each and every time he started something with me, I tried to tell him that we would both get our asses beat, but he still fought with me and then called our parents afterward. Sure enough, every night, Dad would come home and just beat our asses, bad! Mom and Dad never listened or believed me when I told them what he had done and how it had started.

Finally, on a two-night camping trip to Lake Casitas, they would finally see. Dad had checked out a small camping trailer for him and Mom and a tent for us. After finishing up dinner after a day of fishing, I went out to sit by the fire. I put more wood on it, got it going great, and sat back with both feet up on the rocks around the fire pit. It was pretty chilly out, and everyone else was still inside the trailer. I was comfortable and warm, about to fall asleep, when Rick walked out of the trailer. I thought he was going to sit on the other side of the pit, but instead he walked straight up to me, kicked my feet off the rocks, and sat down. I tumbled backward off my seat but jumped right back up. "That's it!" I said. I yanked him up by his jacket, spinning him around, and punched him right into and over the fire and then dove on top of him. It was like a fight scene from a western movie. We rolled through the fire two or three times, collapsed the tent, and broke the picnic table and all the dinnerware and condiments on it. I kept knocking him down and yanking him back up. I was surprised he was taking such a beating, but I wasn't going to let up. That was when I saw Mom and Dad both watching out the window. I thought it was strange they weren't doing anything. I figured this was my chance to end this crap.

I finally punched him so hard that he went flying backward and smashed into the side of the camper, leaving a huge dent as he collapsed and went down. I bent over him, grabbed him by the front of his jacket, and pulled him up. I wanted to smash his face in I was so mad and frustrated. Before I could let him have it one final time, Dad said in a quiet, calm voice, "Craig, stop." I let Rick go, and he crumpled to the ground. When I turned around, Dad was standing there with his belt in his hand. I thought, *We're really going to get it now!* But he just moved me out of the way. Then he pulled Rick up and beat his ass and legs with that belt. I mean he *really* beat him. It's kind of funny now, but I even remember thinking, *Poor Rick!* After that second ass beating, Dad sent him into the trailer, where he made him stay until we left the next afternoon. He told me that he and Mom both had seen what Rick had done and that now he understood what I had been going through. It was finally over, almost.

Rick tried a few more times to start stuff with me, but I would still kick his ass, and Dad would also beat him, but not me, afterward. He finally just stopped. But he wasn't even like a brother to me any longer. We'd drifted completely apart, and I almost never saw him anymore except in the morning and at night and occasionally at school. But even then it was as if he didn't know me. It was as if I didn't have an older brother. I was the big brother and still had to protect him many times after he would start something with other people. I still played ball and hung out with my friends. He never seemed to have friends. After just a year or two we moved to another house off base, and soon after Mom's older sister, her husband, and their two kids moved from Iowa and stayed with us a few days until they found a place of their own. Aunt Betty and Uncle Bill were my favorite aunt and uncle. Their kids, Cathy and Mike, were my favorite cousins, and Mike would become the big brother I didn't have.

We lived closer to the beach now than we did on the base, and we went there often. Mike was three years older than me but let me hang out with him and his friends a lot. He had been racing dirt-track bikes back in Iowa, and he bought an old bike and began racing at a track out by the beach. He took me and would let me ride also. He also got into surfing. He bought a board and would go surfing with two brothers, Dan and Dave. I was only thirteen at the time, but they would let me go with them if I gave them a dollar for gas. They were sixteen and seventeen, and I thought it was just so cool hanging out with them. I didn't have a board but would just sit and watch them until they came in, and then Mike would let me take his board out, a brand-new ten-foot Dewey Weber. They didn't show me anything; I just learned watching them. Back in the early to mid '60s, no one had wet suits, in any season. Fires on the beach were legal then, and when everyone came out of the water, all they wanted to do was get warm. The very first time I went out, I caught my first wave, rode it all the way into the beach, and broke the nose off his new board. I had never been so cold in my life, but I was so excited, so jazzed. I was instantly hooked! I was a surfer, for life.

In 1965 I finished elementary school and would be starting junior high school soon. It was right at that time the Watts riots began. I hadn't really thought much of race relations or problems before this time. Yes, the Hawaiians were tough against haoles (pronounced "howlies"), or white people, but after my first fight all the local kids I knew were all friends. But those riots stunned our nation and shook it to its democratic core. They were quite an eye-opener for me. I had never had a problem with any of the black friends I had growing up; we were all very close. The funny thing was, right at the same time I started junior high school in Oxnard, the Mexicans seemed to just hate us.

I was supposed to go to a new school being built, Blackstock Junior High, but it wouldn't be finished on time, so it looked like we would be going half days at another junior high school close by, E. O. Green Junior High. We would go in the morning from about eight to noon, and the other kids would go in the afternoon from about one to five. A couple of times groups of Mexican guys chased me and threw rocks at me on my way home from E. O. Green, but I outran them and just thought they were bullies. I never had any problems, but it seemed as if white girls and Mexican girls were fighting every single day, just going at it tooth and nail. I got along with everyone.

In October that year my sister, Paula, was born. That was quite a change for our family of three boys. She was Daddy's little girl, and Mom had the daughter she'd always wanted. Less than a year later we would be on our way to Guam.

13

Turtle Rider

Tuna fishing in the Eastern Pacific off the West Coast of the United States, Mexico, and Central and South America is quite different than tuna fishing in the Western Pacific around Samoa, Vanuatu, the Solomon Islands, Papua New Guinea, and the Caroline Islands. In both the Eastern and Western Pacific you'll find tuna feeding on smaller fish. However, in the Western Pacific they feed by themselves, while in the Eastern Pacific they feed with dolphins. In both you can find tuna in strange ways and situations—for example, by a floating log; floating debris; a small abandoned or lost fishing boat; and, in one strange case, a six-foot-long two-by-four piece of wood. All these things have something that smaller fish like to nibble at, such as barnacles or small crabs, and as the items float along, bigger fish are attracted to the smaller fish, and even bigger fish are attracted to those big fish, and so on and so on. Very often at the bottom of that food chain you will find tuna. Sometimes a lot of tuna. Most of the time, though, in the Western Pacific you are looking for foamers. That's where you might suddenly see, very close or far out away from you, a circle of white churning water where the ocean's surface is foaming up almost as if it's beginning to boil. The tuna are attacking small baitfish at the surface, causing the water to foam. And in the Eastern Pacific most of the time you are looking for dolphins. Where there are dolphins, there will usually be tuna below them.

The boats are almost exactly the same, with a large net piled on the stern, or rear, of the boat and a large skiff that has the other end of the net attached to its stern. The skiff is pulled up by a cable to almost vertical and is chained and resting on the back pile of the net. When the boat is close to a school of tuna, or dolphins and tuna, the skiff is released and slides off the back of the boat. As soon as it hits the water, the lone driver starts the engine, immediately turns the boat 180 degrees, and gives the engine full throttle. It looks as if he's pulling the net off the boat and heading away in the opposite direction, but he's actually just sitting there at full throttle holding one end of the net as the larger boat moves away and the rest of the net slides off the mother boat. The mother boat continues on in a circle releasing the net slowly around the tuna. The very experienced navigator, usually steering the boat while the captain is with me in the helicopter, will expertly release the net so that its other end will come off right back at where the skiff is sitting. The ends are closed together, the purse lines are pulled up, and the bottom is closed, hopefully with the tuna still inside.

The one big difference between tuna boats in the Western Pacific and the Eastern Pacific is that the boats in the Eastern Pacific carry five or six small, one-man speedboats. These are actually used for herding the dolphins. Finding, encircling, and netting the tuna by themselves is pretty simple and easy. They are usually feeding and fairly stationary. But with the dolphins on the surface and the tuna swimming together below, they can easily outrun and out-turn any big fishing boat. So whenever we spotted a school of dolphins, we'd try to get the boat as close as possible without spooking the dolphins and making them run. When the skipper thought we were within speedboat distance, he'd stop the boat, and the speedboats would be lowered into the water one or two at a time. The tuna boat always made a set, or released the net, making turns to the left to encircle the tuna, so all five or six speedboats would form up on the right side of the boat next to each other. Once they were set, the skipper, flying in the helicopter with me, would give the order, and the tuna boat would go to full throttle and head for the dolphins. The speedboats would easily stay directly alongside the tuna boat, lined up together using hardly any of their throttle power. As the boat got close, sure enough the dolphins would take off. The skipper would then order the first speedboat, the one farthest from the tuna boat, to go. It always looked almost as if a torpedo had been fired from alongside the boat as the first speedboat raced ahead, leaving a white trail behind it. As it got a certain distance out, the skipper would order a second to go, and it would dart away. He'd send one after another, keeping them a little to the right of the school of dolphins. Once they began to overtake the dolphins, he'd start turning the lead speedboat slightly to the left. As it got farther ahead of the fleeing school, the other boats would slowly begin to turn the dolphins and surround the school. With the tuna boat now close behind and the wind and ocean currents taken into account, the skipper would order the skiff let go, and the net would begin to come off.

In the Eastern Pacific you almost always find the tuna swimming below schools of dolphins, as they feed together on brown balls of small fish, normally sardines. These balls can be very small or enormous, and together the dolphins and the tuna can devour these balls very quickly. Generally you will find two different species of dolphins, spinners and spotters. Spinners are so-called because as they jump out of the water while racing along, they actually spin through the air just like an airplane rolling on its longitudinal axis. You would always hear a groan or an "Oh no!" whenever someone spotted spinners. The crew members kept an eye out through huge binoculars from the crow's nest, and the captain was almost always in the helicopter with me searching for tuna. On the other hand, everyone loved the spotters, so-called because of the spots all over them, because once you put the net around them, they tended to just stop and give up.

When you let the net go and surround the dolphins and the tuna together, you first have to connect the ends of the net together, closing the sides. If whoever's piloting the boat on a set drops the end of the net off right back at the other end, then it can be closed very quickly. However, if for some reason the pilot has his head up his ass, the wind shifts, or the current is stronger than expected, the end of the net might come off too early, leaving the net open. This is called a towline, and it's not a good thing. The winches on the boat have to work extra hard and fast to slowly bring the ends together. With the spotters, who tend to give up and just sit on one side of the net away from the boat, this is not a problem. But with the spinners, who are constantly on the move, it's a different story. They don't stop, and when they come up against the net, they just keep on racing along it until they can hopefully find a way out. If there is a towline, they will find it, and out they will go, with the tuna going right along with them! Most times the speedboats will race over to the opening and circle there, and that will keep the dolphins and tuna inside. At times I would do the same using the helicopter, churning and pushing the water just above the dolphins or sometimes just the tuna by themselves, like a cowboy herding them back into the net.

But even if the net is closed quickly, it then has to be pursed (the bottom closed) quickly soon after, as the spinners continue circling the net going deeper and deeper. If they reach the bottom and it's not pursed, they will go out, and the tuna will follow. As they go deeper and disappear out of sight, everybody just starts praying, and it gets very quiet. More often than not, after a few minutes you'll spot the spinners again—on the other side of the net, jumping and spinning happily away. And of course the tuna are swimming right along with them. That's why the "Oh nos!" It's so frustrating because you're pumped up, thinking you're about to catch whatever amount of tonnage you estimated was in the net. Then it's a huge letdown as that tonnage swims away. The three, four, or even five hours of finding, chasing, letting the net out, and finally hauling all that empty net back on board was for nothing. On the boats they call that a skunk. You could get skunked with dolphins and tuna or just tuna only. Many things could go wrong, and the bad thing was that even when there was lots of tuna around, if you took too long to make a set, you might only be able to make two or three sets in a day, so those skunks could really hurt.

When we made a set on dolphins, no one ever went into the net. Just the year before, one of the crew, trying to expedite the removal of dolphins before hauling in the tuna, had been hanging on the inside of the net when a shark came around from outside the net and bit half of his side off, killing him. After we'd caught everything and closed and pursed the net, the skipper would begin backing down the boat. The net would elongate, and the dolphins would be forced to the back of it. One crewman in a speedboat would tie up to the net and, lying over the bow, would hold down the net and the corks supporting the net line and help the dolphins out one at a time. This could take quite some time.

Seeing all the dolphins in the net each day, I wanted to go in and play with them. The skipper said go ahead, and with my mask, fins, and snorkel, I walked down on the net until it dropped down deep and out of sight. Then I stepped off and swam out. It was so beautiful—endless, ice-blue water. But the sounds! The dolphins, clicking and squeaking, really surprised me. As I'd gone in, I had been able to see them on the surface at the back of the net, but since the net dropped off and bent a little left, I hadn't been able to see them underwater yet. Once I started swimming inside the net, the first thing I saw was the eighty tons of tuna we had just caught circling the net looking for an exit. It was a giant school with all these huge tuna gulping, opening and closing their mouths, and headed right toward me. I thought they were going to run into me, but just before they did, I froze, and they did an instantaneous right turn and headed back the other way. When I finally saw the dolphins, it took me a second to really realize what I was looking at. There were thousands of them slowly swimming, some seeming to hover motionless, all huddled against the net. I went for the left side of that huge mass to a small group and reached out to touch what looked like a half-grown, like teenager-sized, dolphin. He didn't run away from me, but just before I touched him, he opened his mouth, showing his teeth, and hissed really loudly at me like a cat. *You're not supposed to do that!* I thought.

I had reached out too quickly and startled him. So I slowed down, and he let me touch him. He was so cool! I reached over and began to pull the corks supporting the net down to let him out. What really surprised me as I did that was all the others began to gather around me, almost as if they had been through this before and knew what I was doing. I began helping them over and out one after the other. Even though they could easily jump over, they would hesitate right at the net. I would simply grab them by their snouts and pull them over. They would instantly bolt away, jumping as they ran.

I really hadn't been aware of the outcry against the effects of tuna fishing on dolphins until I went out on my first boat. The US government would randomly assign agents, or observers, to fishing boats to monitor and record all sets, netting, and interactions with the dolphins. I had seen dead dolphins in the nets as they were hauled back aboard but couldn't understand how they were being killed. I'd seen one that had had a huge part of its belly bitten away by a shark from outside the net, but that was it. That poor observer, a real nice American guy, about my age, was just despised by the crew. He and I got along fine, though. He was just doing his job. But I was curious: How were the dolphins dying? The crew was very careful with them, and besides, why would they want to hurt them? It was the dolphins, 90 percent of the time, that led us to the tuna!

After the massive pod of dolphins began to thin out as I pushed them over the net, I could see more and figured out what was really happening to them. Some of them were just giving up, as if thinking, *That's it; I'm a goner!* They were letting themselves go limp and sliding down the net to the bottom. They were drowning themselves! Every time I saw one start to slide down and give up, I raced over to it, grabbed it by its snout, and shook it. Each time was like waking it up. The dolphin would have a *Wha … wha … what's happening?* kind of expression, and then it would swim back up. One guy had tried to go out through a hole in the net about twenty feet down and had gotten stuck. I went down there, and with my flippers on the side of the net, my right arm around his fluke and my left arm holding his left flipper, I pushed and tugged together. I damn near screwed up. I couldn't budge him and couldn't hold my breath much longer. Then he suddenly popped out, and we both went for the surface. I had actually grayed out a little bit and had tunnel vision as I caught my breath while clinging to the corks. After a few moments, though, I was fine and helped the last few out. We didn't lose one dolphin on that set! I would do the same on my second trip into the net, but my third trip would be my last time in.

The second time I went in was just off the Galápagos Islands after the net was set on a pretty big school of tuna. As we circled overhead before landing, the skipper said, "We've got a turtle!" I looked down and spotted this huge sea turtle just as he began to dive. After landing, the skipper, so happy with us not losing any dolphin on my last trip in, urged me to go in again. Great day for a swim! I got my snorkeling gear and headed in. I started getting the dolphins out right away, as again they came to me like, *Get me out of here!* I didn't see the turtle the whole time. I thought he must have jetted out the bottom of the net before it had closed. I had all the dolphins out except for one giant bull dolphin. Each time, he would come up to me, but when I'd grab his snout and almost get him over, he would panic and take off swimming around the net with me holding onto his big dorsal fin. It was really pretty fun. He took me all the way around once. After I let go, he circled the net one more time, then stopped right next to me again. A second time, the same thing. On the third time he took off again, I held on to his fin to enjoy the ride. We were circling close to the net, and I was looking down, amazed at how deep I could see and how much sea life there was. It was like if I just focused and unfocused my eyes, I would see something deeper and deeper floating at all these different levels.

When I looked up, that giant sea turtle was directly in front of us trying to get past the net. I didn't even have time to finish an "Oh shit!" when that big dolphin crashed us both right into the turtle's side. It didn't really scare me that bad. I knew sea turtles were pretty docile, but I didn't know if I could be cut by his huge shell or if he might try to snap at me with his powerful beak. When we hit him, I lost hold of my ride, and the dolphin was gone. After all the bubbles cleared, there was my new ride, right in front and below me heading down. He was swimming his heart out trying to get away from me, stretching his neck out and looking back over his shell. "Oh no you don't!" I said as I dove after him. With my big swim fins I caught him in a second. With one of my hands under the edge of his shell behind his head pulling up and the other on his back pushing down, we quickly popped right to the surface. I was lying squarely on his big old shell as he swam straight back to the boat. All the crew on deck were cheering, clapping, and waving, and I waved back. They lowered two big straps down to me, and I quickly slung them around the turtle. I hooked the straps to the crane hoist, and up he went. As I was swimming over to the ladder on the side of the ship to climb out, that big dolphin came over. I didn't touch him this time, though. I swam over to the net with him,

117

pulled it down, and jumped up and sat on the corks. It sank far enough for him to start to head over, and as soon as I thought he was going to go for it, I dove away to the side. It was a good thing I did, because as he flipped his powerful fluke, he was gone like a shot. If his tail had hit me, it would have knocked me out cold.

When I got back on board, they had craned the turtle up out of the way from the guys working on the deck and set him right by my little helicopter workshop up a couple of decks. He was truly amazing—so big, with a beautiful shell. *What a trophy that would be hanging on my wall!* I thought. No sooner had the thought passed through my mind than I said out loud, "What the fuck am I thinking!" This was such an incredible creature and, even at that time, was much older than I could ever hope to be! How could I even think of such a thing? I knew what the crew was thinking: turtle soup! I had heard them talking about it before. Besides, this was an endangered species, and I could go to prison if I harmed it. The observer didn't know yet. He wouldn't come up on deck to check on the dolphin until after the net was hauled in. If he knew, he would definitely report that one, and I'd be screwed.

I sat with him for a second just touching that magnificent shell and feeling so glad I had experienced this with him. What a story to tell! I lifted the back part of his shell up to slide his enormous body across the deck and over the side. "Thanks for the ride, Tony!" I said.

The skipper walked up behind me and said, "You know we really shouldn't keep that."

"Way ahead of you, skipper!" I said. I was half bent over, like I was pushing a giant wheelbarrow. I slid the turtle over to the edge of that upper deck and, with all the power I had left, shoved him over the side. With his head tucked into his shell and all four flippers tucked back along his sides, he almost looked like an enormous seabird diving in to catch a fish. He cut through the surface like a knife at a slight angle and hardly made a splash at all. He shot down like a bullet. I saw his head and his fins come out just before he disappeared into the dark-blue water.

Then, like out of a comedy, the cook walked up in his big white apron sharpening a long, huge knife. He stopped, looked around, and asked, "Where's the turtle?"

"He had another dinner engagement. He went home!" I said.

I would go in the net just one more time a few days later. After landing and tying up the helicopter after a set, I ran down, donned my gear, and jumped in. The dolphins were already bunching up at the back of the net. About halfway across the net a huge outline began to appear out of the dark blue water a little below but right in front of me. *Man, that's the biggest tuna I've seen so far!* I thought. When it fully came into view, I froze in fear. I had seen bigger monster sharks before from the helicopter, but this was the biggest I had ever been close to. He was easily twelve to fifteen feet long. He had a huge, round, fat body and teeth that protruded out the sides of his mouth. I couldn't move. Where could I go? I was dead center in the middle of that large open net. His big vertical tail fin propelling him slowly, he came within about five feet of me. I could see him checking me out, and with a *I'll be right back!* kind of look, he looked forward and headed toward the boat. As soon as he began to disappear from view, I sprinted for the speedboat tied to the end of the net, grabbed the bow, and was on board with one pull-up. I told the guy in the boat, and neither of us used our hands to push on the net or grab the dolphins' snouts. We used the oars to push the net down and got almost all of the dolphin out. I never went swimming in the net again!

Away we go. The second tuna boat I worked on with the turbine-
powered Hughes 500C, which is much better for this type of
work. Notice the line running under the pad that goes up to
the belly hook. On landing, a deck crewman runs up and hooks
the line into the release as another crewman on a hand crank
at the other end winches it down tight. On takeoff, just push
the release button on the cyclic/joystick, and you're off.

Woleai Atoll in the Caroline Islands, part of the Federated States of Micronesia. With our boat waiting outside, up to the left, we took two guys who grew up here in for a visit. They ended up staying. I landed the helicopter on the beach in that little half-moon-shaped part of the atoll on the right. I had an amazing time in the one day I spent there.

After we landed here, it took a little while before anyone came out to greet us. When they came out, the first guy I tried to greet and shake hands with grabbed my hand and brought it up to his face. I thought he was going to take a bite and started to pull my hand back, but he just touched it to his forehead. That was how they greet.

Looking out over the captain, who always flew with me
and ran the whole set, at about eighty tons of tuna caught
after a bit of a struggle to keep them in the net.

Sometimes the tuna tried hard to find a way out, and if we didn't get
the net closed quickly enough, they often found their way. So, at times,
I had to be a helicopter cowboy and herd them back in. I was successful
on this one and got 125 tons turned back around and pulled in.

Leaving the MV *Jeannine* on one of the speedboats for Woleai Island.

Another photo shot over the captain as he directed the boat into a three-hundred-ton-plus school of tuna. Three hundred tons was too much weight for our net, so we had to surgically cut one hundred tons off of the school and then wrap the tuna up with our net.

Using the heavy-duty line used to repair the net, a huge handmade
hook, and a piece of tuna, I caught this big black marlin by
hand, with a little help from the deck crane to land it on the
boat. The marlin's spear nose is just touching the deck.

After dropping off two crew members, I went back to park the helicopter
on the boat. I would return with a speedboat to water-ski in the
middle of the beautiful, shark-infested water of the atoll and sample
the coconut alcohol made from the various family-owned trees.

Early the next morning before heading back out to fish, a couple of the crew and I brought the big skiff back in full of tuna and traded for fruit and of course some more coconut juice!

The tuna really racing for the huge opening as I work my magic.

When my buddies Tigga and Baruka, the boat's mascot dogs, saw any type of birdlife, they knew we would be catching fish soon and they would be getting free tuna.

The Woleai islanders piling up the fish we traded for fruit.

14

Humphrey, the Almost Killer Whale!

Humphrey the wayward humpback whale (named off the cuff by a reporter covering him) came into San Francisco Bay and was first spotted on October 10, 1985, near Oakland, California. He swam up the Carquinez Strait, up the Sacramento River, and under Rio Vista Bridge into narrow, dead-end Shag Slough, about sixty miles from the Pacific Ocean. He became quite a celebrity on every local and national news channel as well as many international news channels. The news crews searched for and followed him every single day of his journey inland.

My helicopter company called him Humphrey the Golden Whale because he made us an absolute fortune with us flying all the media every day. While following him I would have the closest—I mean the absolute closest—close call ever. At that time we only had a contract for one helicopter with Channel 10, the local CBS-affiliated station. We would also occasionally fly for Channel 13, the local ABC-affiliated station. Later, well after Humphrey had gone, we would fly for both stations exclusively. Channel 4, the last big local station, the NBC affiliate, had their own helicopter and pilot. We would end up flying both Channel 10 and 13 during Humphrey's stay and would also fly for all three major national news networks and the occasional international news networks.

By the time Humphrey arrived, I had been occasionally flying a lot of different agencies, such as the FBI, ATF, and DEA, up and down the valley and knew most every major and minor lake and river and many sloughs from the coastal range north of San Francisco up to Eureka across the valley to the Sierra Nevada; east of Reading, California; and south to Yosemite and Sequoia. But mostly I had been flying with various county sheriff's departments on all types of law enforcement operations and with PG&E (Pacific Gas and Electric) flying power-line patrol and carrying maintenance crews wherever needed. I found a lot of really cool spots to fish. I love to fish, and heli-fishing is the best way to get into quiet, secluded spots.

The very first day I flew sheriff crews, their captain came up to me and said, "Don't fly looking for fish or stop to fish!"

I said, "Sure thing," and we took off.

The first thing the guy next to me said after we took off was "You want to go see some catfish?"

"Sure," I said.

PG&E was the same: no stopping for fish anytime! But we took a lot of lunch breaks by rivers, creeks, and small lakes. Everyone was amazed that I could find and spot the best fish everywhere we went. What was really cool, that no one knew, was that I had just done my first tuna-boat trip the year before searching for, finding, and following various marine life like dolphins and whales but mostly tuna. It was much easier spotting fish in the open, clear, blue Pacific Ocean compared to the fairly narrow rivers and even more narrow sloughs with mostly limited visibility into the muddy brown waters. However, various signs made by moving marine life, especially whales, were the same in the ocean as well as lakes and rivers.

None of the other helicopter crews could find Humphrey unless he broke the surface with his head or tail. I found him every day right off the bat, always underwater. After my first day all the other helicopter crews started following me, knowing I would find him. So I would immediately spot him and then, without slowing, keep flying away up or down the river and slowly circle over another spot. They would all come racing over and begin to circle with me. After just once or twice around, I would climb up and away as if I were finished and flying home. After flying out a ways I would turn and make a quick descent back to where I'd last spotted Humphrey. The news crew I was flying could shoot all the video they needed before anyone came back, and that would be it. We always got great shots of him. Of course the other crews would always find me and race over and would get shots as well as we all circled together, keeping our distance between each other. I just loved playing with them every time.

The secret to spotting marine life is simple but can be almost imperceptible unless you know exactly what to look for. Mostly the water was fairly calm, but at times it was windy, and the river surface was choppy with small waves. It didn't make any difference, though; even with waves I still found him. If he moved side to side or turned even slightly, a small ripple would move to either side and away from him. If he was in shallow water, it was more perceptible, but even in deeper water I could still see the ever-so-slight out-of-place movement. The real giveaway, though, was from his horizontal fluke moving up and down, propelling him along. It displaced the water down and then back up and out in a circle. It was a bit like when a stone is dropped into water and the ripples go out in all directions from a small circle. But this was a huge bubble circle with ripples starting out in all directions farther out from the wider center bubble. Yes, if he flipped his tail harder, the disturbance was greater, but even when he was slowly moving along, there was almost like a phantom bubble. It could easily be missed, but it was there.

In the river Humphrey headed in various directions each day, and even people in boats or onshore looking for him had a hard time finding him. The first two days I found him early morning, each time by three faint rings. I could actually see the rings before I even got over him, from a quarter to half a mile away. Other days I would see a single ghost bubble and lucked out guessing which direction he was heading. Each time I would slow down and watch carefully ahead, and he'd come up right in front of me or just a little off either side of me. The main reason the national news crews were calling my helicopter company was because I was finding him first each morning. When he finally ended up in the very muddy Shag Slough, I still found him right away, but as the slough narrowed and he went underneath the little bridge near Rio Vista airport, the slough came to an end, and anyone could find him then.

As in many situations, such as disasters or fires, the looky-loos would show up to see what was happening and to take pictures of Humphrey from the shoreline or in boats. But air space can become extremely crowded and especially dangerous in looky-loo situations, hindering the aircraft that need to be there to do their jobs. In such situations, to keep all the aircraft that need to be there, such as firefighting airplanes and helicopters or any type of aircraft in rescue or disaster relief, safe, the FAA puts up a temporary flight restriction—Federal Aviation Regulations 91.137(a)(3): "Prevent an unsafe congestion of sightseeing and other aircraft above an incident or event which may generate a high degree of public interest." Only aircraft needed for any such operation are allowed into the surrounding airspace. However, accredited media or news aircraft, most always helicopters, can get special permission to fly into these areas. There are usually altitude and distance restrictions depending on the situation, and all the helicopters monitor a special radio channel and remain in constant contact with each other. They all remain well clear of each other as they circle together in the same direction. If anyone wants to get in closer, circle tighter, or even just leave, they give all the others a heads-up first.

As Humphrey hit the dead end of the slough, we would each take turns circling in close for better shots. He was getting more active, and being in shallower water, he was breaking the surface quite frequently. They had begun to hammer on pipes hanging in the water from boats to try to get him to go back out, but the noise only agitated him. Everyone was getting more worried now about Humphrey's health. He had been in freshwater for some time now, away from the saline ocean water he so desperately needed, and his skin was changing color, cracking and peeling.

I had flown into Rio Vista airport, right next to Shag Slough, many times before Humphrey came and knew the guy who ran it. That day I had already flown in and out of the airport a few times picking up and dropping off national news camera crews and reporters. I came out of my last circle around Humphrey, leveled off, and called the airport UNICOM to let them know I was on my way back in to drop off this latest group. I had been looking down and looked up toward Rio Vista off to my left to make sure it was clear before I turned in to land when *boom!* Something violent and loud scared me so badly I jumped. As I did, I squeezed the control so hard that I accidentally keyed the microphone button as I yelled, "Jesus Christ, what the fuck!" The guy who ran the airport had been outside of the UNICOM office watching us and hadn't seen the airplane either until just a couple of seconds before it almost hit me head-on. By the time he had turned and grabbed his mic to warn us, I had already screamed out. He instantly asked, "Craig, are you all right?" It took me a few seconds to realize what had just happened. I thought we had been hit! The wind pressure of the plane passing so close to us and the vortices from the wing making lift rolling off the top of it had seemed to explode on my helicopter. I held on flying straight ahead, not sure if I would keep flying or go down. The controls seemed fine; everything seemed okay. I looked back to my left and saw a high-wing Cessna 172 turning and diving away to his right. He knew he wasn't supposed to be there and was probably monitoring the airport UNICOM, so he likely heard as the guy at the airport immediately asked me if I got the plane's N number, the registration number on either side of all aircraft. I told the guy at the airport I hadn't. The guy in the Cessna dove away, descending as he ran away.

I hadn't gotten his N number, but I had seen his red position light. All aircraft have lights on either side of the aircraft, red on the left and green on the right, to help identify an aircraft's position relative to other aircraft. On airplanes these lights are at the outer end of each wingtip. When I said before that he got so close, I meant it; I actually saw that airplane's red position light not two or three inches out of my window right at my eye level. The wing had gone under my rotor blades and so closely to my face that it was almost like a snapshot of that light stuck in my mind. The Bell 206 helicopter I was flying had a horizontal stabilizer sticking out either side of the tail boom just forward of the tail rotor. I don't know how he missed that. He had to have gone just under it as well and missed it by I have no idea how much. You can't get any closer than that.

I turned back to land at Rio Vista. I was shaking a little as I shut the aircraft down and went inside to take a break. The incident had scared the news crew pretty badly as well. They knew the plane had been there illegally, and they weren't mad at me but hardly said a thing. During their good-byes, as they thanked me, shook my hand, and hugged me, I could see in each of their somewhat-ashen faces that they were pretty shaken up. The guy at the airport had tried with binoculars to get the airplane's N number, but neither he nor anyone else had been able to see it. After a while I calmed down and relaxed. That was the last crew for the day, so I started the helicopter back up and headed home by myself, checking for other aircraft in all directions a hell of a lot more than I ever had before.

They finally dredged under the bridge to make it a little deeper and moved a couple of pilings from the bridge so that Humphrey could squeeze back out of his dead-end trap. Using underwater speakers to play acoustic recordings of vocalizations from the whales' feeding ground, a bright scientist got Humphrey to follow his boat out of the slough. As they approached San Francisco Bay and the water became more saline, Humphrey seemed to get his energy back. He became more excited and started sounding. The boat lost him off and on in the deeper bay, but he continued on out and was finally led out under the Golden Gate Bridge on November 4, 1985. Old Humphrey would come back into San Francisco Bay again in 1990 and become beached on a mudflat just south of Candlestick Park. It would take the United States Coast Guard and the Marine Mammal Center, using a big cargo net, three days to free him before guiding him back out through the gate into the Pacific Ocean again. He must've learned his lesson this time. Though he has been spotted several times near the coast, Humphrey has not returned to the bay again.

15

Boot Camp

When I joined the navy, I had no idea where it would take me. I thought it might be a career for me as it had been for my dad. All I knew about the navy was what he'd done, which was fly around the world having a ball. Little did I know that, within six months of enlisting, I would be on a big aircraft carrier as a jet engine mechanic in a helicopter squadron. I didn't hate it, but it was absolutely not where I wanted to be. I wanted to fly!

Growing up a navy brat was like a prep school for military life. At about five or six years old my dad sat us all down and said from this day forward if Mom or he or anyone at all asked us a yes-or-no question, we had to answer with "Yes, sir" or "No, sir" or "Yes, ma'am" or "No, ma'am." If we didn't, we would get backhanded or slapped. If we answered with a "Huh?" or "What?" then wham, right across the face. Every answer had to be "Yes, sir" or "No, sir" or "Yes, ma'am" or "No, ma'am"! If not, pow! This happened at home by ourselves and even around other people. In front of other people Dad would whack us in the head or butt, grab us by the hair or arm and yank us toward his face, slap us, and tell us what to say. Other times we would get the belt.

Along with that we had chores that rotated every week. Each week he made up a list for each of us of things we had to do. For example, one week I would have to clean the kitchen and dining room and do the dishes. Rick would have to do the living room, vacuum, dust, and clean the windows, and Tony would have to clean the bathroom, take out the trash, and so on. We each had to make sure our rooms were clean and our beds were made. Mom or Dad would check everything like a drill instructor every day when they came home. Unless everything was done and done perfectly, we would get spanked with the belt. At first all three of us boys were in the same room. Then as we got older, Rick had his own room, and Tony and I shared. If one of us didn't do our chores, we would all get in trouble. This led to Rick and me fighting a lot because he would just play around when we came home from school. We had to get all our chores done as soon as we came home, before we did anything else. We were like three little slaves. We also had to wash Dad's car, pull weeds, and cut grass weekdays and weekends too. In later years we rarely got the belt. We would either get the shit slapped out of us or get punched in the face.

So when I went to boot camp, it was just like being at home with Dad but actually easier! They taught us everything we needed to know with little classes and lectures—from how to make our beds and fold our clothes to how to handle our weapons and march. All I had to do was do exactly what I'd been taught and told to do and always answer, "Sir, yes, sir!" Piece of cake! We had lessons all day every day and had to sit with our little notepads and take notes on everything. It really was simple and, as I said, like growing up with my dad telling me what to do, except without the drunken tirades and ass beatings. All you had to do was listen and do what you were told. It was a nightmare for those who didn't follow orders or instructions, though.

When the other newbies and I first got to boot camp, we were sent to Worm Island. It wasn't really an island, but you had to cross over a small river on a bridge to get to it. It sat right next to the marine basic-training base. We were all called worms because we were the lowest-ranked newbies in the navy. After a few days of processing, testing, medical, dental, and uniform issue, our regular daily routine began.

The days began with reveille at 5:00 a.m. and ended with taps at 10:00 p.m. and then lights-out. After reveille we had only minutes for basic hygiene, which they called shit, shower, and shave. We would make our bunks and then stow our gear in our lockers. Then we went downstairs where we fell into formation. From the first day we had all been put into a height line, with the tallest guy in the company at the front right of the formation and the next tallest five guys to his left and then the seventh-tallest guy starting the second row behind the tallest guy and so on. I was the second tallest guy, second guy up front. Then we would march off to the chow hall (also called the galley or mess hall) for breakfast. We would march in formation everywhere we went and then fall out and form a nut-to-butt line into wherever we were going. Nut to butt meant you would literally touch the tips of your boots right up against the heels of the guy in front of you. When he moved forward, you would put your toes right back up against his heels again and keep doing that all the way into wherever you had to be. There was no talking at all in line or when eating. After eating we would race back out to the parade grounds, where we would form up again with our company. We had a flag bearer, usually one of the smallest guys, who would carry our company flag. We were Company 421. He would usually be the first in and out, and when he came out, he would get the flag, race out to the parade grounds, and begin calling out, "Company 421." The parade grounds were huge, and there were hundreds of guys forming up, so that made it a lot easier for everybody to find his own company. At breakfast at five or six in the morning it was also pretty dark.

Everywhere we went, every meal was the same. We marched wherever we were going, got nut to butt, ate or did whatever we had to do, ran back out, and reassembled. Every day we had lectures; did our drills, marching in formation; and had physical training (PT). One of the biggest things they pushed was folding and stowing our uniforms and gear in our lockers exactly as we had been taught, with even our socks rolled up and folded and placed in an exact location. We each had eight pairs of socks, seven of which we never used and one pair that we wore every day. At night, when we showered, we would take that pair with us, place the socks over our hands like gloves, and wash them as if we were washing our hands. After wringing them out, we would hang them over our bunks' foot railings at night, and they would be clean and dry in the morning. Our shirts, pants, and underwear had to be folded and placed in exact locations top to bottom and front to back. We made the bunks every morning. The catch edges—the edges all the way around the sheets that are folded over and sewn—always had to be down, and the blanket had to be tight with hospital corners. Even our bars of soap, razors, and toothpaste tubes had to be placed in an exact position and of course immaculately clean. Not a speck of dust was allowed in, on, around, or under our lockers and beds.

Our company commander (CC), an E-7, just like my dad, would check people occasionally. He had chosen a guy from the company to be the recruit company commander (our leader), but that guy wasn't much help. He was always doing something wrong too. At first I helped guys a little when I could, but so many guys just didn't listen or couldn't learn or didn't really understand and were getting yelled at and in trouble for doing the dumbest things. So for about the first week or so our company commander and sometimes other company commanders would spot-check different people. He warned us that a major inspection was coming soon and that we had all better have our shit together. I was trying like hell to stay under his radar. I didn't want him to even know I existed. He had briefly looked through my stuff once but had never said a word to me or even looked at me. I was pretty confident that everything was okay with my gear and all my stuff. I was also in the very last bottom bunk in the back corner of the barracks. Out of sight, out of mind! Yes!

A day or two later, after we'd gotten up, shaved, and made our beds, I was just about to get dressed when a big metal garbage can flew through the door and banged down the floor (the deck), spilling all the garbage out before it slammed into the wall right in front of my bunk. The guy who had thrown it came in along with two CCs from other companies right behind him yelling and screaming at everyone to get to our inspection positions. The second two guys stopped right at the front and waited while the first guy came about halfway down the barracks on my side and stopped. Each company had about eighty to ninety recruits, and the bunks, one up and one down, lined both sides of the barracks from end to end. Each barracks was three stories tall, and our company was on the third floor of this particular barracks. Once we were all in our inspection positions, backs against the wall next to our bunks, lining both sides of the barracks, in parade rest, legs about two feet apart, and hands folded behind our backs, the carnage began.

You could not move a muscle or talk in parade rest. If questioned or spoken to, you would come to attention and answer every question or order first with "Sir, yes, sir." I wasn't really scared, maybe more nervous than anything else, worried that I might have forgotten something or done something wrong. These guys, exactly like my dad, were really enjoying their little power trip. They tossed clothes around the room and even chucked mattresses and bedding out the open windows as they moved from man to man, locker to locker, and bunk to bunk. Before long guys were beginning to cry. They had to do push-ups, run up and down the stairs, or run in place. Not one person had anything right, and each was having his personal things thrown at him with the CCs screaming right in his face. One guy had washed all his socks the night before and rolled them back up and put them in his locker wet. While he was standing at attention, one of the CCs began throwing those wet, rolled-up socks right into his face. And I mean throwing like a pitcher with a full windup and follow-through with the CC's outstretched arm coming to within about six inches of the guy's face. The guy bawled out loud each time he was hit. It really had to hurt. As the CC threw each one, he screamed, "You … stupid … ignorant … son … of … a … bitch!"

I was getting more and more nervous now. Two guys had gotten caught talking and were dragged up to the centerboard, a long table that ran down the middle of the barracks with picnic-like benches on both sides for writing and studying. They were told to stand up on top and come to parade rest facing each other nose to nose. The others CCs had stopped just so everyone could watch what was to happen to these two guys. The CC pushed their foreheads together and told them to keep their heads together. He told them to start backing up. They only backed up about two feet from each other, keeping their foreheads together, but you could tell it was hurting them like hell. "Now," he said, "start talking," which they did, though I could barely hear them. The CC screamed, *"Louder!"* which scared the hell out of them, and everyone else, so much that the two guys started crying and almost fell over and the rest of us all jumped about a foot. The two guys started talking much louder. "And don't stop!" the CC yelled. They didn't until it was all over.

The CC who had started in the middle on my side was just about finished tearing up the bunks and lockers next to my bunk when my bunkmate, who was in the upper bunk, reached up and picked his nose. The CC caught him out of the side of his eye and screamed, "What in the fuck do you think you're doing?" as he ran over and grabbed him by the front of his T-shirt. Ripping my bunkmate's shirt, the CC yanked him out of parade rest and over to the centerboard. He pulled my bunkmate up to the top with him, yelling, "You know goddamn good and well you do not move at parade rest!" He made my bunkmate stand at attention as he jammed his right index finger up his nose. He told him to repeat, "I will not move or pick my nose while at parade rest!" Screaming, he added, *"Loudly!"* My bunkmate sobbed as he did so until the end as well.

The CC came back over to our bunks and lockers, and now I was a little scared. As he'd come down the barracks, he'd been tearing up the top bunk and locker first and then moving to the bottom bunk and locker. When he came back over by me, he tore up my bunkmate's gear and threw everything out of his locker, not really even looking to see if it was in order or not, just doing it out of spite for what my bunkmate had done. I began to think that just because my bunkmate had picked his nose, this guy was not going to look at my stuff either after I'd worked so hard to make it perfect, or so I'd hoped. *I'm screwed,* I thought. But after he threw almost everything out of my bunkmate's locker and bunk, most of it out the window, he stopped and seemed to calm down and take a breath. He glanced first at my locker, started to look at me, and did a double take back at my locker. He bent down and, with his hands on his knees, started looking at everything really carefully. He measured and checked everything, not pulling anything out or throwing everything around the room but just moving things to see what I had done. The whole time he had a *This can't be right* type of look on his face. He actually looked as if he was getting angry again because he couldn't find anything wrong. After he had worked his way down my locker and looked through the last drawer, he closed it gently, as if he didn't want to mess anything up inside. But I also saw him mouth, "Fuck!"

He looked up at me in frustration. Then he looked down at my bunk. When he looked at me again, he began to smile. I suddenly realized I hadn't checked the catch edges on the sheets or blanket this morning when I made the bunk up. I thought, *Oh no! After all that . . .* My expression must have changed, because he got an even bigger smile on his face. He knew exactly what I was thinking. He grabbed all the bedding and said, "Aha!" as he ripped it back, exposing all the edges of the sheets and blankets. I couldn't believe it. They were perfect! It was almost as if all the guns misfired at my firing squad execution. What a relief! He threw the edges back down and this time said out loud, *"Fuck!"* He yelled at me, "Come to attention, and get your ass over here!"

I snapped to attention, took about three steps to get over to him, came to attention again, and said, "Sir, yes, sir!"

He got right in my face and said in a pissed-off, growling voice, "Do you write letters back home to your mother?"

"Sir, yes, sir," I said.

"Then you get your ass over there, sit at the centerboard, and write your mother a letter!"

"Sir, yes, sir," I said. I grabbed my stationery and pen, ran to the centerboard, and wrote a letter to my mom telling her what had happened and was happening as I sat there.

The inspection was only about halfway through when they finished on my side. I wrote my mom, my girlfriend, and my friends as I watched for the next hour as these CCs trashed everything and made guys cry, do exercises, or run around the barracks with their weapons above their heads. Things were flying everywhere. I ducked a couple of times as things flew by me or hit the guy standing above me picking his nose. After it was over and everyone was cleaning up, I finished up my letters and went back to my locker. The CC I had talked to must've told our CC, because he came over, looked at my stuff, looked at me, and said, "Wooton? I didn't even know you were in my company." My cover was blown!

Everything would be okay and work out just fine, though. I simply continued on doing everything I was told and supposed to do and maybe went a little more overboard than I needed to, but I never had a problem, not one! Soon after we left Worm Island and went over to a more relaxed routine. We still had lectures, marched, and had inspections, but it was much, much better. Soon after we moved into our new quarters, everyone had to participate in work week, which was when everyone had to go out each day and do just about whatever needed to be done. Some people—most people actually—went mess cooking, where they would go to the mess hall and do whatever was required, mostly cleaning and washing. Others cut grass and trimmed hedges, and others painted buildings. I was the only one who didn't have to go anywhere. Our CC made me stay in every day and help everyone with any problems they had. Mostly it was basic stuff like where things were supposed to go, how things should be folded, and even just how to make the bed correctly. But I also helped guys with everything from shining their boots and their weapon to learning marching maneuvers and the ten general orders you had to know by heart. I was helping guys with some very easy things, going back to the very beginning of our training, and with others I was helping them to finally get their stuff together.

The CC was also graded or scored on how well his company did in everything, so he loved me. I got free Cokes and candy bars every day in the barracks as I worked to help these guys out. I would help somebody, take a break for a while, help somebody else, and take a break for a while; it was pretty cool. On one of my breaks one day, I was leaning out the window watching a company of marines running along the fence right outside the window. When they saw me, they sang in cadence, "Look to my right, and what do I see? A faggity squid looking at me!" I flipped them the bird and said, "Fuck you!" They instantly came to a stop, broke the formation, and charged the fence. They screamed at me, cussing, telling me to come down and what they would do to me if they could get me. Thank God for the fence and the fact that I was up on the third floor of the barracks. Those eighty or ninety gung ho guys literally wanted to kill me. Break over!

I got along well with all the other guys. A couple of guys were a little closer friends than others, but I really didn't have a good buddy through my time there. Time went by pretty well, and things went smoothly for me all the way through boot camp. One of the neatest things that happened to me came at the very end. At the end of recruit training, three recruit awards are given out in each company. One is the honor-man award, which is awarded by the CC and almost always given to the recruit CC. Then there's the academic-achievement award, given to the recruit with the highest test scores. Those two awards went to our recruit CC. But the last award was for outstanding recruit and was decided by all the guys in the company. The night before graduation we all gathered together to pick who was to win the award. I was kind of leaning against a locker, mostly out of view from most of the guys gathered in the center of the barracks. Three or four guys' names were recommended by different guys, and our recruit CC wrote each one on the barracks blackboard. I agreed with most all of the recommendations; those recruits were all pretty cool guys and did pretty well. Just before we started to vote, some guy yelled out, "How about Wooton?"

A lot of guys asked, "Who's Wooton?"

Another guy yelled to me, "Craig, step out here."

It literally brings me to tears every time I think about this, but as soon as I turned around the corner and everybody saw me, everyone immediately yelled out in unison, "Yeah, him!" I couldn't believe it! I was shocked and totally surprised. They all voted unanimously for me, and that was that: I was the company's outstanding recruit.

The next morning I went down to the base theater with all the other companies' award recipients to meet the commander of the recruiting center. The first thing he told us was that we were all supposed to automatically receive a meritorious advancement, which would have meant I would have come out of boot camp an E-2 instead of an E-1, one rank above the lowest enlisted rank, but unfortunately President Nixon had put a freeze on all military advancements. That was a real disappointment, but we would get a commendation letter placed into our files. One by one, we all had our pictures taken with the captain as he presented us our awards. Then we were off to our graduation ceremony.

That was December 23, 1972. My father, who was now the chief of maintenance for a helicopter squadron at Point Mugu naval test station, had gotten permission to fly down the next day to North Island in a helicopter and pick me up and bring me home. After breakfast the next morning, I got a taxi to the docks next to downtown San Diego and took a navy ferry across the bay to North Island Naval Air Station, where my father and two pilots were already waiting for me. We hopped in, they fired it up, and soon after takeoff, one of the pilots got out and told me to come up and take his place. They let me fly all the way back. That started my thoughts of possibly flying helicopters someday. What a cool way to head home! When we landed, my girlfriend was standing on the ramp waiting for me. Just after Christmas and New Year's I would be off to jet engine school in Millington, Tennessee. My unknown future was on its way!

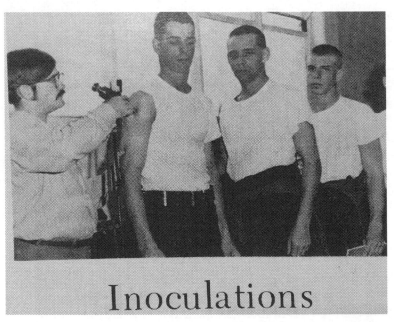

Inoculations

One of the first up for shots.

I am standing third from the right in this photo. I
spent a lot of my time coaching and helping a lot of
the other guys in the company with their gear.

Passing in review graduation day. I am up in
the front row, second from the left.

C. R. WOOTON
Outstanding Recruit

After being chosen by all the other guys in the company,
I received my commendation from the commander
of the training center for outstanding recruit.

16

Three Doomed Flights

I don't call these three incidents close calls. Avoiding these disasters was more like fate, something that was meant to be. They didn't just go by; they were flights I wanted to take but wasn't able to. All three ended in tragedy.

The first was on the set for *Twilight Zone: The Movie.* I was swamping, driving our biggest fuel truck to refuel our big Bell 204 helicopter when needed. The filming site wasn't that far from our company in Rialto, so I could drive out and back each day, and the helicopter would do the same. Like on many other jobs, I would be able to fly left seat if no one else was needed up front. At first they only had two camera guys and two stuntmen on machine guns in the back, so I flew with our director of operations on the first day.

The premise of the film is a racist white bigot having his life flipped around. As in the old TV *Twilight Zone* series science-fiction style, roles are reversed, and the bigot is the persecuted one. He spends time as a black man in the South, a Jew in Nazi Germany, and finally a Vietnamese being hunted by imperialistic Americans. Realizing now what he had been like, he tries to redeem himself by saving two Vietnamese children under fire in a small Vietnamese village. Unfortunately something went terribly wrong during the filming of this part of the movie. The set was a fake Vietnamese village built up against a fifty- to one-hundred-foot cliff next to a small creek. Using a bulldozer, they had dammed up the west end of the creek to make the creek swell up and look like a bigger river. The actor was to pick up the two small children and carry them across the river to safety. The whole while, explosives would be going off all around them, the helicopter would be hovering nearby overhead with its spotlight shining down on them, and .50-caliber machine guns would be blazing.

I only got to fly the first day. After that they decided the assistant director should be up front, so I was out. The second day I watched the helicopter hover over the river, close to the cliff, as they blew some test explosives. The blasts, coming from the mock village built right up against the base of the cliff, only had one way to go because of that cliff face: right out at the helicopter. I was standing up against the cliff, a little ways away from the village setup, across the river from where the cameras were when the explosions went off. They only used two explosive pyrotechnic devices, but they were much bigger than any of us had thought they'd be. The helicopter was rocked so violently I thought it might come down!

When they landed to refuel, the director came over to talk with us. I told the pilot I thought that the explosions were way too dangerous. The director immediately chimed in, "That was nothing. Wait until you see tomorrow night!" Right then, I would've said something if I were pilot in command, but I wasn't. Our pilot didn't say a word as he tended to work in the cockpit. I really thought he would go over later and talk about it with the director, and I assumed he had.

We arrived on the set the next afternoon but didn't get to the planned scene until very early the next morning. When the filming started, there were smaller explosions from the village as the actor screamed and yelled at the hovering helicopter. Back in he went to pick up the two Vietnamese children. Carrying the children, he began walking across the makeshift river. The helicopter was hovering off to their left, half over the mock village and half over the water, with its spotlight shining down on them and .50-caliber machine guns firing. The actor struggled carrying the children across the hip-deep water. You could tell he was having a hard time and getting tired. As he got about halfway across, the director told the pilot, "Lower, lower, lower!" Then a split second after that, he yelled to the pyrotechnics guy, "Now!"

The explosions started in the mock village just behind the actor and the two children. Boom, a pause for only a second, then boom-boom in quick succession. Just after the third explosion the helicopter started moving forward and left and then began to spin to the right. It circled directly over and around the actors as it spun at least three times and then moved to their right side. They had no idea the helicopter was out of control above them. The incredibly sad thing was that as the actor struggled in the water carrying the two children, he lost his balance and fell forward to his knees. He lost his grip on the little girl in his left arm but still held the boy in his right. He was fighting to pull the girl back up but only got her up to about his stomach when the helicopter crashed on a small piece of land not underwater and rolled to its left, its blades striking and killing all three of them. Had he not fallen, he would've probably been clear of the blades' arc when they struck the water.

The blades hit the adult actor just below his shoulders, flinging his shoulders and his head back across the river. The little boy lost his chin and his arm before his head also flew off. The girl half underwater must've been protected somewhat, as she was not fortunately not sliced to pieces, but she was still hit with enough force to kill her. All six people in the helicopter had minimal injuries, and no one else on the set was hurt.

I was called to speak to lawyers several times at the crash scene and was told I would probably be going into court for the trial against all who were charged. Fortunately, I never was. I was flying for Channel 13 when the trial was coming to an end. They knew I had been there and did a TV interview with me once. I couldn't say much, though, because the lawyers had ordered me not to say anything then. At the end of the trial Channel 13 had me on again, and I was able to tell much more of what had happened and what I thought. It was a very unnecessary, tragic accident.

To get the special effect of a huge fireball explosion like we all see in the movies, the pyrotechnics people use five-gallon white plastic commercial paint buckets. They place their pyrotechnic device in a bucket filled with sawdust from wood cuttings soaked in gasoline. Investigators determined a heavy plastic lid from one of those buckets, most likely from that third explosion after the actors entered the water, was blown outward away from the cliff right at the helicopter. It struck and damaged the tail rotor, causing the helicopter to spin out of control and crash.

The second doomed flight happened soon after the first while I was still working for Western at Rialto airport. Next to Western, on the east side of the huge fenced-in compound, were two other companies connected in a long row of hangars. Half were owned by a company that repaired and refurbished fire trucks, and the other half were owned by two wealthy gentlemen who used all the space to house their toys. They had every Harley Davidson, almost every model of Cadillac and a few beautiful vintage airplanes, including a Beechcraft 17 Staggerwing, which I think is one of the most beautiful planes ever built. The Staggerwing is a tail-dragger biplane. Most biplanes have their upper and lower wings directly above and below each other, but the Staggerwing has the upper wing positioned back a little farther, connected to the lower wing with slightly slanted, thick struts, one on each side. It is just so cool with its sleek, tapered front windscreen, huge propeller on a big radial engine, and cowling-covered main landing gear.

They had a mechanic/pilot who worked on and took care of everything. He and I had become friends and talked often. He was about my age, maybe a little older, but we didn't hang out with each other. He was a great guy and super nice to me. Around the time I had begun flying the Bell 47, he came out one day when I was getting ready to take one for a test flight. He asked if I could take him for a ride sometime, as he had never flown in a helicopter before. I asked, "No one ever offered to take you for a ride here before?"

"No!" He added, "All your other pilots seemed like such pricks. You were the first cool guy I met!"

I asked if he was free now.

"Hell yes!" he said.

"Hop in, but I want a ride for ride in that!" I said, pointing to the Staggerwing parked in the open hangar.

"You got it!" he said.

We only flew for about ten or fifteen minutes, and I let him take the controls. He was like a little kid when we got back. He was so happy. As he started back to his hangar, I said, "Just let me know when you're going to fly that Beech again, okay?" He smiled and gave me two thumbs-up.

Months went by. I had seen him take off in that Beech ten or more times with never a word from him. Soon the two gentlemen's collection was getting too big, and they needed a new toy box. They moved into a big new hangar on the east side of the airport next to the north-south runway. We faced the east-west runway from our compound. Not long after they moved, I had to deliver a fifty-gallon drum of oil to another company next door to them. I saw my friend outside working on a new aircraft they had. "When you going to give me the ride you owe me in the Staggerwing?" I asked as I walked up to him.

"How about a ride in this instead?" he said.

"Holy shit! Are you fucking kidding me? Hell yes!" I shot back at him. It was one of the United States Navy's and the United States Air Force's primary flight trainers from the early 1950s. It had a gigantic radial engine, tandem cockpit (student up front and instructor in back), and tricycle landing gear. I had always wanted to fly one of those or even something vaguely similar, but they cost hundreds of dollars for just minutes of flight time! "Really, promise?" I asked.

"You bet," he said.

"Okay, but if I see you take off again one more time without coming to get me, I'm going to be really pissed off!" I told him.

He reached out, shook my hand, and said, "I promise!" as he put his left hand over his heart.

"Bitchin'!" I said. I hopped back on the forklift and drove back down the taxiway to my company.

The very next day, late afternoon just about quitting time, I was checking everything before leaving when I heard that big radial engine coming down the runway. No mistaking it; it was the only one on the airport. When it finally came into view from behind the gentlemen's old hangars, I was standing out on the ramp by one of our helicopters. The company chief pilot was with me, and I even said to him, "Son of a bitch, there he goes again! He promised me a ride the next time he flew it!" As he flew by just out in front of us, I stretched out my arms in a *What the fuck?* gesture. I couldn't tell if my friend saw me or not as he climbed away; he probably did, though. As he turned and headed north, I turned, walked over to my car, got in, and headed home.

I had just walked into my apartment and was changing clothes when there was a knock at the door. One of the mechanics from our shop, an ex-marine and a good friend of mine, was standing there and said the T-28 had just crashed. We raced over to the crash site. We parked and walked out into the field where it had gone down. The police had already taped off the scene and were keeping everyone out. At that time I was playing softball with the police department in a city league and knew the guy who was manning the taped-off area, and he let us in.

Some witnesses told the police officers that the plane had tried to do a loop but hadn't made it. I could see where the wingtip had first hit the ground as my friend had tried to turn out of his horrible mistake, the loop maneuver. The giant radial engine had left a huge crater where it had smashed into the ground. The aircraft had crumpled into a ball as it had cartwheeled several times, trapping my friend and one of the co-owners of the company inside. They were cut to pieces by the razor-sharp, broken aluminum body. The coroners were just bagging my friend's severed head as we walked up. The firefighters had had to use the Jaws of Life to open the aircraft like a tin can to get them out.

I have no idea who was flying. I don't know if the co-owner was licensed to fly or not, but I really don't believe my friend caused this accident. He was a good pilot, and he was just so conscientious and careful. We'll never know. But whoever yanked that stick back and started that loop was not aware of the aircraft's limitations. *Know your aircraft and its limitations!* How many times have I said that? The T-28 needs a minimum of two thousand feet to complete a loop. They were flying between twelve hundred to no more than fifteen hundred feet above the ground when they started that maneuver.

The third doomed flight would happen a few years later up in Rancho Murieta, California, near Sacramento. Rancho Murieta airport is a small private airport owned by a wealthy businessman. He had a beautiful Beech King Air, a twin-engine turboprop, that he used for business. I flew as copilot in it when needed and absolutely loved it. However, he was getting busier, flying much more and carrying more passengers. He wanted to step up to a private jet. He needed something bigger and faster.

When you start shopping for a jet, all the aircraft manufacturers know, and their salespeople will bring their jets right to your front door. Soon some really nice jets began to show up each week. It was quite a deal too. Yes, they showed you the aircraft inside and out and of course flew you around, but they also brought lots of gifts and wined and dined their hopefully soon-to-be customer. A big, super-nice twin-engine jet came in one day for a scheduled appointment with the airport owner. However, he had been held up out of town and couldn't get back until the next day. Our office was in the airport fixed-base operator (FBO), and when the two pilots and sales manager came in, we struck up a conversation. They invited us out to see the jet, and it was like the plushest limo you could imagine inside, just absolutely gorgeous. The cockpit was, of course, equipped with the latest technology and all the bells and whistles. One of my bosses asked them to lunch and told me to come along. They were really cool guys and a lot of fun. We got back to the airport. They had decided to spend the night and meet the airport owner back here in the morning. However, they couldn't leave that big, beautiful, multimillion-dollar plane out on this unsecured airport with no hangar to lock it up in. So they were going to fly over to Sacramento International Airport, where there was hangar space for them.

We walked out to the aircraft and were just saying good-bye when the sales manager asked if we would like to come along. "Yeah, I'd love to!" I said. My boss said he couldn't because he had a meeting to go to in about half an hour. I asked the sales manager if they could wait just a moment while I checked to see if I could get a ride back first. "Sure, we'll wait for you," the sales manager said. Our other pilots were gone except for Brad, but he would be going on a flight shortly also. It would only be about a ten-minute flight to Sacramento, but it would take almost an hour by car to get over there from Rancho Murieta. With no way back, I couldn't go. So I went back out and told them thanks but declined. "No problem, maybe tomorrow," the sales manager said as he closed the door. They started up, taxied out, and took off. One of the fuel boys and the secretary from the FBO came out on the ramp with my boss, Brad, and me. We knew what was coming next. Every one of these sleek rockets that had come in to demonstrate their aircraft would take off, bank left, head downwind, and then from a couple of miles out turn final and come screaming right over the runway on a high-speed pass.

Sure enough, after a few minutes, here it came, maybe fifty to one hundred feet above the runway. My exact words to my boss were "That sure doesn't seem very fast to me!" He agreed as it went by completely quiet and not very fast at all. Just after they had gotten past midfield, whoever was flying pulled the nose up and began a left roll. I expected a fast flyby with a quick snap roll and to see it shoot away. Instead it did a really slow, wide barrel roll. I instantly knew they were in trouble. Just as they reached the top of that roll, upside down, they began falling. They continued to fall through the roll, and I heard the engines spooling back up to full throttle before the aircraft became level. The pilot, I'm sure instinctively, was pulling back on the yoke to climb, which was stalling the aircraft and only making it fall quicker. With its nose up easily forty-five degrees or better, it disappeared behind the trees next to the river that ran along the south side of the runway. A huge fireball followed.

There was no way to get to the crash site because of the river. Brad and I both started running to the hangar. He said he would get a bucket and start hitting the fire we knew would be going already in the dry brown fields on the other side. I said I would go to take a quick look and see if there was something I could do, which I knew there wouldn't be, and then I was going to call Channel 13 and pick up a crew. I got off first and in just seconds was over the crash site. The tail section was the only part recognizable as being from an aircraft, everything else was just small, scattered debris. The three guys on board were obviously dead. The two pilots were right in the middle of the wreckage with their clothes completely burned away, and the salesman had been thrown away from the fire a couple hundred feet forward and was lying on his back in the grass still in his suit and tie. I called the station and picked up a waiting crew.

When we got to the crash site, I shut down the aircraft as the crew started filming, live on the scene within minutes. I walked over to check it out close-up. Like I said, nothing was recognizable except the tail. It looked as if somebody had dumped a bunch of trash and then set it on fire. Most every crash I flew into was the same. Both pilots were burned really badly, but it must've been a really quick flash fire. Their clothes were completely gone, and yes, they were burned, but not like I'd seen in other crashes where people had burned for a longer time. One was lying facedown; the other looked almost as if he had tried to get up but been caught in that quick, intense fire and been frozen. He was lying on his stomach with his head up, looking straight ahead, his chin resting on his forearms and elbows. He had a perfectly circular hole in his forehead where he'd obviously smashed into the instrument panel when the aircraft hit, and one of the round gauges had been driven into him. As I walked out to where the sales manager was, he didn't look as if anything had even happened to him. His suit looked pretty much intact, but he'd obviously hit something on his way out also. His face looked as if it had been taken out, smashed to pulp, and put back in.

All of us who had seen the crash were called in to talk to investigators and the aircraft's company people. Turned out, when this particular company did their high-speed flybys, they would throttle back before they reached the spectators so this nice, quiet jet would pass by. Then quickly they would throttle back up, do a snap roll, and be gone. The manufacturer's investigator said he thought these guys had throttled back too early, gotten too slow, and throttled back up too late. They'd been doomed as soon as they'd begun that roll.

17

Ed the Elephant

One of the first things I found out at the library was that Myanmar had fifty-two species of venomous snakes. I thought they might have tigers, which they didn't, though there might be some up near India where we would be flying, but they did have leopards and bears. They also had a third of the world's elephant population. But in general, the country seemed much like any other Asian country I'd been to in the past.

Once we started flying I checked everywhere for any type of wildlife but didn't see anything for days. After reading about all they had here, I sure wasn't seeing any of it. After about a week, while flying on my own during lunch, I started getting a pretty serious high-frequency vibration. I'd felt it begin a couple of days before, and it had gotten progressively worse. Just to be on the safe side, I thought I'd better land somewhere and check it out. I spotted a small clearing off to my right on one of the many small rivers that ran along my flight route. As I circled around it once, to make sure it was safe, I saw, just a couple hundred feet down the river from where I wanted to land, an old guy with this huge, hardworking elephant pulling around big downed teak trees and piling them up. I went ahead and landed on the spot I wanted. I was a little concerned now that it might be his property, and I didn't know whether he would be all right with me being there. I really needed to get down, though, and determine that all was well with the aircraft just for my own peace of mind. I guess I would find out soon enough. I landed and shut the engine off and, using the rotor brake as quickly and smoothly as I could, brought the rotating blades to a stop because, just as I thought, here came the old guy riding on top of his elephant.

I didn't know what to expect but didn't want to hurt either of them with the fast-spinning blades. I got out to greet him as he came strolling up to me with his big old elephant. It was a little intimidating and scary. I had only seen elephants in zoos and of course always at a distance. But there was just something about this big gray guy. His face and the look in his eyes seemed almost happy and childlike. The old guy was really very nice and spoke pretty decent English. He slid down off his elephant and said his name was Aung. I told him my name, and he asked me if everything was okay; if I needed anything, any help of any kind; and if I was hungry. I said I was okay, but he gave me a couple of bananas anyway. I asked him what the elephant's name was, and he said he hadn't given him one. *Ed* suddenly popped into my head: Ed the elephant. "Hi, Ed!" I said. It was funny because I just happened to have some shelled salted peanuts that I always brought for something to snack on anytime I flew. I asked the guy if it was okay to feed his elephant a few. He said no problem, and as soon as I pulled out a handful, the elephant instantly went for my hand. Before I could even stretch out my arm to give them to him, he grabbed some with his trunk, curled them up into his mouth, and munched them down. So, just to be funny, I stepped back a couple of paces, turned around, and placed a couple into my flight suit pockets before turning back around and walking back over to the elephant. Sure enough, he started sniffing me from head to toe until he found all the peanuts. I thought that was pretty funny and amazingly cool. But I had to get back to work.

I told the old guy why I had landed and gave him a step-by-step explanation as I opened up the engine cowling and began to check what I expected to be the problem. It was actually very comical, both of them standing right there next to the aircraft listening so attentively as I talked. The old guy had his mouth wide open, and they both would move their heads in unison following my every move, with the elephant cocking his head occasionally like a little puppy dog, wondering what I was doing. As I expected, the rear engine mount was the problem. It wasn't damaged, but the bearings in the mounting points were getting loose and would have to be replaced soon. It would be okay to fly safely for now, though. I buttoned everything back up, walked over to Ed, gave him a few more peanuts, and told the old guy thanks so much for checking and making sure that I was okay. I asked if I could stop again sometime just to say hi, and he said sure thing. As I got in, Aung and Ed turned and started to walk back to work. I waited till they were well clear before I started back up. Just as I'd thought, or feared, Ed stopped and turned around. I'm sure he wanted some more peanuts, or maybe he just liked his new friend. Aung instantly got in front of him as he started toward me and made him stop. I quickly lifted off and waved good-bye. They both stood right there and watched me until I was out of sight over the trees.

So the very next day at lunch I brought some sandwiches and coffee for Aung and more peanuts for Ed. I landed the helicopter a little ways away from them but didn't shut down this time. I just walked over to him, gave him the coffee and sandwiches, and said thanks again for the other day. I had put the peanuts in the bottom pocket of my flight suit before I'd landed, and when I got up to the old guy, Ed instantly started sniffing me from my neck all the way down to the pocket with the nuts and found them! What a crack-up, what a cool animal. Of course he was huge. He had an amazingly soft trunk and loving eyes that actually seemed to twinkle. And as big and powerful as he was, he was so gentle. Whenever he touched me, he seemed to be doing it ever so softly so as to not hurt me. After feeding the peanuts to Ed, I turned to walk away. Ed began to follow me back to the helicopter. Aung was pulling on one of the ropes tied around Ed trying to hold him back, but Ed was just pulling him along as if he was nothing at all. I stopped, turned, raised my arms, and yelled stop. Ed instantly stopped, and his facial expression completely changed. I've seen many pictures of elephants with watery eyes, but he actually looked as if he was going to cry, as water really did well up in his eyes. He took one step back, and I turned back, jumped in the helicopter, and took off. When I looked back, he was still standing there watching me fly away. I felt terrible! It was as if I'd just broken some little kid's heart.

A couple of days went by before I went back to see them again. I brought lunch again and of course the peanuts and was planning to stop and stay awhile. As I circled around to land, Ed was already watching me and turned and headed toward me while I was landing. I landed a little farther away this time and shut the aircraft down. While we were eating lunch, the old guy told me that Ed had been watching me for the last few days every time I flew by. I was a little worried, as was Aung, that when I landed the helicopter, Ed might come too close. He was like a little excited puppy that knows he's going to get a treat soon. So I had landed each time a little bit farther away from them and turned the tail rotor away from the direction they would be coming. Ed could actually walk underneath the rotor blades, but if he were to raise his trunk or his head up, he could hit the blades. And sure enough, each time I started coming, he would turn and leave whatever work he was doing. The old guy wasn't angry at me; he thought it was kind of funny, and he could actually hold Ed back if he needed to. But, as I said, he too was worried about the rotor blades and knew I was being safe by landing a little farther away.

I probably stopped and had lunch with them another four or five times before I left. Old Ed became my good buddy. He was always as excited to see me as I was to see him each time I came in to land. I flew by where they were working many times every day but didn't always see them. One time, when I couldn't stop, I just circled them a couple of times, waved, and flew on. Aung told me Ed would perk up and get excited as soon as he heard me coming and would stop everything even if he couldn't see me. When he could, he would stand there and watch me. If I didn't land and flew out of sight, his big ears would drop, and he would sadly turn and get back to work. To not distract him from his work, I made sure not to circle around them if I wasn't going to land. I loved watching him work. He was so amazingly powerful and seemed to move effortlessly while pulling those huge teak trees. He would drag them around as if they were twigs.

I was going to be leaving soon. Days went by, and I hadn't seen them. On my very last flight coming back late in the afternoon I saw them again and landed. I couldn't stay long, because the government had a rule that we couldn't fly at night (after sunset) out over the jungle, so I couldn't shut the helicopter down and left it running. I ran over to them, and Ed, with his happy puppy face, was again as excited to see me as I was to see him. I said good-bye to the old guy and gave him a really nice flashlight I had and the last big bag of salted peanuts I had for Ed. As I fed Ed a handful of nuts and patted his trunk, his face changed again, and his ears actually dropped! He raised his trunk up as if he was going to start sniffing me again but instead laid it over my right shoulder and against my face. I wrapped my right arm over his trunk and held it and rubbed it while holding my left hand up against his face. He was holding me, so gently keeping me there. I could feel he didn't want to let me go. He seemed to know this would be our last time together. I stepped back, and he let go of me, his trunk sliding slowly off of my shoulder. As I backed away, I held up my hands one more time just to make sure he would stay, then turned and ran back to the helicopter. I actually had tears in my eyes as I lifted off. I turned and, flying right over them, waved good-bye.

18

Guam-Bound

My old man's next duty station was Naval Air Station Agana, Guam. I was really looking forward to going and ended up absolutely loving it there. It was very similar to Hawaii but without the hotels and tourists and maybe a little more humid. It was a pretty simple, quiet little island, thirty miles long and three to nine miles wide. Not much there, but it was beautiful. Dad was there for nine months before we got there and built up how cool his three boys were to his buddy's daughters on base. They were all looking forward to meeting us, and apparently all the guys our age were jealous and were waiting to kick our asses.

We left for Guam on Tony's eleventh birthday, August 12, 1966. He actually missed his birthday because we crossed the international date line heading west and arrived in Guam on the thirteenth. Dad was cool, though, and had one of the new Schwinn Stingray bicycles waiting for him. Dad knew the girls were waiting for us but also knew the boys' plans as well. He had arranged for everyone to come to our house for a pizza party the day after we arrived. It was so cool. We all had so much fun, and all the guys got along with us just fine.

We didn't have to worry about the guys on base, but everyone, guys and gals, was telling us how much the Guamanians hated us and were going to kick our asses when we got to school. We would be starting school in less than two weeks and wouldn't really get to meet any of the local kids till then. The kids on base really had me worried. They said the guys all

159

wore big belts with huge steel buckles that they would take off and swing around to hit us with. The guys also wore platform shoes with three or four more soles attached to the bottoms and steel taps, as in dance-shoes taps, on the toes to kick us with.

I took it all with a grain of salt, but I was still a little scared. Sure enough, when I arrived at my third junior high school, Barrigada Junior High, there were all these guys out front waiting for us, all with greased-back black hair, right out of the '50s, only they were Guamanian and not white. They were screaming, "Fucking haoles!" I thought that was only in Hawaii! As soon as we got off the bus, they came at us with their belts off, ready to start swinging. I'll never forget what happened as the first guy came after us with his belt. I had dropped my school stuff and was ready to go with a couple of my new friends next to me when this girl, actually the base's executive officer's daughter, jumped out, knocked the guy's belt out of his hands, and stood on it. That was so cool, but it only stopped him. The others just went around her and tried to surround us. Right then it was as if every male teacher in the school, Guamanian and white, exploded through everybody, got between us, and forced the Guamanian boys back.

Everything seemed to calm down, and we went to our classes. I still got dirty looks from all the guys in my class, and I knew something was brewing. It was funny: all the Guamanian girls were just the opposite. They were all devout Catholic girls and absolute sweethearts. They were so nice to me the whole time I was in school. At about third period, I was told I needed to turn in a medical form that I had forgotten in my locker. The teacher told me to take it to the nurse's office and then hurry back. I had just pulled the form out, closed my locker door, and turned to walk away when three big Guamanian guys blocked my way.

"Where are you going, you fucking haole?" the biggest one asked.

I instantly grabbed him by the throat and slammed his head and back hard against my locker. It scared the other two so badly they jumped off the concrete walkway into the grass. "You're fucking with the wrong guy!" I said with my face right in his.

Wide-eyed, he nodded his head up and down three or four times, muttering, "Okay, okay, okay."

I turned and walked away, waiting to be jumped from behind, but nothing. *Did I actually just do and say that?* I asked myself. No one ever bothered me again, and all the Guamanian guys became my good, good friends.

The second and third summer in Guam my parents couldn't find a babysitter for my sister, so I volunteered. I took care of her every day for those two summers. She was such a little doll. We went to the pool, park, and movies almost every day. In the rest of my free time I built model airplanes. They hung covering my ceiling and on every wall in my room. I played ball again, but now I was playing with guys who were all a year or two older than me. I had pitched a little but mostly had played first base because I was left-handed. But now I was in danger of being put on the bench with only the outfield left open for me. The other guys were just so much bigger and better than I was. Rick tried playing ball again as catcher but quit after the second day. That was the only spot left, so I volunteered to be catcher. I loved the shit out of that! It was lots of action, and I was good at it. I had a pretty good arm, and I was accurate and pretty fast. At practice one day, the guy leading off third base turned his back on me as he walked back to base after a pitch. I threw the ball to third to get him out, but the third baseman had turned away also, and the ball flew into left field. After that hiccup, I called a meeting with everyone and told them to never take their eyes off of me whenever I had the ball. They never did again. I used a right-handed catcher's glove backward on my left hand all through practice until our very first game, when the coach gave me a brand-new left-handed catcher's glove. It was great. I picked off three guys that night before their coach wised up. I got two of the guys, one at first and one at third, as they looked away and nonchalantly headed back to their bases. The last was on second base leading off with his hands on his knees, bent over to spit. Zip! "You're out!" the ump called. To this day I still remember that guy's face, the look of disbelief as he was caught there with his hands still on his knees. It was the best season of my life. We won all sixteen games, and I was chosen most outstanding player.

The night after our last game all our parents took the coach out for a drink, and all of us went to my house to drink. We mixed all the booze in my parents' pantry with cherry Kool-Aid. It was my first time drinking, and I chugged down three or four glasses of the spiked Kool-Aid. I was sick for three days, and to this day I will almost gag just smelling whiskey.

One of the coolest things while being in Guam was my age. I was old enough to where I could do more and get off base. Some of my friends could drive, and we went everywhere—visiting beaches, boonie stomping (hiking in the jungle), spelunking, exploring caves, going all over the island. The base had a teen club, and we had dances almost every weekend. My favorite thing to do was go to Ipao Beach, also known as Gun Beach because of the Japanese guns still in place from World War II. Our house was up on a plateau next to the runway that looked right down on Ipao. I could be there in minutes. It was a big half-moon bay with nothing but palm trees completely covering it. There were a few palm-leaf-covered huts you could barbecue under or just relax in out of the sun. That beach is now completely packed with hotels. I would snorkel there almost daily. The front half of my body was fairly tan, but my back half was dark, dark brown from floating around facedown in the water almost every day.

The Vietnam War was going hot and heavy right then, and living next to the runway was the perfect place for an airplane geek like I was. Every day B-52 bombers would depart and return to Andersen Air Force Base at the north end of the island, flying right out in front of us over the water. Also every day, nonstop, bombs for the bombers were brought up in huge trucks from where they had been shipped into the naval base at the south end of the island. I would also start my first job in Guam, only fifteen years old, at Fjord's Smorgette, a smorgasbord restaurant, with my best friend PS. Though I only worked there a month or two before my family left, I really liked it.

In January 1969 Dad decided to take a break from flying and be a recruiter for the navy. He picked Dubuque, Iowa, for his next assignment. So after only a few months at my first high school, John Fitzgerald Kennedy High School, we were off to good old Dubuque.

1968 FINENANA YEARBOOK STAFF

10 students signed up
aree ninth graders and
ere quickly found to
.7.

k start and $800.00
abscription sales be-
sponsors and adver-
other $200.00 pushing
of the $1,000.00 goal.
improve the 1968
ing from soft paper cov-
r and decided to in-
m 64 to 76. This means
than the 67.
obor. Mr. William and
he Island Photo Service
hot over 1,500 indi-
a students for the year-

mittees were formed
th, and 9th grade photos

Me on the yearbook staff at Barrigada Junior High School
in Guam. I really liked being a part of that staff!

19

Tuna-Boat Bounce

There are four conditions or configurations that can be hazardous to your health while flying: high altitude, high temperature, high humidity, and high aircraft weight (operating at an aircraft's maximum weight). Combined, these factors can cause potential problems, such as limited power and performance. Even though I had to fly under three of these four conditions while working from tuna boats, the flying was pretty simple and basic. Being at sea level canceled the first condition, but being in the South Pacific Ocean meant it was almost always hot and humid. We always topped off the fuel tanks before each flight, and the aircraft was loaded with the usual instrumentation and radios as well as extra navigation and marine radios, seal bombs, two big guys, survival gear, and the two big whale dicks, the two huge hotdog-looking floats. So we were right at maximum allowable weight every takeoff.

Actually, we would maybe be a little bit over the allowable weight each takeoff, but after just a little flying, we would burn quite a bit of fuel and drastically reduce our weight. If the boat was at a good speed, heading into the wind, I could get the helicopter light on the floats; ease the stick forward; and, with the wind blowing up and over the bow and the pilot house, get that extra bit of lift and get away from the boat. Once off, if necessary, I could push the nose over more and build up lift very quickly. You don't take off directly over the bow, ever. If you lost power and went into the water, the boat would run right over you. Though the helipad sits squarely on top of the pilot house, the markings for landing and taking off and tie-down points are angled about forty-five degrees to the left of the bow. You take off and clear away from the boat at a forty-five-degree angle. Once away from the boat, if need be, you can turn parallel to it for more lift. On landing you approach from the right rear of the boat and land into the wind on the deck using the same angle from which you left. After two or three hours of flying, you burn off most of your fuel, and your landing weight is not a problem. You wouldn't want to land full of fuel, at max weight, especially with no wind, the boat being stopped, and high humidity and temperature, but I did exactly that, barely!

I was afraid something might happen sometime and I would be forced to land in just such conditions. On one flight, just after we got off and started to make a set on some tuna, one of the guys in the engine room was seriously injured. They had to shut the engines down, and the boat came to a stop. I knew we really needed to stay up to burn off at least a little more fuel, but this guy also might need to be flown somewhere for help, and the sooner we got down, the sooner we could assess how badly he was hurt and whether I would have to transport him somewhere. The skipper was actually more concerned about losing the fish and the damage that might have been caused to the boat's engine. He wanted to get down immediately and asked me if we could do it safely. I didn't really think so. We were just too heavy. But I said I would try.

I had done lots of confined-area landings in the mountains, into the trees, before and knew that if I kept my speed up and power managed until the last possible moment, I could make it. The problem with such landings was that when you got below the treetops, the wind that had helped generate your lift would suddenly be stopped or blocked by the trees. If you didn't have your power already coming in, you would lose lift and settle into your own downwash, which would literally push you down into the ground faster. It's called settling with power. On this day it was dead calm, with no wind; it was midday and hot and humid as hell; and we were way too heavy! I got a good long start away from the boat, turned, and lined up like any other approach but with a little-steeper angle and a lot more speed. As I got closer, I gradually slowed, still staying faster than normal, and added power so I wouldn't have to add a lot at the bottom, which was where I would begin to settle. I only had a postage stamp to land on. The helipad on top of the pilot house was only about twenty to twenty-five feet wide and maybe thirty to thirty-five feet long, and there were also various engine exhaust pipes, wires, antennae, and radar nearby. No running landings here! I didn't want to settle just short and crash into the side of the boat, and I didn't want to come in too steep and fast and overshoot and go off the boat on the other side. As I got closer and lower, it was looking good; it looked like we were going to make it. I was aiming for the right front edge of the landing pad. Thank God I did. I was slowing, adding power, and was almost there when the collective in my left hand, which controlled the power or angle of attack and the lift of the blades, stopped! It hit the stop; it was all the way up, and there was nothing left.

The helicopter began to shudder, and I could actually hear the lift being lost from the sounds the blades were making. We started to fall like a rock. With a sickening feeling I held the cyclic steady in my right hand, resisting the urge to push forward. We were still about ten feet up and falling. We hit, as I would see from the marks on the floats later, exactly half on and half off the deck. We bounced just like a huge rubber ball because of those big, ugly, wonderful floats! I thought for sure that they would explode. I don't know how they didn't. We bounced just once and landed dead center of the large *H* in the middle of the helipad. That extra speed and my aim had saved our asses. If I had aimed for the center of the helipad, that one bounce would've taken us right over the other side and into the water. Amazingly the helicopter didn't have one bit of damage. The floats were fine and the frame perfect, no bends or cracks anywhere! The crewman, it turned out, wasn't hurt as badly as it had first seemed. A few small stitches and pretty good bandaging, and he was fine. The engine had been damaged a little but was repaired soon enough by the engineer.

Most every flight was normal flying, with uneventful takeoffs and landings. The landings were potentially most hazardous but fun and challenging. Most of the time the boat, with satellite weather information, avoided most all bad weather. We had a little rain almost every day, which was a good natural helicopter freshwater wash, and occasional good-size swells, but mostly we operated in fairly calm conditions. Even in calm conditions there were always swells. We could expect swells to come in three- and sometimes four-wave sets. While sailing along, we would go through smooth spots and then go up and down, one, two, three times, and then it would be smooth again. Almost all boats had stabilizer systems that prevented most side-to-side rolling but not pitching, nose-up-nose-down motion. So when the boat was heading into the wind and into the swells, as it almost always was when recovering the helicopter, I would see as I approached to land the up-and-down pitching—one, two, three—and then the swells would stop and smooth out. All I had to do was time it, set up my approach, and slow as I got close. At the end of the last downward pitch, as the boat came back up, leveling off, my goal was to be right alongside the helipad. I could then just move over the deck and set the helicopter down. I didn't try to hover and stay over the deck too long. I went in and put it down as quickly and as safely as I could. It would not have been good to be hovering over the deck thinking I was about to touch down just to have the deck suddenly drop twenty or thirty feet away from me or, worse, come screaming back up at me when I was just above it pushing down on my controls.

20

United States Navy

I wasn't sure if I would make a career out of the navy and be a lifer like my father was. I had wanted to be a pilot from a young age and thought I could do it in the military, but to be a pilot in the military you had to have a college degree. My folks couldn't afford college for me, and of course I couldn't afford it either, so I went into junior college right out of high school in hopes I would be able to transfer to a four-year college after two years. I did okay for about six months until President Nixon got me, actually a lot of us.

I was in the last draft of the Vietnam War the year I graduated high school, and my number was pretty low. I was very worried about having to go. I would if I had to, but who really wants to go to war? A lot of guys were going to college just to avoid the draft. If you were taking a minimum of fifteen credits of classes, which I was, you were deferred from the draft. It wasn't really fair, though, that all the rich kids could go to college while all the people who couldn't afford it were being sent off to Vietnam. Nixon suddenly changed the rules and said there were no more deferments; everyone was going!

Even though the war was winding down, I was afraid I was going to be called in. I figured if I was going to go, I would rather have a choice of what I was going to do. We were watching live TV broadcasts of the fighting every night at dinnertime just days before I was going to go into the military. I wouldn't know until after I got out of the military, returned to college, and met an ex-army guy in class that the United States Army took guys with only a high school education as warrant officers flying helicopters. I was still just a kid, had been around only the navy all my life, and knew nothing about the other branches of service. I was actually really pissed at my dad because he knew of that program and never told me, even though he knew how much I wanted to be a pilot. He had us all kind of brainwashed and wanted us to go into the navy. He was also a recruiter for the navy for some time. He just wanted to continue the navy tradition our family had. If I had known about the army program, I would have been gone in a heartbeat!

But my main thought at that time was if I couldn't be a pilot now, I would learn all I could about all the aircraft systems so that when I did become a pilot, I would be a much better one. That would turn out to be so very true. After taking all the military tests before I joined, I thought that, of all the things to choose from, jet engines were what I wanted to go to school for. Piston-powered aircraft were just about nonexistent. Even the propeller- and rotor-powered aircraft the military had were powered by turboshaft turbine engines. All others were powered by thrust-powered turbine engines. I had no idea at the time that even new navy ships were being powered by turbine jet engines. So after boot camp, I was off to jet school in Millington, Tennessee, right down the road from our first little chicken farmhouse. The memories flooded back each time I drove past going to and from Memphis. Though that pretty little house still stood with its beautiful front yard, the two big elm trees had been cut down, leaving two huge stumps in the yard, and the fields and chicken coop my old man had built behind the house were long overgrown with weeds.

I liked jet school. It was much more relaxed than boot camp of course but still had a few restrictions. Regular reciprocating engines, or gas-powered piston engines, were all fairly simple then: intake, compression, power, exhaust, four strokes of the piston. Jet engines were similar in a way: suck, squeeze, bang, and blow. They were actually really simple, just with thousands more moving parts and exceptionally more power. There are many sizes of engines of course depending on aircraft size. We learned the basic principles of all jet engines and worked on an A-4 Skyhawk engine, the Pratt and Whitney J52. In the course of our class we took the engine out, did some maintenance on it, put it back in, and started it up. We always heard the engines running up way out on a secluded part of the base, but we couldn't see them. That was the final phase of each class finishing up.

When we finally went out to do our final phase and run the engine up, I was picked to go first. We would each take turns in the cockpit using all the hand signals we had learned, monitoring all the gauges, and communicating with the ground crews starting it up and shutting it down. That A-4 is a tricycle-gear aircraft with one wheel under the nose with tall hydraulic landing gear that makes it sit nose high on the ground and the two main gears under the wings, one per wing. The aircraft was chained down at various points all around it, and the wheels were choked, with big pieces of wood in the front and back of each wheel. None of us had seen this running-up procedure before. We'd learned all the steps from start to finish in class, but the instructor had never told us what was going to really happen. I got in, did all the checks, gave all the appropriate hand signals, and fired up the engine. After it settled in at idle, I made sure all was well with oil temperatures and pressures. I could feel the awesome power that engine was producing even at idle! I signaled all was well and was signaled back to go to full military power, full throttle. I had really been waiting for this, and, while watching to make sure all gauges were in their proper ranges, I firmly pushed the throttle smoothly all the way to the stop.

I was not prepared for what happened when the throttle hit that stop. The nose gear contracted, and the nose dropped about four feet instantly. It scared the living shit out of me! The noise was phenomenal even with the headsets we were all wearing, but the vibration, the power, was unbelievable! I was sure it was going to break the chains and I was going to be airborne. This all happened so quickly and scared me so badly I was about to pull back on the throttle when I looked out at the students and instructor standing nearby and saw them all busting up and bent over laughing and pointing at me. He had told them all after I got in what was going to happen and to watch me. Sure enough, my reaction, as all other first-timers in the cockpit, was hilarious. After I realized I'd been had, I relaxed, and the instructor let me enjoy my few extra moments. I loved it; I wanted to be set free! I could only imagine this little sports car zipping around through the air being propelled by so much awesome power. I was signaled to throttle back and then shut it down after it had cooled. I got out, and the other guys took their turns. I don't remember watching any of them go through this final test. I was in another place dreaming of flying something like this and what it must be like. I was jealous of the pilots that would be flying things like this. I didn't want to work on these aircraft; I wanted to fly them.

I knew I would be going to a helicopter squadron, but I didn't know where yet or whether I would be able to fly as a crew member or not. Our instructor asked me if I wanted to go to search-and-rescue (SAR) school or to engine school. If I went to SAR school, I would come out and be a crew member but would know only basic systems on the aircraft. So I would basically be a gas station attendant for the helicopter. I still had my mind set on flying someday and still strongly believed the more I knew of any aircraft could only make me a better pilot, so I told him jet engine school. My next school would be for the T58-GE-10 engines used on the helicopters I'd be working on. I really wanted to learn them first, and my instructor said I could be a crew member after engine school too. So off I went to T58 school. The only problem was that neither the instructor nor I had any idea of the difference between an HC and an HS helicopter squadron. HC is the designation for a cargo helicopter, and HS is the designation for an antisubmarine helicopter. I was heading to an HS squadron, which carried only two crew members, two sonar operators in the back searching for submarines. I would not be flying.

My first duty station was in Imperial Beach Naval Air Station located at the southern part of San Diego, California, right up against the border with Mexico and only about a mile from the beach. I would go to Helicopter Antisubmarine Squadron 10 (HS-10), which was a training squadron for all operations of the H-3, the big twin-engine Sikorsky helicopter exactly like the one the United States Marines fly the president in but loaded with sonar screens, sonar dipping devices, and magnetic anomaly detectors. I learned about the T58 engines, which I really liked, and all the other systems as well as the corrosion control required because the helicopters constantly operated over the ocean, flying and hovering low to dip their sonar gear into the water to search for submarines.

After a few months I finished my training and simply moved to the other end of the airfield to HS-8, the "Eightballers" squadron. I hadn't even touched any of the H-3s yet, and I would first have to work on the line as a plane captain, essentially a gas station attendant for helicopters, and learn more about the aircraft before they would send me to the jet shop. Each squadron had an electrician shop, airframes and hydraulic shop, jet shop, and the parachute rigger shop. I set a record by becoming the fastest person ever to make plane captain in any helicopter squadron on the base. It took most everyone else three to six months; I did it in one month.

The cool thing was that my training was over and I was finally able to relax and settle into a normal military life. It was actually exactly like a regular nine-to-five job. The only difference was every six days I would be on duty and couldn't drink (or do any other drugs) or really go anywhere, not far anyway, because I was on call if needed. However, I found out right away that everyone was getting high all the time. I didn't really drink much, maybe at a party or out dancing; that was about it. I had smoked weed a little after high school and with a guy in Millington, but I was so surprised at how much literally everyone was drinking, smoking, and doing every type of drug you can imagine. Most of the lifers only drank, but they drank a lot! Everyone else smoked; many smoked and did other things. In my first four-man barracks room, the very first night, my roommates kept dropping little innuendos until I finally said, "Why don't you guys just ask me if I want to get high?" They all busted out laughing and brought out the pot. They started to stuff a blanket under the door, but I told them I wasn't comfortable smoking in the barracks. None of them had a car, so I offered to drive us to the beach to get high. I loved that beach, and we would go down there many times to get high. It was an open, uncrowded, really pretty beach, and you could literally walk across the border into Mexico from it.

But these guys were getting high all the time—before work, on breaks, at lunch, and definitely after work. The base was really small with a small runway for helicopters only, no airplanes. They would drive around the perimeter road around the base and get high two or three times a day. I partied with them a little at first but not much, because I was in love with a girl, my high school sweetheart. I would drive the couple of hours it took to get up to where she lived every chance I had. I wasted so much time and energy and an awful lot of money over the next three years, thinking we had a future together, only for her to dump me when I went on my first Western Pacific (WESTPAC) cruise for six months. Besides going to see her, being so close to the beach, I began surfing a lot more, and I was in the water almost every single morning or afternoon, sometimes both.

I was in heaven! I was going surfing all the time. All the San Diego beaches were great, from Imperial Beach—which was really great most of the year and uncrowded and was right on the border, so you could sit in the water and see a bullring in Mexico—up the Coronado strand, over the Coronado Bridge, around to Point Loma, and on to Mission Beach, Cardiff, and Encinitas, a surfer's paradise. Being just minutes from the Mexican border, I could cross into Tijuana and get over to the coast, and there were literally hundreds of spots to surf. They were all called "the Ks" because of the kilometer signs that showed distance traveled into Mexico. K-41 and K-51 were my favorite spots. I could get to them from my house in thirty to forty-five minutes, and most often there was no one else there and almost always great waves. That was as far south as I would go until after I got out of the navy. With all the cafés/restaurants I could get all the Mexican food I wanted—five-cent tacos, enchiladas, tortas sandwiches, and of course cheap Mexican beer! After about a year I changed to night check, the night shift at work. More often than not we would be done early, and I could sleep, still get up early, and have a full day in Mexico or San Diego before having to head to work. I stayed away from Mexico on weekends, though. All the gringos would come down, and it would be too crowded. Not to mention the crazy tequila- and beer-fueled gringos!

The part I didn't like about the navy would begin only three months after I arrived at HS-8. It sounds kind of silly, going into the navy without having a single thought about being aboard ship, but it honestly never crossed my mind! All I had ever known about the US Navy was what I'd seen at the beautiful naval air stations I'd traveled to with my father. He was flying all over the world in those big four-engine, propeller-driven C-121 Super Constellations and having a ball. Going out to sea and living and working on an aircraft carrier was a total shock to me. Life on a carrier now is night-and-day difference from what it was back in 1973.

The first carrier I set foot on was the USS *Oriskany* (CV/CVA-34) but not to go out on, just to off-load all the equipment our squadron had on board from its last trip overseas. The Big O was going to be decommissioned. It would later be stripped and sunk to be a man-made reef off the Florida coast near Pensacola. However, we would soon fly three or four of our helicopters north to Oakland, California, and board the USS *Ranger* (CV-61) for a two-week crew qualification cruise. "Cruise" makes it sound nice and luxurious, but it was far from it. I would deploy on many short cruises and two thirty-day Rim of the Pacific (RIMPAC) cruises on board the USS *Kitty Hawk* (CV-63) and the USS *Constellation* (CV-64). They were all exactly the same: five thousand guys (no gals back then), all always in a bad mood because none of us wanted to be there and living in pretty dismal conditions. My final cruise was a six-month WESTPAC cruise aboard the USS *Kitty Hawk*.

There were some pluses to being aboard ship of course, number one being that my surfboard and I were being transported to some pretty cool surf spots around the Pacific Ocean. The sunrises and sunsets were amazingly beautiful and clear. The ocean was incredibly beautiful, blue and green in good weather and gray with choppy, wind-whipped waves in bad weather. I could feel the ocean's power reverberate through the ship as it rose and descended on the enormous swells. I could watch the sea life for hours and hours—the flying fish that seemed to skitter and flutter in all directions, making way for this giant floating city; dolphins always seeming to be racing us off the bow; thousands of sharks; occasional whales; and an abundance of birdlife almost everywhere we went.

The nights, when we weren't at flight operations, with cool breezes blowing over the flight deck and countless stars visible, were indescribable. The ships at night ran pretty much blacked out, except for a few red lights, which were harder for an adversary to see, and on a clear, moonless night you could see the stars from one dark horizon of the ocean to the other. The Milky Way was so clear I really began to ponder how we fit in this endless universe; how really, really miniscule a speck we truly are on this rotating rock floating in the vastness of space and time; how the mere eighty to hundred years, maybe, of life we have is only a blink of an eye compared to the billions of years the universe has been here. This, the nature I was surrounded by, I truly loved. But the twelve-on and twelve-off, mundane, routine, everyday living with unhappy, lonely people, like me, was not good.

The living conditions back then were pretty crappy. No, life aboard a carrier wasn't a cruise. Sleeping quarters were small and tight and were all old even then, and it seemed as if the toilets and showers were always breaking, dirty, and smelly. But the food? The food was supposed to be the most important thing aboard any ship. If the food was good, morale was good. If not, everyone was miserable, and morale was at a low point. A very, very low point!

Now in the navy the galley, or mess hall, not a restaurant, had people who were rated, and they all had a specialty like me. My rate was aviation machinist's mate, jet (ADJ). Today the people are known as culinary specialists (CSs), but back then they were mess management specialists (MSs), and there weren't many on navy ships. So the ship would take guys from certain divisions on the ship—guys from the ship were called "black shoes" and guys from aviation squadrons were called "Airdales"—to help cook, serve, and clean up. And guess who these people were! They were usually the lowest-rated, undesirable fuckups each division or squadron wanted to get rid of. I had heard stories in boot camp about the guys who had been taken from each company to go mess cooking for two weeks and all the things they did to the food. The stories were bad enough on their own, but a couple of guys they took from my squadron told me it was all true. Guys spit into the food, blew their noses into it, and added who knows what other secret sauces!

What could you do? You had to eat, but it was hard not to think about it. The most important morale booster on the ship, and it sucked. I never looked forward to it. There were two messes on the ship, one fore (in the front) and one aft (in the back). The fore mess had regular breakfast, lunch, and dinner, but the aft mess had just small stuff like grilled cheese sandwiches and hamburgers. The ship also had two snack bars that sold Coke, candy bars, and other snacks. With five thousand people to feed on board, the two messes were always full, and we had to wait in long lines every time we ate. Many other guys from my squadron and I would go to the snack bars more often than the mess halls. The snack bars were always the busiest and would run out of all the good stuff very quickly. Without fail, when it was hot out, everything was hot in the mess, drinks included. When it was cold, everything was cold. But I had to eat and grudgingly did so. I lost a lot of weight each time I went aboard ship.

Working on the flight deck was kind of cool, though. We were almost always busy, and that kept our minds off of everything else. The work was pretty exciting, and though we were an antisubmarine squadron, our helicopters still flew search and rescue at times. Our helicopters were always the first ones off and the last ones on because we had to fly plane guard. Plane guard meant that during flight operations one of our helicopters would always hover just off the port (left) side of the ship heading into the wind in case a pilot ejected from an aircraft and went into the water. It could then quickly swoop in and pull the pilot out. Our main shops were on the forward end of the hangar deck down below, but during flight ops guys from each shop would work from rooms, more like compartments, on the port side of the angle deck. That was where the aircraft landed and where our helicopters took off from and landed as well. Anytime our helicopters were operating, we maintenance guys would all stand on the catwalk that went around the edge of the flight deck right by our shops and wait to be called if needed. Pilots and crew had hand signals for whichever shop—hydraulic, electrical, engine, and so on—maintenance person they needed. We didn't have any radio communication with them.

Mostly we maintenance guys, in green shirts, waited while the plane captains, in brown shirts, handled all the wheel chocks, tie-down chains, and red-flagged safety pins to be pulled out and shown to the pilots. The landing signalman enlisted (LSE), after clearing the area, signaled the pilots for takeoff. Landing signalman officers (LSOs) were the officers on the aft part of the flight deck signaling all the airplanes on landing. There were hundreds of other people all over the flight deck doing all sorts of jobs and wearing various colors of shirt. The plane handlers wore yellow shirts; safety, white; fuelers, purple; and weapons and firefighters, red.

The ship was like a small city in itself, with its own zip code and its own huge, very busy airport on top. Ships were and still are one of the most dangerous workplaces on earth. Guys are often blown down by propeller or jet exhaust, and at least one guy was blown overboard on every trip I was on. Sometimes guys are killed. Once, it was one of our guys. When a plane captain couldn't remove one of the safety pins that prevented the landing gear from being retracted or inadvertently collapsing while on the deck, one of the mechanics from the airframes and hydraulic shop was called up on deck. He couldn't remove it either. I don't know why he did what he did next. We all knew that if a pin couldn't be removed by pulling on it with one hand while applying pressure moving or shaking the rest of the linkage with the other hand, there was most likely a hydraulic failure in the system. I'm sure in the excitement of operations, with the helicopter running and aircraft waiting, unable to take off until the plane guard was off, he wasn't thinking correctly. He took a big screwdriver and a hammer out of his bag, and with a few bangs of the hammer against the screwdriver, he drove the pin out. The landing gear immediately collapsed and began to fold up into his face. The aircraft began to roll over and crushed him up into the wheel well. The pilot prevented further damage and possibly more deaths from occurring by immediately catching the helicopter and stopping it from going completely over. He held it in a semihover, still sitting on the other landing gear, while flight deck crews raced over with pallets and mattresses and stacked them up under the collapsed gear support just inboard of the wheel well. After enough were placed to safely hold the helicopter up level, the pilot reduced the controls enough to settle firmly and shut the aircraft down. They pulled the landing gear down, locked and pinned it in place, and took the poor guy away. There was nothing the corpsman could do for him; he had been so badly crushed.

The thing that was really amazing was how much drinking and drug use went on aboard every ship I was on. People were getting busted right and left for both but mostly for drinking, probably because hiding bottles or cans of alcohol was a lot harder than small amounts of drugs. The first time I smoked on the boat was with a French guy who was like an exchange sailor, and he knew all the best places to avoid detection. He took me to this out-of-the-way passageway that had a hatch on the deck in the recess of the wall. When he opened it, I was amazed! It was one single shaft that was thirty or forty floors down to the engine room. It was an emergency fire escape from the single opening in the engine room all the way up to the hatch we were going into. I went in first down about ten rungs of the ladder. He came in next, stopped just above me, and closed the hatch. He lit a joint, and we passed it back and forth, hanging there so high above that engine room hatch it was just a dot. When we finished, he popped the hatch above us, and we walked through the hangar deck and out to get some fresh air. There were two small decks that stuck out from each side of the carrier that had huge cleats on them for tying up while in port. You could walk right out to them from the hangar deck, and it was very rare anyone else was ever out there. That was the best place I discovered to smoke pot. The only people who came out there were people who wanted to smoke cigarettes, and you could just stand at the aft end and act natural, like you were holding and smoking a cigarette, and the wind created by the ship moving through the water would carry any smoke and smell away.

Not long after I started working in the jet shop in San Diego, they sent me to aircraft intermediate maintenance depot (AIMD), which I really dug. In the squadron most all we did was check and lubricate fittings and change oil filters in the rotor transmission and engine. We might change out engine blade actuators or ignition systems, but I wanted to get into more of the inner workings of the engines. This was it! We got engines in that were damaged or in for timed maintenance. We would stand them up on their noses in a special stand and tear them down from the exhaust, section by section. Those T58s were powerful little jet engines but not huge like the Phantom F-4's engines. Upright in their stands, the T58s stood only five or six feet high. There were hundreds and hundreds of nuts and bolts, clips, oil rings, blades, bearings, and so on. We would take them all the way down, repair or replace any broken or worn parts, and then build them all the way back up good as new.

After about six months I knew that engine pretty well, and they decided to send me out to be a test cell operator. The test cell was way out on the far end of the base away from everything and everyone because of the noise. I loved that! We checked in at the AIMD office each morning and then headed out to the test cell site. There were only five of us out there, and it was so cool. Unlike the bigger thrust-powered aircraft engines that would be run up in huge test buildings, the T58 was a shaft horsepower jet engine with almost no thrust. It had a very hot exhaust but wasn't quite as noisy. The suck, squeeze, bang, and blow of a normal thrust jet engine is turned around a little in the shaft horsepower jet engine. After the bang part of the cycle it's blown backward to internal turbine wheels that send power to a gearbox that, in our case with the helicopter, drives a huge transmission that turns the rotor blades. We ran them up outside on small towable trailers with two-man booths on the back that housed all the controls.

The next time I went back aboard the *Kitty Hawk*, I was the T58 test cell operator with AIMD. The AIMD had a huge compartment on the aft end of the hangar deck of the ship where all the different aircraft engines could be torn down, rebuilt, and then tested on the huge test cell on the fantail, the very aft of the ship outside. The big engines were slid onto and mounted to giant rails that faced fore and aft with a huge test cell booth off to the side. Every jet engine from all other aircraft on the ship could fit on those test cell rails except mine. I had the little towable trailer test cell parked and tied down on the hangar deck, and whenever I needed to test an engine, I would just roll it into the shop; mount the engine on it; roll it out to one of the giant elevators on the side of the ship; and take the engine, test cell, and all up to the flight deck. It was cool too because after I towed it to the aft part of the flight deck, with engine exhaust pointing overboard, chained it down, and chocked the wheels, that aft half of the flight deck would be closed, off limits to everyone else except for me and my helper.

When I was free, I would help other crews on their engine teardowns and buildups as well as in the booth doing their run-ups and testing. There were two giant, deck-to-overhead (floor-to-ceiling) steel blast doors that opened out to the fantail. Each door was about two feet thick and about ten feet wide. They were supposed to be able to withstand a direct hit from any of the aircraft on the ship if any were to go too low below the flight deck on approach, for whatever reason, and slam into the back. I hoped I wouldn't be in there to test the doors if that ever happened! I loved helping out the guys on the big J79 engine for the F-4. What an awesome engine that was! I loved running it up on that test bed with afterburner going at max power and watching that huge flame, beautifully cone shaped and as long as the engine itself, blasting out the back. The J52 in the A-4 we'd run up back at jet school had seemed powerful to me, but it was nothing compared to this. You could feel the J79 literally shaking everything around you, as well as your whole body, and it was very intimidating standing next to that. It almost seemed as if we were pushing the ship along faster.

Most of whatever could be thrown overboard, biodegradable trash that would not be harmful to the ocean, was brought back to the fantail and dumped over. At times, when we were taking breaks or just had nothing to do, we would lay out on the test bed relaxing in the sun, and we would see the master-at-arms (ship police) bring case after case of alcohol and bags of all types of drugs, but mostly lots of weed, to be dumped overboard. All the bottles and plastic bags were emptied of their contents and recycled. One day another guy and I were standing and leaning against the back railing of the fantail. We were talking, more daydreaming than anything else, and watching the giant, white, bubbling trail being left behind us by the churning propellers when these two masters-at-arms came out. They started dumping pounds of marijuana over the railing just to the right of us. They kept pulling bag after bag out of this huge box, cutting the bags open and dumping them one at a time. I immediately noticed that the marijuana wasn't all going into the water. The wind spiraling around the fantail was whipping it all over the place. Most of it was pooling up a little to their right, and they didn't seem to notice. My friend saw it too and looked at me. We both smiled and looked back aft out to the horizon without a word, as if we hadn't seen a thing.

When they finished, they gathered up all their recyclable trash and left. We stood there for a moment, a little in shock. Then I signaled for my friend to follow me. We casually followed the masters-at-arms a little bit down the hangar deck as they went all the way to the other end. We went back to the railing and waited a little longer, making sure no one else was there or was coming. My friend bent down to check the marijuana out while I grabbed a sheet of paper from a clipboard sitting on the run-up test bed and handed it to him. He started scooping and brushing the marijuana up onto the paper. This floor was immaculate—freshly painted, free from rust, and swept and mopped every day to prevent the powerful jet engines, which could suck a person into their intakes at full power, let alone any type of foreign object debris, from sustaining any damage from things such as nuts, bolts, screws, paint chips, and so on. Each engine always had a mesh safety screen attached to its intake before run-up to prevent anything from being sucked in. The engines' power was amazing: even when we would run an engine up in the rain, we would see little waterspouts form up from the water on the deck and spiral up into the engine! When my friend got all the marijuana up and showed me, I was really surprised. It was a lot more than either of us thought. He had a package of rolling papers on him and started to roll it all up right there as I made sure the coast was clear.

He got two big fat joints rolled up with all that—one for him and one for me! We had nothing to do for the rest of the day. He wanted to smoke, and so did I. This was the day I would smoke in one of the craziest, most dangerous places you can imagine. Up to my left was a spot I had been curious about and had always wanted to climb up to and check out. On the aft end of the flight deck, used for approach and landing, the deck rolled or tapered down. Called the "round down," it provided a less blunt, or rounder, surface if an aircraft should strike it or clip it when coming in too low on landing. A little to the right of center line, just below the round down, a small platform jutted out aft. Sitting on this platform was a small gray dome that housed part of the landing-system guidance electronics. There was a single ladder just to the right of the AIMD shop doors that led up to a door on the platform that opened up to a space between the round down and the gray dome. I knew it was supposed to be locked because I'd seen many guys go up to work on it and had seen the masters-at-arms occasionally climbing up to check and make sure that it was locked.

I told my friend to watch out as I quickly climbed up to check. It wasn't locked! It opened as I pushed up on it, and I quickly jumped up and signaled him to come on up. When he was about halfway up the ladder, they called everyone to flight operations and ordered the aft doors closed. My friend froze for a split second, but I signaled to him to come on faster. He got in, and we closed the door and sat on it just as the guys came out to make sure the fantail was clear and to close the doors. They were already beginning to turn the ship into the wind, and aircraft were running up. We waited until we heard the first planes being launched off before we fired up our joints. After only two or three tokes, the first jet was coming around to land. It was such a rush as the aircraft got closer and closer and the noise got louder and louder until, with an enormous blast of warm air pressure, it passed almost right over the top of us just a few feet away. After that first jet, I thought this really might not be a good idea after all. But after the next few jets, even with that *Oh shit, oh shit, oh shit* feeling as each jet got closer and we got blasted with the almost tornado-force wind along with the smell of the hot engine exhaust, the excitement kind of overruled the fear.

The pot was really good! We were getting really stoned and laughing so hard we were crying, both of us knowing we shouldn't be there but absolutely loving the excitement of the moment. Just about then, in between aircraft landing, we heard a hatch on the starboard (right) side of the fantail open and close and then heard someone coming up the ladder. Still laughing, covering our mouths with one hand, we braced with our backs against the ship and our feet against the dome, and with our other hand we pushed up on the bottom of the round down to force our butts down tighter on the small door. Sure enough, we could feel whoever it was pushing up on the door. But it wasn't going to budge with the weight and pressure we were putting on it. We both almost lost it, struggling to hold back our laughter. The guy obviously assumed the door was locked and slowly started climbing back down the ladder as another aircraft was turning on the final approach for landing. When we heard him finally close the hatch, we lost it completely! We exploded with laughter just as the jet blasted over us. We had to catch ourselves quickly, though; we were laughing and crying so hard someone could still possibly hear us as the jet did a touch-and-go and the engine noise subsided. There were probably people up there near us only yards away. When we finally stopped laughing and caught our breath, I said, "I think we'd better get the hell out of here!" He agreed, and after the next jet passed over we quickly scampered down the ladder, through the hatch, and into the hangar bay. No one even saw us as we slipped back in and went down to have lunch!

Going aboard ship became pretty routine: twelve on and twelve off, two weeks per trip. That was about the average time we would spend at sea even on our six-month cruise based at Subic. Go out and come back. The only other place the ship went after we got into the Philippines was Hong Kong, and I stayed there on a beach detachment while it was gone. I had two very scary close calls in the Philippines. On every trip, though, I always took my surfboard and had some great surf experiences all around the Pacific. Back in San Diego it was normal nine-to-five work, and I really enjoyed my job. I had moved out of the barracks and rented a small house just one block from the beach. I had become a local, had made lots of new friends, and was surfing and partying a lot. I had seen a lot of drug use in the navy and seen a few lives destroyed by drugs. I had done a lot of different types of drugs and would continue on after the military and into college.

With all the drugs I did, I was very lucky that they really didn't get me. I would eventually drift away from it all, thank God! But I sure did a lot for a while in my early and mid twenties. I still wasn't drinking much; I liked to smoke weed, which, unlike drinking, meant no puking or hangovers the next day. I had done LSD and mescaline and actually really liked them until they began to be cut with different types of chemicals that completely changed how they made you feel. I loved cocaine! At parties with other people it was so much fun. Mushrooms were great. Each time I did them I was out hiking or trekking through the forests, along rivers, and around waterfalls, and my friends and I always laughed our asses off every single time. I was partying a lot, but fortunately I was smart enough to know that drugs were not only illegal but also way too expensive and obviously not healthy for you, especially heroin!

I had walked in on guys shooting up in bathrooms at parties in San Diego but was never really around heroin, and no one I knew did it. That would all change after the ship came back from Hong Kong. I hated just going to the hospital and getting a shot. There was no way I was going to stick myself with a needle for anything, especially heroin. It was so cheap and so pure a lot of the guys I knew bought huge bags of it. They looked like big fat two-pound bags of white sugar.

When the ship went to Hong Kong and I stayed on the beach detachment to take care of the helicopter being left behind, I had to spend two nights in a temporary barracks until my permanent room would be ready. The temporary barracks was a big ten-man room, but there were only three guys in it. On the first night I came in late after eating dinner, stowed all my stuff in my locker on the other side of the room from them, and wanted to get some sleep. I hopped in my bunk, but all three guys, from various places around the United States and from various squadrons, wanted to talk and had a million questions. All three of them were nice and cool, and I really enjoyed talking to them, but they just went on and on. I thought they had been doing some speed or meth or were wired up from drinking too much coffee. Eventually the subject of drugs came up, and I said, "Yeah, I get high. I like to smoke."

"Oh yeah!" they said. "We can get some killer weed! We can get anything!"

We just talked and didn't do anything that night. They went on and on, and I eventually just nodded off.

The next day after work I raced back to the barracks to change clothes and get some money. The movie *Jaws* had just come out, and they were going to be showing it for the first time tonight at the base theater. I had just enough time to change, run out, and get the bus to the theater for the first showing. A lot of guys were still working, so the first movie wouldn't be crowded, but the next two would be. When I went upstairs and went to push the door to my room open, it stayed put, and I slammed my face into it, expecting it to just swing open. There wasn't a lock on it, and I instantly thought, *They're getting high.* I heard a little commotion when I hit the door and surely startled them. I whispered, "Hey, it's me, Craig; it's okay!"

I heard one of the guys say, "He's cool; let him in." Then I heard a locker and a bunk bed being slid away from the door, and they opened it. I went in, and they immediately closed it and slid the locker back in front of the door.

There were three new guys in the room, and two were standing by a table in front of my locker looking a little nervous. Again, one of the guys I knew said, "Don't worry; he's cool!" One of them opened the empty locker next to mine and pulled out a leather pouch and a long piece of rubber that I thought was a deflated tire inner tube. As one guy pulled a bag of something out of the pouch, the other guy began to wrap the rubber around his upper left arm. Shit, heroin. I stopped; I couldn't get to my locker.

The guy wrapping his arm with the rubber asked, "Can you help me with this?"

Trying to be cool, I just said, "Naw, man, I don't want to do that."

He quickly shot back, "Just hold this while I shoot it. You don't want any?"

Again I said, "No, man, I just want to get my clothes and get out of here. I've got to catch the bus."

The expression on his face changed, and now he looked like he was getting a little worried and thinking that maybe I wasn't so cool. "Okay, okay," he said as he let the rubber loose from his arm. "Just try this." He scooped a small amount out of the bag and made two little lines with it on the table. It looked like coke, and just to make them happy and move, I said okay. I took a half-cut drinking straw he handed me and did two quick snorts, one up each nostril. Then I took off my shirt, reached around him, opened my locker, grabbed my money and a clean shirt, and headed for the door. The other guys were already sliding the locker from in front of the door. Out I went. The door closed, and I heard the locker sliding back into its locking position.

I ran down the stairs and out the front door just as the overcrowded bus was coming to a stop right in front of the barracks. I was still buttoning up my shirt as I jumped on with just enough room for me and two other guys behind me. As the driver closed the doors, the heroin hit me. It was like nothing I had ever had before. It was amazing. I felt so wonderful, beyond wonderful! It was like I was in the best place in the world, with all these wonderful guys with me. I loved everyone! I wanted to talk to everyone and tell them how I felt. But my very next thought was *So this is why so many lives are ruined by this stuff!* I could honestly understand how easily someone could so quickly be taken by the power of this drug. It was the best bus ride ever and the best movie also. I soon came down and knew I wasn't going down that path, but it would take one more incident to really open my eyes.

When the ship came back from Hong Kong, I started hearing the stories of heroin. So many guys were coming back with it. Big bags that would cost thousands of dollars back in the States were less than a hundred in Hong Kong. Some guys bought hash; others, cocaine; but, for the price, most guys bought heroin. I had hooked up with one of the guys from the electric shop before everyone had gone off to Hong Kong. He was a good-looking, intelligent guy that I smoked with occasionally and had become good friends with. He said he had bought a little of all three as well. I told him about snorting heroin and how I felt about it, and he just laughed. He told me he would save a good line of coke for me. I said, "Cool!"

After a few days we were back at sea again. I was back on night shift again, temporarily with the squadron. They would be shorthanded in the jet shop on this trip, and I would be with them until we returned to Subic in about a week. I would be back in AIMD on our return. On the second night out, just after midrats (midnight rations), the night shift's dinner, I was sitting in the shop down on the hangar deck all by myself. In comes my friend with a big smile on his face, and he said, "I've got a present for you!" I knew exactly what it was and instantly got a big smile on my face too. He sat down and started to lay out two big fat lines when they buzzed me and all the other shops to head to the flight deck. We were about to begin flight operations. Because our helicopters were first off, my friend and I had to hurry. He already had a dollar bill rolled up and quickly did one line. He handed it to me, and I did the other. He was already on his way out and up as I cleaned off the table and my nose.

My first thought as I crossed the hangar deck to the hatch and ladder that led up to the flight deck was that the stuff didn't taste like coke. It was about five or six decks up to the flight deck and then across the deck or under it to our spaces on the port side. About halfway up, a wave of semi-euphoria but mostly stomach cramping and aching nausea made me stop and grab my stomach as I uncontrollably puked all over the side of the bulkhead. I instantly felt much better, but as soon as I got on deck and crossed over to our catwalk, I puked all over the deck right in front of the E-7 chief in charge of the maintenance crews. "What the hell did you eat, Wooton?" he asked. Almost everything I had eaten was all over the deck. Someone opened a seawater valve and instantly hosed it all over the side. I couldn't stop puking, though, and soon there wasn't anything left to puke out; I was just dry heaving. I got really scared that I might die from whatever the hell it was I'd just snorted.

The chief said, "I've seen this before. You've got some kind of food poisoning. You get down to the dispensary and see the corpsman!"

"Okay, I think you're right. Sorry!" I said as I headed back down.

"Don't worry about it. Just get taken care of," he said.

I was so glad. There was no way I could've worked up there, but there was also no way I was going to the dispensary. They would surely know what I had really done, and I would be busted. I could tell I was really high, but I was so sick and so scared and my anxiety was so high I thought my heart was going to stop! I happened to run into one of the cool guys from the hydraulic shop on the day shift on his way to stand a four-hour fire watch. I explained what had happened, and he told me, "Definitely do not go there!" He told me to go to his bunk and just relax.

The day-shift guys were in a different compartment from mine, but I knew where his bunk was. He was on the bottom of a rack of four bunks, back in the corner of the compartment. All the lights were out, and everyone was asleep, so I quietly slipped into his bunk and closed the curtains. I instantly felt safer and began to relax.

I must have just blacked out moments later. I don't even remember falling asleep. I woke up in the pitch black of that bunk from a horrible dream of doing drugs and going too far. I thought I was dead! I flung my arms out from my side. My right hand hit the bunk wall with a loud bang, and my left hand hit the curtains, giving me a glimpse of the red lights in the compartment. I let out a huge sigh of relief and quietly slipped out of the bunk and compartment. I'd slept exactly four hours. As I walked over to the hangar deck's open elevator door to get some fresh air, I ran into the guy whose bunk I had been in. "Shit, man!" he said. "I'm so glad to see you. I thought for sure you were a dead man! I've never seen anyone as white as you were. You looked dead!" I guess I really was lucky because I'd felt like that then, but as I sat there in that cool early-morning breeze, I felt amazingly great. A little like I had been hit and bruised in the stomach, from the puking I'm sure, but I was fine. Actually, I was really hungry and asked him if he was hungry as well. He said he'd been on his way to the mess hall when he saw me, so off we went.

I would later learn that the guy who had given me the drugs had quickly run out of his coke and thought I would like a line of pure heroin instead! He too was glad to see me. He had heard the chief telling someone I had gone to sick bay for food poisoning, and he'd known right away what it really was. He had spent all night worrying that he might have killed me.

I still got high and smoked weed, and I saw heroin brought out many more times, but I would never, ever touch it again. Later occasionally I would do small lines of coke at parties with people I knew well, but I was a little nervous of even that, and of course I always tasted it first. But weed would almost get me in huge trouble before my last cruise was over.

Those four years in the navy were the longest years of my life. Though more often than not it was like a nine-to-five job in many ways, it just wasn't for me. I knew I needed a college education, and mostly I still wanted to fly. I would work and surf in San Diego and Mexico Monday through Friday and then go up to see my girlfriend Saturdays and Sundays. She swore she would wait for me when I left for my last cruise in 1975 and marry me when I returned. When I came back six months later in December, she had run off with someone else. I was heartbroken beyond description, and though I still worked and did well, I was devastated. I surfed a lot, and that helped, but the best thing for me was actually starting college three months before I was to get out in 1976. I had to concentrate on school of course, but new friends, college life, the parties, and so on, all helped. It would still take me almost two years to really get over her. I would soon see, though, that that was the best thing that could've happened to me. If I had married her, my dreams of flying would most likely never have come true. But my short military career was now over, and I knew where I was headed!

Me in Pearl Harbor with the *Arizona* memorial behind me. This photo was taken during my first RIMPAC (Rim of the Pacific maneuvers) on the *Kitty Hawk*. The whole exercise was thirty days with a couple of days in Hawaii.

Me (*back row, seventh from the right*) with my graduating class at the US Navy's jet engine school in Millington, Tennessee.

21

A Simple Trap

The thing I really liked about Initial Attack, emergency first response team, was the diversity of things that would come up. Though I did enjoy firefighting, having so many different things come up in a day was really cool. You could be called to rescue a climber, a construction worker on a tower, or lost children or adults; assist at vehicle and aircraft crash sites; and on and on. Though most calls had happy endings, some were not so happy. All the aircraft accidents I went to were fatal except for just one, where we were called to find a downed aircraft. Luckily the pilot was in radar contact, so we had a pretty good idea where he'd gone down. After a fairly short search, we saw the plane, intact, in a small clearing in the trees. He had done a great job getting it in there and had stopped before hitting the trees at the end. We simply landed, picked him up, and got him home.

One of the strangest, funniest calls we were sent on was way up near a small secluded mountain town, a little northwest of Lake Tahoe. We weren't the first on the scene. Local firefighters were already there. They wanted us there just in case the situation turned sour and we were needed to transport someone to a hospital quickly. What we saw after we shut down and went into the small restaurant was very funny and heart wrenching at the same time. A little boy, no more than four or five, had tried to reach up into a candy machine and grab a candy bar. Apparently, his mother had said he couldn't have one because he had been a bad boy at dinner. While she was paying for their meal, he had gone back and stuck his arm up into the machine to grab a candy bar and had gotten stuck. He was screaming as if there were some kind of monster slowly nibbling his arm away deep inside the machine.

The first rescuers there, the firefighters, had tried to ease his arm out gently, but each time they barely moved him, he would scream louder and say they were hurting him more. They couldn't open the machine, because his arm was behind a huge set of fairly sharp louvers; opening the door could pull his arm into them and possibly seriously cut his hand or arm. As we stood back and listened to the boy scream and cry louder and louder, the firefighters whispered back and forth that it was time to bring in the chain saw to cut the machine open and free him that way. I wanted to say something but thought I shouldn't butt in, as it was their rescue. They brought in this giant chain saw, and the kid really started to freak out when he saw that, especially when they tried to put protective gear and a face guard on him. I couldn't take it any longer. I asked the firefighters if I could try something, and they said, "Please!" I think his screaming was getting on everyone's nerves.

I walked over to the boy and got down on one knee. He was still screaming as I whispered in his ear and asked him if he was still holding the candy bar in his hand. Still screaming, he nodded yes. I whispered, "Let go!" He did so, and his arm immediately slid right out! The firefighter holding the chain saw up, ready to fire it up and cut away, dropped it down to his side and rolled his eyes. They all kind of went, *Duh!*

The funny thing was I had learned this little trick while I was in the Philippines stationed aboard the USS *Kitty Hawk*. The naval base in Subic Bay was surrounded by beautiful green mountains and hills. Outside the gate of the base was Olongapo city, which was made up of hundreds and hundreds of brothels and bars. I had avoided it for a while but finally went out to see the copy bands I had heard so much about. They were really amazing! They could play music from all the famous bands—rock, country, anything. I was really into Led Zeppelin and ZZ Top at the time, and a few places had bands that copied them perfectly. You wouldn't believe it; they were really that good. The best thing, though, was the beer!

Good old San Miguel beer! It was five cents a bottle, and some bars would sell it for two or three cents to get the guys to come in.

One of the very first places I went to was a favorite place of a friend of mine. He finally talked me into going with him after a couple of beers at the base club. The base clubs were okay, but they were pretty boring. I wasn't really a bar guy anyway and didn't drink much. The bar he took me to was definitely more exciting, though, and the very first band I saw was really cool. There were little barbecue grills, hibachis, outside every single bar we passed with meat on sticks, like little skewers or kebabs. I wasn't sure what the meat was; I thought it was beef, possibly chicken. I told my friend I was hungry, and he said he'd get me something. He went out and came back with four sticks for each of us. It looked like beef but what kind, I didn't know. I was game, and hungry! I had tried many things—sushi, raw horse, rabbit, squirrel, alligator, and more—and really liked them all. I ate each one piece by piece. They were absolutely delicious, exactly like a very tender, lightly salted tenderloin or filet. "Come on," I said, "tell me. Beef, right?" When he told me it was monkey meat, I really wasn't too surprised. I had seen lots of monkeys everywhere, especially on the base in the forested areas. But I was completely surprised how delicious and tender monkey was!

After a couple more bottles of beer, I walked out and bought a couple more skewers. The guy cooking them was a middle-aged guy, sitting outside with his young daughter sitting next to him, pulling the meat out of a small cooler and putting them on the sticks. I asked him where he got the meat and how. Shoot it, bow and arrow, trap? "Trap," he said. Then he told me that they used *coconuts* to catch the monkeys. You could get the monkeys anywhere; they were like rabbits were back home. But using coconuts to catch them? My first thought was *Throw them at the monkeys?* No! When he told me how he trapped monkeys using coconuts, I was surprised at how simple it was. He would cut off just a small part of a coconut and drain the milk. He would attach a rope or chain to the coconut, then secure the line to a tree. He said that you could put the coconut anywhere, in the tree or on the ground, but that the ground was best, the easiest. Then he placed a peanut inside—a simple double-nut, shelled peanut. The hole he'd cut was just big enough for a monkey to squeeze its hand into. But when it grabbed the peanut and made a fist to hold the peanut, it would not be able to get its hand back out. "You're kidding, right?" I said. He swore it was the absolute truth, and I completely believed him. He told me that all the monkeys could get free if they just let go of the peanut so their hands could slide out, but they never did. They would scream and jump around yanking the coconut to the end of its line, but they would never let go. That was how I knew how to free the little monkey from his candy machine!

22

Getting Blasted

How do we really know how many close calls we've had in our lives? My brothers and I were kids doing crazy things—playing with fire; climbing on top of tall buildings; swimming in the ocean around Hawaii without knowing how to swim; learning to ride bicycles for the first time and finding a hill to go down as fast as we could go; and becoming new teenage drivers and driving like maniacs, day or night, not ever knowing how many people or things we might have just missed or that missed us by who knows how much. I don't know how many close calls I had as a child, but I know that I've had many close calls as an adult that could've ended very badly!

One of my first and one of the scariest close calls I've ever had was in the Philippines when I was in the navy. I had taken a little leave into Guam while crossing over on the ship to the Philippines. When I reported back and went into the jet shop, I found a note telling me to come down to a certain level in the ship to meet the guys in the surf club. I had no idea there was even a surf club on the ship. I went down there and found out there were a bunch of guys in the club that worked on the flight deck. They'd seen me jump on the helicopter with my surfboard when I'd flown into Guam. They were all pretty cool and had been on tours to the Philippines several times before and had found a lot of different surf spots. The very next weekend they were going to a place called San Miguel, and they wanted me to come along. San Miguel was a little town a few hours north of Subic Bay where the navy had a small communications station.

195

Subic Bay was absolutely gigantic. It was a huge naval ship facility as well as a naval air station with a long runway running right next to the bay. The communication base at San Miguel was maybe two or three blocks long by two or three blocks wide, and it sat right next to the beach.

Unfortunately, there were a couple of problems getting to San Miguel. The only way to get there was by a local bus—not a bus as you would imagine but a very large open-air van the locals called a Bonka bus. It seated only about ten to twelve people, but you could load lots of stuff on top. It was great for carrying our surfboards. The other problem was getting to San Miguel from Olongapo could take anywhere from three to four hours. Olongapo was the city just outside the east gate of the base, over the Perfume River bridge. We must've made two hundred stops each time we took the bus out and back, but it dropped us off right outside the gate of the communication station. All we had to do was carry our surfboards and gear inside, show our ID cards, and walk a block or two to the sand dunes leading to the beach. The very first day, as we approached those sand dunes, I could see the spray over the top of the dunes from the waves breaking on the beach before we were even close. I knew the waves were going to be big, and they were. They were probably eight to ten feet but beautiful breaks, nice rolling, easily rideable waves, and I had a blast! I knew I was going to be spending a lot of time here.

That was the only time I went with other people. It seemed as if every time I could go again all the other guys were busy doing other things or had to work. I took the local bus a few more times but then stopped, for a couple of reasons: (1) I hated all the stops and the time it took just to get there and come back, and (2) our squadron commander had ordered us not to travel on any kind of local transportation far from the base. There was a Muslim guerrilla insurgency going on at the time that was south of us but worrisome enough that he didn't want us taking any chances. However, just a day or two after we had been warned not to go, someone told me about a naval bus that left every morning around five or six in the morning and drove directly to San Miguel. They would take sailors back and forth as well as food and other supplies. The very next weekend, Saturday morning, I was at the bus pickup point at a secure north gate reserved only for military vehicles. I showed my ID card to one of the marines guarding the gate as well as the driver, who was a local Filipino guy, and hopped on the bus. I was the only one on the bus that morning all the way to San Miguel. It only took about an hour, and it was great.

I never told anyone I was taking the bus every day, because I was afraid I might get in trouble, but seeing how it was a navy bus and I was only going to another naval station, I didn't think it would really be a problem. After a trip or two back and forth on the Bonca buses, before I'd started riding the navy bus, I'd begun leaving my surfboard with a local guy. On my very first day surfing in San Miguel, I had noticed about a mile down the beach a bunch of coconut trees clustered together right up against the water. Right next to them, I could see what I was sure was where a river emptied into the ocean. River mouths are often great surf spots with a left break on one side of the mouth and a right break on the other side. So on my next trip back, I walked down there, by myself. In the middle of this beautiful grove of coconut trees sat a little grass shack on stilts. There were a lot of pigs and chickens running all around. I didn't know who lived there and felt that I shouldn't bother them, so I just went down by the water, dropped all my gear, put on my bathing suit, grabbed my board, and hit the waves!

After about thirty or forty-five minutes I looked back at the beach and saw a little Filipino kid sitting next to my bag. I didn't think much of it. I waved, and he waved back. I thought he probably lived in that little shack. I turned around, caught another wave, and rode almost all the way back into the beach. As I was turning to get out of the wave, I saw that the little guy was gone, and so was my bag! I immediately paddled in as fast as I could, threw my board down, and ran up toward the shack. He couldn't have gone down the beach toward the base because it was all fenced off and he could've never gotten that far without me seeing him. And he couldn't have gone the other way because there was no way he could have crossed that river. He had to have gone back to that shack. When I got up there, I met the owner, who had come out wondering why I was running up and down the beach so quickly. His name was Chris Amanonce, and we would soon be very good friends. I told him what had happened. He said he hadn't seen the little guy come by and didn't know who he might be. We looked around, and I did find my bag. My clothes were still there, as well as my wallet, minus all the money, which really wasn't that much. The boy had taken all my snorkeling gear, though—very expensive fins, mask, snorkel, and diving knife. He'd also taken my extra ankle leash, spare fin, and wax for my board, but the worst thing was he'd taken a bag of weed that had been so hard to find and was so good. But at least my ID card was still in my wallet; my ID was one of the most important things I would need to get back to the ship.

The funniest thing was that Chris was angry at me. "Why didn't you come up and leave your things with me?" he asked. I wish I had gone up, introduced myself, and said hello when I'd first gotten there. He was an older guy, with a very young wife and two beautiful little girls, about four and six. From that day on I would leave my surfboard with him and have an easy trip up and back on the bus each time. For the next few months I would travel up to see him every weekend, often staying overnight with him and his family. He told me how he had planted all those coconut trees many years ago just before World War II. It was such a beautiful spot with those big, tall coconut trees, but it was also deadly dangerous. The very first time I sat down underneath one of those trees, he warned me—yelled at me, actually, startling the hell out of me—to sit only under the trees where he had gone up and cut the coconuts down. No sooner had I gotten up after he told me that than a huge coconut fell silently and hit the sand, right where I had been sitting, with a loud thud. Those things are big enough and heavy enough to actually kill you if one should hit you in the head. From that day on I knew where to walk around all his trees and which I could sit under and which I could not.

Each time I came I would bring him extra batteries and flashlights as well as other various tools and things I knew he needed. He loved it; it was like Christmas for him. And of course I always brought things for the little girls and his wife. He had a Bonca boat that he used to go out fishing every morning. It was just an outrigger canoe, but it had a big V6 engine in the middle with a long shaft and a propeller on the end out the back. I had seen some islands just off the coast from the first day I'd come to San

Miguel. I had been curious as to what they were and who might be out there. He told me all about them, that there was no one out there except for usually only one person who, at certain times, might be out there to take care of an old Spanish lighthouse built hundreds of years ago and to service a modern light that had been installed. I asked him about the waves, and he said there was a big point that stuck out at the north end of the biggest island. The waves came in, wrapped around that point, and broke into the bay.

One Saturday morning he took me, my surfboard, and all my new snorkeling gear out to that island. It was amazing! He couldn't take me all the way into the bay because there was a reef that surrounded the island there, but I didn't mind. I just grabbed my gear, which I had in waterproof bags, jumped on my board, and paddled into the beach over the reef. I could not believe how absolutely cool that was. No one else was there. I could walk around the whole island in about an hour, and a perfect stairway from an old waterfall led me about two hundred feet up to a plateau where the old lighthouse was located. After going around the island and checking out the lighthouse on top, with an absolute beautiful 360-degree view, I went down and put on all my snorkel gear to check out the bay and the reef. I could already see the waves were great, but I wanted to check out the bottom to see how dangerous the rocks might be and if there were any sharks. Chris had already told me that he didn't think there were any sharks there, but I wanted to check. Each morning I surfed near his place, I always checked with him or any of the other local fishermen about the sharks. They went out fishing early every morning before sunup and always knew if sharks were there or not. Sometimes they warned me not to surf, and I wouldn't.

I didn't find any sharks in the bay. I paddled out to the outer edge of the reef, where the seafloor dropped straight down with no bottom in sight into deep, dark blue water. I did see sharks down there. I turned around back into the bay, which was only about five to ten feet deep in its deepest spots. I found lots of beautiful shells, which I collected, and went back to get my surfboard. I had one of the most amazing surf days of my life! I rode some of the best waves I've ever ridden, all alone on my private little island. That night I went up and spent the night in the lighthouse. The next morning I surfed for an hour or so, and soon Chris came to pick me up. It was only about forty-five minutes to an hour each way, and I was back at San Miguel in time for lunch at the cafeteria on the communication station. I got on the bus and was back in Subic before dark on Sunday night.

We would be leaving soon and heading back to the States. A week or two before I was to leave, Chris and his family, as well as some of the girls from nearby, all got together and had a going-away barbecue for me and a few of my friends I brought. He killed his biggest pig and buried it in a huge fire pit. They covered the pig and left it to cook overnight. We drank beer and partied all through the night. In the morning I got up early and surfed by myself while the other guys slept. None of them were surfers. Chris, his wife, and her mother dug up the pig. Then they cut it up and laid it out in front of us on palm leaves about twenty or thirty feet long. We had the best feast you can imagine!

I would have only two more chances to surf again before we were to leave, but the next time I went up to surf and visit Chris again would end up being my last. When I got on the navy bus at Subic, I always positioned myself in the very back, on the right side, by the emergency exit door that went out the back. There was a long emergency bar with a big round plate on it. It wasn't a handle but an emergency exit door release. You simply smacked the round plate, and the door would pop off. It looked just like the release you would see on the old dunk tanks in carnivals where you would throw a softball and try to hit the round target to release the seat and make the person sitting there fall into the tank of water. So should something happen, if we should crash or, God forbid, any of the Muslim guerrillas should attempt something, I could hit that release with my left elbow and be out the door in a heartbeat. Little did I know how important that little bar would be.

I had another great surfing day at Chris's place. I had gone up all by myself Sunday morning and surfed all day and was heading back to Subic in the early afternoon. Since no one else went up from Subic to San Miguel, no one else was on the bus going home besides me and of course the bus driver. We were about halfway back, traveling through part of the road that was really dense with jungle cover. There were no houses or shacks anywhere nearby, and I almost never saw cars going in our direction or passing us going the other direction. It was funny; each time we'd gone down this road, in the back of my mind I had always kind of thought that this stretch of road would be a bad spot, or should I say a good spot, for an ambush of some type. But on this trip I didn't give it a second thought. I had been down this road so many times by now, and the thought of leaving soon and heading home occupied my mind.

I was never able to sleep on any kind of transportation. About the only time I would get sleepy and nearly fall asleep was when I was driving! On this trip back I was dazing, kind of dozing and daydreaming at the same time. I was a little sleepy from getting up so early and surfing all morning. I was getting a little hungry and thirsty as well, and I was just looking down and reaching into my backpack to pull out something to drink when the driver suddenly slammed on the brakes. I was instantly slammed up against the seat back in front of me, twisting my neck a little bit as the sudden stop bent me over the bar of the seat in front of me. No sooner could I get the "What the fuck!" question out of my mouth than the front bus doors exploded open and not by the driver using the handle. Glass and metal shattered into the bus, spraying all over the driver, followed almost immediately by at least two obvious gunshots. Without hesitation I hit the emergency exit handle with my left elbow. The back door literally flew away, and as I leaped from the bus, I heard several more shots fired. I knew that they were being fired in my direction because I could hear them going by and hitting metal on the bus.

As funny as it may seem, as I immediately hit the ground running, my thoughts were of all the Godzilla and monster movies I'd watched as a kid where the monsters would come through the town and people would run straight up the street, never turning or ducking into a store to hide or taking a side street. After only about ten steps, I instantly turned left, busting through jungle foliage. I then ran about twenty or thirty more yards into the jungle, made another abrupt left turn, and dove in among a bunch of small palm trees and palm leaves. It couldn't have been more than five or ten seconds after taking cover that I could just make out three guys with rifles running past where I was hiding, heading in the direction I had taken from the road. I lay perfectly still and listened as the sound of them crashing into the jungle grew weaker and weaker. I knew I couldn't stay there because they would probably soon realize I'd turned one way or another and would be coming back to find me.

As quietly as I could, I slowly got up and out from my cover. I hesitated for a few moments, listening to see if they were coming back or if there were possibly others who might have been with them. I had no idea how many there might be. It was dead silent. The noise at the bus, the shots, and everyone running into the jungle had silenced everything. Even the monkeys and birds, that were always squeaking and squawking and making noise, had gone quiet. I started walking away, keeping myself about ninety degrees from the direction they had run off to and keeping myself parallel to the road where the bus was. Watching my step and being as careful and as quiet as I could, trying to keep from stepping on anything that might give me away, I literally tiptoed away as quickly as I dared. I had only walked a few minutes when I began to hear them shouting as they headed back. I instantly dove for cover again, praying and hoping they had given up and would just leave. I couldn't see them through the jungle, but I could hear them pushing through. I learned there were in fact other guys at the bus, as when the men in the jungle shouted, others at the bus shouted back. I had no idea what they were saying, of course, because they were speaking Tagalog, the Filipino language, but I'm sure they were saying something like "Where the fuck is he? Have you seen him? Did he come back this way?" Suddenly, one of them began to fire his gun. I just about jumped out of my clothes. It scared the living shit out of me. He only fired a few shots, and I could hear the bullets going through the jungle off to my left. I squirmed and tried to get into the dirt and down as low as I could. There was no movement for a while, silence. Then, bang, bang, bang! My heart nearly leaped out of my chest. This time I could hear the bullets crashing through the jungle on the other side of them away from me. I thought for sure the next shots would be coming my direction, but they didn't fire again.

I lay frozen, listening as they moved back toward the road. I could tell they were still searching for me because I could hear them stopping and rustling through the jungle—move a little bit, stop, check again, over and over. I strained hard watching for them through the jungle cover, but I never saw them again. When I heard them move far enough away from me where I felt safe again, I quietly started heading ninety degrees in the direction away from the bus and the road. I was still too close to them and wanted to get as far away from them as I could.

I walked as straight as I could in the direction I hoped would take me farther away from those guys. After about thirty or forty minutes of stopping and listening, stopping and listening, I turned and headed toward where I thought the road would be. Not much farther from the spot where we had been attacked the road made a ninety-degree turn to the right, and then it was almost a straight shot back toward Subic Bay. I couldn't believe my luck: it wasn't but about another thirty minutes later that I ran into the exact road I was looking for! I still hadn't seen one house or shack or any cars from either direction. I stayed hidden in the jungle and just waited, hoping I would see a car or military vehicle that might pick me up. No more than ten or fifteen minutes later a car passed, but I didn't trust it enough to step out and try to wave it down. Then I saw a military ton-and-a-half cargo truck coming down the road. I waited until it was almost right on top of where I was to make sure they were military guys before I jumped up and waved my hands to stop them. They quickly slammed on the brakes, looking very startled and wide-eyed at seeing a white guy come out of the trees!

There were only two guys in the truck, and they slid to a halt right next to me. The guy on the passenger side opened the door, jumped out, and yelled out, looking up and down at me, "What in the fuck happened to you!"

I said, "I was just running away from some guys that were after me. Could you give me a ride?"

"But what happened to your side?" he asked.

That was when I looked down and saw that the left front side of my shirt, from the second button down from my neck and across to my left side was gone. I had a bunch of small red spots on my side that looked like pieces of something had hit me, and there was a big bulge sticking out of my bottom left abdomen where I could feel something was stuck inside of me. Whatever it was had gone inside of me, and then my skin had folded over and held it in place. I hadn't noticed it or even felt it until I saw it at that moment. Adrenaline flowing, I had been so intent on trying to get away and so scared that I hadn't realized I had been hit. I'd been too busy looking for a way out and looking up behind me as I ran.

The passenger grabbed me by the arm and said, "Let's get the hell out of here and get you to a hospital!"

The driver took off and sped all the way back to Subic Bay. I still couldn't relax and kept looking in both rearview mirrors as we raced down the road back to the base. Now that I knew I'd been hit with something, I began to feel a little pain, but it wasn't terrible pain. It felt as if I'd bumped into something while running and had just bruised my stomach. It was hard to concentrate and answer the questions that they kept asking me in rapid succession. I'm sure I must have seemed a little freaked out to them, but I was just so sure that those guys after me would come up behind us or be waiting for me up ahead of us. I couldn't stop checking the side-view and rearview mirrors and looking ahead back and forth on both sides of the road.

When we reached the base, the driver went into a gate that he wasn't supposed to be using and was only for certain traffic coming out of the base. One of the guards stopped us and began to tell us we couldn't come in that way, but then the driver told him that I had been "blasted." The guard came up and looked in the window. As soon as he saw me, he jumped back and said, "Jesus Christ, go up this street, take the first left, go down about two blocks, and you'll see the dispensary on the left."

When we got to the dispensary, both guys jumped out and wanted to help me down and put me on a stretcher. I told them I was okay and walked in by myself with them following. The driver, before I could say anything, told the nurse at the front desk, "He's been blasted!" She immediately ran around the desk and led me into the emergency room. My wound really looked worse than it was. From each room we passed as she led me down the hall, doctors would jump out and run after me asking what had happened. So when they got me in to check me out, I had about five or six doctors around me.

I laid back, and as one of the doctors began to clean me up with antiseptic and cotton around where I'd been hit, what had been inside of me fell out onto the bed. It turned out to be a smashed 9 mm bullet that had been partially broken up. I don't know where the bullet hit when they fired at me, but it must have ricocheted off something—the seat handrails, the side of the bus, or whatever. The smaller pieces of it had ripped my lower shirt away and kind of splattered me, and the biggest part had gone into me about an inch or two. I knew the bullet had to have hit something first because I knew what that 9 mm would've done to my stomach had it hit me directly. I was really one lucky son of a bitch! The funny thing was I hadn't even felt it when it had happened.

There was nothing else the doctors had to do for me. I didn't even need stitches. They just cleaned the wound up, taped a gauze bandage on my side, and sent me back to the ship. It wasn't so easy back in my squadron. At first everyone was angry at me because we had been warned to not go out there, and they talked about a court-martial. But after seeing I'd been hurt and seeing how my shirt had been blown apart, which made it look worse than it really was, they decided not to do anything. They also knew I wouldn't be going back again.

Security came to talk to me soon after I got back to my squadron, but there wasn't a lot I could tell them except what had happened to me after the attack had started. I didn't know how many guys there were, who they were, or where they'd come from. I didn't know what had happened to the driver, and I didn't even know exactly where the attack had taken place. The security guys all knew which road led to and from San Miguel communication station, but that was about it. They hadn't even heard about the bus yet until they heard it from me. So after talking to me for just a short time, they raced off to go find out what had happened. They said they would get back to me.

It wasn't until about a week later they finally came back to talk to me again. I didn't have anything new to tell them. They didn't believe the attackers were Muslim guerrillas. They thought the guys were probably just a gang of robbers, and they thought the driver might even be involved. It turned out he was still gone, and apparently there had been a lot of money on the bus that he was supposed to be delivering to Subic Bay. And that was it! I wasn't in trouble with my squadron, nothing was ever brought up about it again, and I never talked to security again either. To this day, I wonder about that driver. I really wonder if he was involved or not. With the way he sort of swerved as he slammed on the brakes and we quickly skidded to a stop and how he looked with both hands on the wheel in the brief moment I saw him as I looked up, I just don't believe he had anything to do with it. So where is he? I know security had all his information, where he lived in town and so on. Did he really get away? How much did he get away with, if he did? Or is he still out there somewhere, possibly buried in that remote jungle I spent a few hours running around and hiding in, scared shitless?

23

Dubuque, Iowa

From Guam my family flew to Osaka and then San Francisco. Dad had ordered a new Chrysler New Yorker, and we picked it up in San Francisco and drove first to see his brother in Colorado. I bought a thin Pendleton jacket there, and I was okay with that for a couple of days, but man, was I in for a surprise when we got to Iowa. We pulled into Dubuque on February 1, 1969, my sixteenth birthday, just as a cold front came in and heavy snow started to fall.

The next day I would start school, and I was supposed to catch the bus, a city bus, not a school bus, but buses were for dorks (that's what we called nerds back then). I had wanted to take driver's ed classes in school, but they were all full, so I would have to wait to take the class in summer. So, wearing hard wing-tip dress shoes, thin slacks, a thin long-sleeve shirt, and that Pendleton jacket, I headed for school on foot. Now, you always hear old folks say, "When I was your age, I used to walk five miles to school in the snow, barefoot!" I actually did that day, though not barefoot. Here I was, straight from warm, humid Guam to Iowa in a snowstorm with a wind chill of –30 degrees Fahrenheit that day. When I got to school and went into my first class, the teacher said, "Let's welcome our new student. What's your name?"

"I nane is Cag ooton!" I said with my lips and jaws frozen. Got a good laugh from everybody, though. The teacher was cool and let me thaw out. I couldn't talk for thirty minutes.

Dubuque was a trip. That place really was exactly like the '50s, with people still wearing two-tone saddle shoes and clothes just like those in the movie *Grease*. But many kids had come out of that and were full-blown hippies. Dad was really patriotic and against long hair and hippies. Many antiwar protests were taking place everywhere and in Dubuque as well. I had by this time become more of a free thinker myself and began to doubt many of the things that were happening in our country and in the government. I was very patriotic, still am, but had my own opinion of things. I was a surfer guy, and that was very different there, but I made a lot of good friends with the '50s people, the sports jocks, and all the hippy kids. I fit in best with the hippy kids.

The second or third day there would be the last time anyone would confront me again for being the new guy. Two guys, who both looked like Fonzie from *Happy Days*, came into the locker room while I was sitting on a bench getting dressed after a PE class. They started to threaten me, one bending down almost in my face and the other pushing a push broom against my feet. I was only sixteen but had hit 6ft. 1in. that year. I wasn't big really, but I knew I was taller than these guys. With the one guy still in my face I stood up and stepped on the brush with my right foot and stomped down on the long wooden handle with my left foot, breaking it in half. The guy with the broom was trying to pull it free when I snapped the handle, and he crashed backward into a row of lockers. It scared the other guy so bad he jumped back a foot or two, and they both stood looking at me wide-eyed and mouths open, just as all the other guys before them had done, as I said, "You guys together might kick my ass, but I'm going to really fuck you both up first!" I don't know where that came from. They both stepped back farther as I walked out between them. They didn't become my best friends, but they always acknowledged me in the hallway between classes as we passed. As in all high schools, word got around fast, and, again, no one fucked with me any longer.

This would be the first time in years that I wouldn't play sports. Soon after we got there, a new Mr. Steak restaurant opened near the big four-lane road that led in and out of Dubuque. I walked through the snow, much warmer this time, interviewed for a busboy job, and was hired. A few days later I was working there at a dollar an hour. I worked awhile as a busboy, then went to dishwasher, then assistant cook, and finally head cook. Cooking was cool because the grill kind of stuck out into the restaurant, and we had to put on a show for the customers. We had special words for everything: order up, eighty-six that, and so on.

I was making a lot of money but wasn't spending much. Mom had bought a second car to drive to work, a 1952 Chevy. She had borrowed fifty dollars from me once, and rather than pay me back, she asked if I would like to have that car instead. Heck yeah! My first car! I was pretty shy at that time. I had bad acne and was so self-conscious about it. Most everyone else did too, but no one really cared. I knew a couple of girls liked me, but I didn't start dating until I went out with one of the waitresses at the restaurant. The first drive-in movie I drove to, illegally with no license, was with one of my guy friends. Kind of strange, but I didn't care. I thought it was so cool being able to drive myself. My first date with a girl in that old Chevy was a blind date. The assistant manager from the restaurant set me up with his girlfriend's friend.

Dubuque was called the Tristate City because after you drove over the Mississippi River bridge, if you turned left, you were in Wisconsin; if you went right, Illinois. Iowa was a dry state, no alcohol sold anywhere on Sunday. In Iowa and Illinois you had to be twenty-one to drink, but you only had to be eighteen in Wisconsin. We went left over that bridge a lot. Even though I was only sixteen, I was so tall no one ever questioned me or asked for my ID. On that blind date I was driving us in my Chevy to a club about an hour into Wisconsin that my friend said was really cool. We never made it. I didn't know the oil light in my car was out, and there was no oil in the engine. I didn't know you were supposed to check that. All of a sudden it was as if somebody slammed on the brakes, just for a second, then let off. I hit the steering wheel, and the other three were also thrown forward. The car skidded just for a second and then continued on. I was holding onto the steering wheel just looking at everything. I didn't know what the hell had happened. Just a few moments later, the brakes locked up, and we skidded off the road into a field and came to a stop. The engine, without oil, had literally melted inside and frozen up. That was the end of that car and that date. We had to wait for hours for a truck to pick us up and tow the car back. Never saw that girl again.

Dubuque was really special in its way. Yes, there was lots of fishing and hunting, and though it wasn't a small city, it had that small-town feel. Everyone seemed to know each other. In Oklahoma and Tennessee I don't remember the seasons changing; we weren't in either state very long. After Hawaii, California, and Guam this was really the first time I got to see the changing of all four seasons. Winter, though cold and gray, was actually beautiful also. I loved going on sledding parties on Goats Hill at the snow-covered golf course and taking sleigh rides with friends. Spring meant an amazing transformation of colors and smells. In the summer there were parties and barbecues in the parks and by the Mississippi River. Autumn meant hayrides and huge bonfires. But the sports, wow!

In all the other places we'd lived they of course had basketball, baseball, and football, but sports were always a summer activity, not seasonal. A high school baseball game might have a fraction of the grandstands full. Basketball or football sometimes had more. In Dubuque the sport fandom was amazing. Baseball would draw a lot of people, but basketball and football, unbelievable! It seemed as if the whole town came out for games, with the gym or stadium overflowing with people standing all around, and that was just on the home team side. The visitors brought their city as well! It was really wild, with the two sides cheering back and forth at each other. "Beat 'em! Try it! Beat 'em! Try it!" On and on. The closeness of the people was very special to me. Most of the people there had lived in Dubuque their whole lives and had maybe traveled thirty or forty miles away from Dubuque. They had never seen mountains or the ocean, let alone any other part of this great country or the world.

In 1970 airplane hijackings were happening more and more, and the government started the sky marshal program to put armed marshals on board aircraft to prevent hijackings. They needed military people with combat and weapons training at first until they could train civilian marshals. My dad volunteered and was accepted. So in November 1970, after less than two years in Dubuque, Dad was off to sky marshal school, and we were on our way back to Oxnard and my third high school, Hueneme High School.

The Wooton family, now with Paula, in Dubuque, Iowa. I (*on the right*) was already six foot one at just sixteen.

24

The Emerald Triangle

After I came back from my first tuna boat, I called my best friend Brad and asked him if he wanted the job. They still needed a pilot and had begged me to come back, but I was done. When I'd left to go on the tuna boat, Brad had still been just an A&P (airframes and power plant) mechanic, and they hadn't been letting him fly. It turned out he'd left soon after I'd gone on the tuna boat. He'd hooked up with a couple of guys in Sacramento, California, one a personal injury lawyer and the other an ex-cop, who had started a small helicopter company on their own. When I finally found him there, he said he was really happy and told me to come up. They needed another pilot, especially a certified flight instructor (CFI), and I had gotten my CFI as soon as I had come back from the boat.

I had thought that when I came back from the boat trip, my old company would let me fly full-time for them, but they only wanted me to come back as a facilities manager again. I wasn't about to do that, so I told Brad I would give him thirty days and see how it went, and off I went! I absolutely loved it up there and really liked the two guys I worked for. The area was really beautiful for one. There were lots of rivers and lakes all around, and Sacramento was close to the Sierra Nevada mountains and Lake Tahoe as well as just a short drive to San Francisco. The very afternoon I pulled into the airport Brad and one of my new bosses were about to fly five passengers to San Francisco. Of course the owners had heard about me, but I hadn't been checked out to fly anything yet. The boss said, "Why don't you fly with Brad? I don't feel like going!" I said sure. I hadn't been in Sacramento an hour (actually I hadn't even gotten to Sacramento yet, having driven into Rancho Murieta just east of Sacramento), and I was already piloting a brand-new Bell L-3.

It was really great to see Brad again. I had only known him a year or two, but we had hit it off and become good friends from the moment we'd met. We both had this dream to fly. He was an A&P mechanic, and I was an ex-military helicopter mechanic. I didn't want to get my civilian A&P certificate because I was afraid and sure I would get stuck being only a mechanic and not be able to fly. He confirmed that after I met him. He had gotten his ratings, as I had, and hadn't been able to get a flying spot either. But here we were now flying one of the coolest helicopters in the industry on a beautiful full moon evening, heading in to land on a pier in San Francisco Bay.

When I got there, they only had the LongRanger, a regular JetRanger, and a small Hughes 300C. The 300 was used for various small jobs but mostly for training. We used the two Bell JetRangers for everything else—power line patrols, long-line lifting, construction, firefighting, police work, TV news, and more. We flew Channel 10 (CBS) news and occasionally Channel 13 (ABC) news. We had big Channel 10 logos that we could slide in and out of mounts on the side of the 206 whenever they called. It wouldn't be long before we would have two helicopters each dedicated solely to Channel 10 and Channel 13.

One thing we were doing a lot of was police work. None of the sheriff's or police departments in Sacramento, Placer, El Dorado, or Humboldt Counties had an aero division yet. We were flying for all of them and soon had to purchase more helicopters. The one thing we were doing with them a lot was looking for weed. Marijuana gardens were everywhere. All the cities in Northern California were busting more and more people with pot possession, and the police knew it was coming from local growers. So they all wanted helicopters constantly. We started flying marijuana patrols, searching for pot gardens and training new pilots for such patrols at the same time. In a couple of years that would lead to all of the police departments having their own helicopters.

When we first started flying, weed was grown out in the open like row crops. Instead of rows of corn it would be rows of pot plants. Marijuana was everywhere. However, in time the growers moved under cover of trees or man-made covers and went from huge plots to smaller ones with plants scattered all over. The laws for possession of marijuana (and all drugs) at that time were still pretty stiff. People busted for growing marijuana on their property could lose everything—their land, their houses, their cars, their boats, their trailers, and more. Anything that was on the property could be confiscated when law enforcement swooped in to bust them. So the growers began to plant gardens on government land—in national parks, on Bureau of Land Management property, and, most of all, on Department of Forestry land. As long as you weren't in the plot of marijuana when law enforcement showed up, there wasn't much they could do to you unless they had some sort of evidence of you having anything to do in the growing or cultivating of the marijuana. The people we would see near the plots always maintained they were just hiking through.

But problems cropped up soon after growers began to grow on government land. Real hikers, hunters, fishermen, and campers were stumbling in on many of the gardens and were being shot at, threatened, or harassed. It was becoming unsafe to go almost anywhere outdoors. Then there were the "pot pirates" who looked for these gardens to steal the pot. Many of the growers began to live on or near their gardens to protect them, and they were all pretty heavily armed. This was when the Campaign against Marijuana Planting (CAMP) program began. CAMP was made up of California's police departments, sheriff's departments, and highway patrol as well as the FBI, DEA, and ATF. We might fly the sheriff's department in the morning, the Federal Bureau of investigation in the early afternoon, the Drug Enforcement Agency midafternoon, and Alcohol, Tobacco, and Firearms in late afternoon.

I was amazed at how much marijuana was being grown all over California, especially in Northern California around Humboldt County. In the area around Thailand, Laos, and Cambodia they grow poppies for heroin production. It's called the Golden Triangle. Humboldt County was known as the Emerald Triangle. Every day we flew patrols looking for gardens. You couldn't just fly into any garden you saw and try to raid it and cut it down. You needed lots of equipment and tools and lots of manpower and backup behind you. We would fly the patrols for a few days and pick the gardens that we would end up busting. But there were gardens everywhere! We would see anywhere from ten to thirty gardens a day. And that could be in a fairly small area. I realized right away what a lost cause this was. We ended up busting just a fraction of what we saw in the few years that I flew all over Central and Northern California.

When I flew the police, or whatever other agency, into a garden, we very rarely saw anyone at the site. The few times we did find people nearby who we knew were the farmers, they always had the same old line: "We don't even know what marijuana looks like!" The agency guys of course questioned them but could never hold them for anything and just let them go. They would cut all the pot down and load it into huge nets. I would fly over, hover down with a long line, and lift out these net loads of big, beautiful marijuana buds, taking them away to be burned. Often I would see the growers standing somewhere nearby watching as I took all their pot away. After all that hard work, their pot was all just being flown away. They looked stunned, bummed out, sad, depressed, and angry as hell! I got flipped off more than a few times.

The growers didn't have to be there. The growing had become so sophisticated. They used car batteries to run timers that watered and fertilized the gardens automatically. They had huge wooden or plastic tanks and drums full of water and fertilizer as well as huge mulch piles. It was really high tech, very scientific, and professional. These guys were growing fabulous gardens, some of the best pot in the world. Another DEA worry was the potency, the THC content, of the marijuana was climbing. The farmers were learning, getting better and better at growing. They were also getting very good at hiding their gardens.

When the growers first moved into smaller plots, they used small, thin black rubber PVC pipes for watering that ran for acres. This hurt them until they finally wised up. They just laid the pipe out on the surface, and it stuck out like a sore thumb. That was how we found a lot of the gardens at first. We could easily see the black lines through the trees or brush.

Sometimes the lines would run a thousand feet or more down the sides of mountains or hills. Follow the line, and you'll find the pot. Word got out fast, and it wasn't long before they began to cover the pipes. It got harder and harder to find gardens. Sometimes we would get tips; sometimes we would see cars, people, or activity that wasn't normal for the area; sometimes we would just get lucky.

Once, out in the middle of nowhere, an FBI agent with me said he really had to take a piss, so I landed in the nearest clearing in the trees I could see. The other two agents and I sat there with the helicopter running while he was taking a leak. Then he suddenly tapped me on my left arm and signaled me to shut the helicopter down. Right behind the helicopter was a huge garden that was almost completely invisible underneath the trees and the brush. The agent had seen an out-of-place hint of green sticking out of the brush just about his eye level back in a few yards. After I shut down the helicopter, we literally had to crawl on our hands and knees through man-made tunnels in the undergrowth beneath the trees to get to this gigantic garden and all of its amazing self-maintaining systems. This was huge, and these guys wanted it right now. They called back to the staging area to let everybody know what we'd found, and they stayed there to begin work on it as I flew back to get more equipment and more agents to help.

The main thing I remember about that particular garden was just how well it was hidden. You could not see it from the air. I flew back in to the same spot and dropped everyone off with all their gear, including the nets they would load the cut plants into. I flipped on my long line and lifted off to begin flying everything out. I hovered over to where I figured they were, but I couldn't see a thing or any of the guys. After a moment or two I called on the radio, and one of the guys said, "Come left, come left, come left, and stop! Do you see me?"

Looking all around to my left, I said, "No!"

"Look out at about ten or eleven o'clock!"

It was so funny. About forty or fifty feet ahead of me and to my left a little bit, I could see a hand. Just a hand barely sticking out of the brush. "Gotcha!" I said. He was standing up with his arm stretched straight up, and that was all that he could get out of the brush. I had gotten pretty good at using a long line by this time. I eased a little forward and left and slowly lowered the heavy steel hook right into his hand. I slowly lowered the helicopter as he pulled the line out of sight into the brush. A few seconds later they radioed to tell me to lift, and out popped this fat load of giant buds. I flew the load back to the staging area, lowered it into the back of a large truck, and then flew back for another load, repeating the process over and over. Each time I flew back I knew generally where I needed to be but still couldn't see anything. Eventually, however, out of the brush appeared a hand waving a red handkerchief, and I spotted it right off the bat.

All the loads I brought out from the gardens were destined to be burned in big, specially built incinerators. The first time I flew pot out to be burned was in Oroville. I was flying for the sheriff's department, and they had a huge incinerator behind the station building. The funny thing was the city jail was right next door, and they had set the incinerator back in the corner of the parking lot right next to the fence of the jail's exercise yard. On the very first day they fired it up, the inmates played it cool and stayed back until it was fully loaded and burning away, the smoke blowing directly toward the exercise yard. Then they all came down and clung to the chain-link fence, sticking their noses through and inhaling as much of the smoke that they could. They were actually getting high. The next time I flew in, the incinerator was gone.

One thing I learned fast doing these searches and raids was to watch my ass. From the beginning we all knew of a few booby traps being left for anyone coming into a garden on the ground, but we learned more and more as we flew. After all the searching, the various departments would decide which gardens we were going to raid. It was rare that we would assault one by air. Of course it was great to look down into a garden to see if anyone was there, but it was much better to have guys or gals on the ground who could do a much more thorough job of checking and clearing any problems. Plus, I could carry only a few guys. It really depended on how isolated or far from any access roads the garden was, but we did raid by helicopter at times. Normally various teams would assemble close enough to walk in, and we would circle off low and in the distance, far enough not to be heard. When the call came to hit it, we would zip in, do a quick recon, look for any obvious traps, and give the all clear or not. Of course we couldn't see everything hidden from the air, but we would check the best we could.

Most farmers didn't really want to hurt anyone. Others had been burned by pot pirates stealing their plants a few times and so set pitfalls, holes dug in the ground with wooden spikes at the bottom and then covered over with branches and leaves. I saw two gardens with trip wires rigged to the triggers of double-barreled shotguns aiming out of the gardens. Again, such traps were rare, but one day, in just one garden, I got the shock of my life. I was to fly two teams, one after the other, into a very remote garden, just at sunrise. I did the first high-altitude recon. It looked clear, and I swung around to make a low approach. I was flying a Hughes 500, a very fast but smaller helicopter with a smaller blade diameter that I could get into tighter areas with. The plot, surrounded by high trees, had a cutout on one side where the trees were lower. In this kind of work you want to get in, get down, and off-load the guys as quickly as possible, and that cutout was my best path in.

Flying from the left side in the Hughes 500, I was coming down from the recon in a spiraling left turn, watching the plot the whole time. Just as I was beginning to level out and shoot down into the slot, I caught a glimpse of light, a reflection. I yanked back on the cyclic and immediately banked hard right at the same time. I scared the shit out of everyone and actually almost lost one guy in the back. We always flew in with all doors off so everyone could see better and egress quickly, and the guy behind me was just reaching to unbuckle his seatbelt. He went almost completely out of the helicopter but was saved by his loose safety belt. After all the "What the fuck was that?" from everyone, I came around into a slow hover and came right up to the gap between the trees. Sure as shit there were six to eight strands of wire stretched across the gap through the trees. Later I would learn it was piano wire. The team leader yelled for me to just hover straight down in. I decided against going into the site, said, "No fucking way," and went to a small open spot about twenty yards away and hovered down into land. The team jumped out and headed for the garden. I immediately took back off, quickly picked up the second team, and returned. I took off again and circled overhead to make sure our guys were okay and the perimeter stayed clear of anyone.

After a while the team leader called back and, in a nicer, kinder voice, told me to go ahead and land and walk in. He wanted to show me something. I landed in the small open spot and walked into the site. The first thing he said to me was "Thank you so much for deciding not to land!" What he showed me next shocked the hell out of me. Besides the piano wire strung through the trees there were other helicopter booby traps. They looked like giant mousetraps, but they were helicopter traps about two feet wide and about three feet long with spring-loaded rectangular arms. In the spot where you would place the cheese on a mousetrap, the spot that would trigger the spring-loaded arm that slammed down on a mouse's neck, was a big metal plate. Of course the helicopter itself wouldn't catch the plate, but the downwash from the rotor blades on that metal plate would trigger the arm. The arm would flip over and slam down on one end of another plate balanced like a seesaw. As that end slammed down, the other end, with firing pins, nails, or screws attached, would slam up into the primers of a row of shotgun shells mounted on a small rack and pointing up. The shotgun shells would have blasted straight up at us and could have easily hurt or killed someone and would have definitely damaged the helicopter, very possibly damaging the blades enough to bring it down. I thought I was cautious before, but boy, did I become more cautious after that.

On lots of flights with various law enforcement agencies I would fly out and pick them up in the morning and then fly back home at night. But on jobs farther from home we would fly out of base camps or the local sheriff and police stations, which were heavily guarded and kept our helicopters safe. Sometimes we would spend the night at the base camps or in hotels nearby. One night up in Humboldt County, after dinner and a few bottles of beer with a lot of the guys from all the agencies, a mechanic was driving another pilot and me back up into the hills to our compound and LZ in the base camp. It was pitch black out and quiet, with not another car on the road in either direction besides ours. Or so I thought!

A pickup truck had come up behind us with its lights out. In the cab and in the back were four or five guys with bats and ax handles. The first we knew they were there was when the rear window in our truck exploded inward and shattered all three of us with small pieces of broken glass. I don't ever remember jumping like I did at that moment. I was tired from a long day of flying and just finishing a great meal when *bang*! I instantly thought we had hit something, but everything in front was okay. Just then the left side-view mirror on the driver's side was smashed away. That was immediately followed by the guys smashing huge dents in our cab roof and screaming and shouting as they pounded the whole left side of our truck. As they pulled up farther, they began beating on the hood, and the front window soon spiderwebbed and shattered. It didn't come out, but we couldn't see shit out the front. Next the driver's window did the same. Luckily it didn't come out either, or the driver might have been the next home run. He gunned it, and we slowly began to pull away from them as they continued to beat our poor truck and scream every dirty word imaginable. As we slowly moved away, I looked back and got a glimpse of three of them in the back of their pickup truck. I had seen them before: one was from the grocery store, one was from the hardware store, and the last was from the gas station. I don't know if they were the owners of the places where I had seen them, but they probably were.

We were only about a mile from the base camp when this happened. There was only one way up to or down from the base camp on this road. The guys quickly backed off, did a U-turn, and were gone on their way back down. Just before we reached the gate at the top of the hill, we were met by a couple of FBI guys who had come out after hearing all the shouting and banging. They jumped in a car and raced down after them but soon came back. They hadn't seen anyone whatsoever but had seen some side trim, our smashed side-view mirror, and bits of broken glass all over the road. We hadn't gotten a plate number or even seen what kind of truck it was. We were too scared shitless! When we got out of the truck, it looked as if it had gone through a hailstorm on the left side only, from the front to the back, almost exactly from the middle of the hood and roof all the way down to the tires.

It was actually a little funny really, once we got up there and had some time to calm down. I don't think they really wanted to physically hurt us. They could have easily done that! They could have swung through that back window and gotten each of us easily, and another hit or two on the driver's door window would surely have brought it in and made him easy prey. And the road going up that hill ran along a cliff that dropped off hundreds of feet, far enough that with just one tap of their truck into ours, we would have gone over and most likely been done for. They were just trying to scare us off.

From the beginning of my flying for that government program I had felt a little guilty, kind of hypocritical, because I smoked and here I was helping eradicate all these gardens. I never told anyone who I'd seen that night, and those guys knew that I knew but hadn't said anything. I saw them each a few more times before my flying in Humboldt came to an end, and each time they just smiled and winked at me. But it really hit me that night that we weren't just hurting the pot growers; we were hurting everyone. The butcher, the hardware store, the bakery, the grocery store, the small mom-and-pop shops, the gas station, everyone in the community depended on the growers. The growers' livelihood was directly tied to their livelihoods. We were never bothered again. The compounds had always been guarded because of the aircraft, but we never went out again without armed guards with us or following us.

Though CAMP would last many years longer it would eventually end. I knew it would, just as most other projects across the country have failed trying to eradicate marijuana. I'm not saying I'm for or against marijuana; there is just too much, grown by so many, in so many different areas, indoors and outdoors, that it cannot possibly be stopped or even controlled. I was so amazed at the thousands upon thousands of large and small gardens I saw in just the small area of the country that I flew in. I can only imagine what else there must be growing all across this big beautiful country of ours!

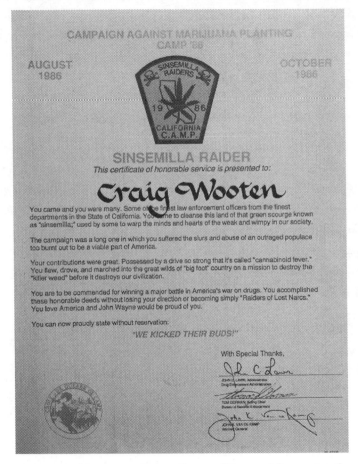

My somewhat comical certificate of honorable service for participation in the Campaign against Marijuana Planting (CAMP) program. As has happened quite often throughout my life, my last name is spelled wrong, *en* instead of *on*.

25

If It Bleeds, It Leads

Electronic news gathering they call it. Being a news pilot and flying for TV news stations was kind of Hollywood. My name was in the credits every night, I was on TV quite often, and it was pretty funny to be recognized by so many people almost everywhere I went. However, the twenty-four hours on call with a pager on my belt got old, and the news director was always trying to kill me. This chapter's title really does sum it up: the more death and destruction, the better.

Within my first year in Sacramento I was pretty much Channel 13's main pilot. One of the first calls I received from the news director at two in the morning was to go up into the dark mountains, at night, in a blizzard, in my single-engine helicopter and find a lost boy in the woods. No shit! Now, aircraft today are pretty reliable, but I had already gone down three times, once in an airplane and twice more in helicopters with engine problems. Up in the mountains, over trees, in a storm, flying over basically a black hole? If you have an engine failure, you're dead! I asked, "Is this a joke?" He sort of stuttered something, and then I hung up. I found out the next day he had immediately called my boss after I'd hung up on him. After he'd told my boss what he wanted and what I'd said, my boss had told him I had no business flying in conditions like that at night, especially in the mountains. Then my boss had hung up on him too. That wouldn't be the last time I would tell the news director no.

A few years later, when I was leaving Sacramento, they had a going-away party for me, and the news guys and gals gave me this great poster-size picture signed by everyone. Every single one of them came up to me that night and thanked me so much and said I was the only one who had ever told the news director no. They had flown with other pilots before, apparently on some pretty scary flights they shouldn't have even been on, that shouldn't have been flown at all. Get the story and scoop the other stations, that was number one!

The scoop was different most every single flight. It was always something pretty exciting. I covered some awful things and some very humorous things. One of the worst was one of the doomed flights I almost got on, when a private jet crashed doing a flyby over our airport while I was outside watching it. After making sure I couldn't do anything to help the crash victims, I immediately jumped in the Channel 13 helicopter, called the station, and picked up the crew. We were first on the scene. As we fed footage of the crash scene back to the station via microwaves, the camera panned to the three charred bodies in the wreckage. The first words I heard back over the station radio were "Oh, crispy critters!" As bad as it sounds, as cruel and heartless, believe it or not, humor like that was a way for the news people to deal with seeing horrible things like this crash almost every single day. Through the years I too have seen so much death, not just on the news teams but also in other flying I've done. You have to do something to keep yourself from going crazy!

Another very bizarre story was when police stopped a guy who had run a red light. As the police officer was writing the ticket, he smelled something terrible coming from the guy's trunk. He ordered the guy out and had him open the trunk. The driver was a carpenter, and in the trunk there was nothing but his big toolbox. He opened it, and there were two severed hands and feet inside. "Well, everyone knows a carpenter always needs an extra pair of hands!" a news reporter said. Of course the guy was arrested, taken to jail, and locked up. He didn't say a word for a few days. Then in various interviews, he started dropping subtle hints as to the location of whoever's body those parts had come from.

One day while I was on another story the news director, always monitoring the police radio bands, called me and asked if I knew of a certain quarry in a certain area in the mountains. He didn't have a name, but I instantly knew exactly where it was. I picked up another crew, and we were there an hour before the cops showed up. It was deep in the trees up against a mountain. It wasn't used any longer, but it still had a huge pit that was filled with emerald-green water. I couldn't land right by the pit because of all the trees, but there was a road that led from the pit to a parking spot a few hundred feet away that had been cleared of trees for all the large trucks that used to go in and out of the pit. I landed back in the far corner and shut down as the reporter and cameraman started searching around the tree line. I got out and was just tying my rotor blades down when a smell hit me. By this time I had been to so many crashes, fires, murders, and so on, I knew very well the smell of a dead body. The wind was blowing from over my right shoulder, directly from the quarry itself. They continued to circle the trees checking as I slowly sniffed around, heading toward the quarry. The smell instantly got stronger, and I called them to follow me. "Do you smell that?" I asked.

"Smell what?" they said together. They had never smelled that smell before, but once you do, you'll never, ever forget it. There is no other smell like it.

I followed the smell straight down that quarry road to where the road stopped and dropped off down into the water. As soon as I looked over the edge, directly below where I was standing was a big, rolled-up carpet half in and half out of the water on the rocks with two legs sticking out with both feet missing. Scooped that one too!

A comical incident occurred when I was flying the news at the same time I was flying all the different law enforcement agencies trying to eradicate the marijuana that was everywhere. With CAMP heating up, the news stations were calling us almost daily to cover all the stories. Channel 13 wanted me to fly a crew out to interview some of the Placer County sheriffs. It was mostly just a PR event for the sheriffs at their headquarters. They showed the hundreds and hundreds of pounds of stacked and ready-to-burn pot that they had confiscated. After filming the incinerators doing their job to get rid of the pot, the crew did a few interviews, and we were on our way back to the station.

On the way back they asked me if I knew where some pot plants might be. I didn't know of any nearby, but I was seeing it every day that I flew with the sheriffs. "No, I don't, but I'll bet we can find some!" I told them.

"All right!" they both said together.

It only took about five minutes flying back south to Sacramento along the Sacramento River before I spotted some. There were about ten patches spread out but fairly close to each other. They weren't real easy to see, because they were planted close to the river, where everything was green. Up in the hills marijuana was super easy to see it if it wasn't camouflaged because everything else around it was so brown and dry. But these were big plants and had been growing for a while. I was flying at about a thousand feet when I pointed them out, but, like most everyone, the reporter and cameraman couldn't see them. I told the cameraman to just start filming and said I'd point them out as we got lower. There were no trees down on the delta, so there were no hazards or possible booby traps, and there was no one around the plants or anywhere nearby. About forty or fifty yards out in the water were two guys in a canoe sitting and fishing with their poles in the water, but there was no one else.

At about five hundred feet I slowed and circled. "See it yet?" I asked.

"No, where?" they asked.

I told them to just keep watching and not stop shooting. I went all the way down and hovered right next to these big plants, and they said, "We can't see it in all the bushes!" I circled around a couple of the patches and then thought I'd better get my butt out of there. Of course they had never seen marijuana before, and, worse, the poor cameraman was looking through his viewfinder, so he could only see black and white.

"We didn't see anything!" the reporter said.

"Just wait until we get back to the station, and I'll go over the video with you," I told her.

"Whoa!" was the first thing everyone said as soon as the film, in color, came on in the editing room. I pointed out the spots of marijuana, and they all freaked out when they saw all the huge marijuana leaves flapping around in the downwash from my rotor blades as I hovered around those plants.

"Holy shit, I can't believe I couldn't see all that!" said the reporter. No sooner did she finish saying that than another reporter came in and told me I had a phone call. I thought it was probably my company wondering where I was, but it was the Placer County sheriff.

"Hi, Craig, how are you?" he asked surprisingly nicely when I answered the phone. After I told him all was well and asked about him, he then said, "Craig, would you please not fly the news folks down on the gardens again?" Unknowingly, we had blown a stakeout! The two guys in the canoe were sheriff deputies waiting to arrest the growers when they showed up, but obviously I'd scared them off.

"Whoops, sorry!" I said.

I loved everyone I flew with on my news-gathering flights. They were all great people and still great friends!

My chance of a lifetime to fly a B-17 bomber
on a Channel 13 news story.

After the really cool B-17 flight for Channel 13 news.

Covering a fire for Channel 13 just east of
Lake Tahoe on the Nevada side.

26

Teaching Japanese Students to Fly

When I was offered a job to teach Japanese men and women how to fly in Tokyo, I jumped at the chance. Another adventure! I didn't speak a word of Japanese. In fact I had been studying Spanish for years and always thought I would be flying somewhere in South America or Mexico. My first tuna-boat job had been with all Spanish speakers, except for the captain, who was Polish, and three Polish guys he had hired. My Spanish had come in handy then, but I never used it again after that. I'd been to Japan only once while I was in the navy. We'd stopped on our way overseas on my first WESTPAC patrol, but it had only been for two days. I had tried to take my surfboard on a train to a place some local kids had said I should go, but boards hadn't been allowed on trains then. So I'd taken my board back to the ship and taken a train to Tokyo for a few hours. That was all I knew of Japan.

Now, fifteen years later, I had a choice of contracts to sign. I could go on a six-month or one-year contract. I didn't know much about Japan really. I knew they were becoming an economic superpower and were buying up properties all over America, but that was about it. So, to be on the safe side, I signed a six-month contract. If I didn't like it, well, I could be back sooner. Japan turned out to be one of the most amazing, cool, and fun places I had ever been in my life. I loved the people, and they treated me like a movie star. I waited too long to renew my contract, and when it came time to go back, another pilot had already signed up for a year after

230

me. So I had to wait another year, but I made sure I was next to go back again when his contract was up. And I haven't left since.

When I first told my folks I was going, the first thing my father said was "Oh yeah! Go there and find a woman who really knows how to take care of a man!" My first thought was *Yeah right, just what I need!* In my travels in the navy and even when I was younger in Hawaii and Guam, all the bases I'd lived on had been surrounded by bars and hookers. Unfortunately that was kind of the image I had of Asian women. But when I came to Tokyo, I was in for an absolutely wonderful shock. The women were the most beautiful I'd ever seen anywhere in the world. They weren't only beautiful; they were also intelligent and very, very elegant. I was getting whiplash everywhere I went. *Holy cow, look at her! Wow, look at her! Ouch!*

Now, you have to understand the time: January 1990. There were very few gaijin, or foreign guys, in Tokyo at that time. I really didn't know it then, but when I look back now, I was a good-looking, thirty-six-year-old, single pilot / flight instructor. I really did feel like a movie star. Everywhere I went, busloads of schoolkids would wave and shout out the window, "Hi, gaijin-san!" I would be sitting on a train or subway listening to my little Walkman with my earphones in and get a tap on my shoulder. There would be just a knockout girl sitting there who would ask, "Can I speak with you and practice my English?" Hmmmm, let me see. Okay! Everywhere I went, every single day, people would literally stop and stare, and I would simply smile and say, "*Ohayo gozaimasu*" ("Good morning"), "*Konnichiwa*" ("Good afternoon"), or "*Konbanwa*" ("Good evening"), the only phrases I knew, and wave to them. I loved it.

On my first day the company's office manager picked me up at the airport, drove me to the office in Tokyo, and then took me to my temporary apartment at a Weekly Mansion. With just the little bit that I saw of Tokyo that night, the very next morning I was able to make my way to my new job at the pilot school on my own. My little apartment was quite a ways from the office. When I say little, I mean little! Though it had a small bathroom and shower and a little kitchenette, I could literally reach my arms out and just about touch the walls on either side. They would move me into a bigger temporary place a week later and then to my nicer, newer, permanent apartment a week after that.

I had to take a train from my place in Nippori to Ueno Station, which was just one stop away, and change to a subway. For a few days I had a hard time finding the subway line each time I got off the train and went down into Ueno Station. That very first day, after finding my subway line and purchasing a ticket, I went down to the platform to board the subway. It was absolutely jam-packed with people! It seemed as if hundreds of small lines of people were lined up to get into each car of the subway. I got into a line. At each door of every car these little guys in caps and uniforms with white gloves pushed and crammed in as many people as they could before the doors closed. It kind of freaked me out. I didn't want to be crammed in with all those people. I kept stepping out of line, not sure if I wanted to do this. Finally, I said no way and went up and out of the station to get a taxi.

I knew the name of the area where my office building was located and told the taxi driver. When he got me down there, I recognized the area and had him stop. When I got out of the taxi and began to walk down the street, there was an old woman sweeping out in front of her just-opened store. She was looking down sweeping, and when she looked up and saw me, she did a double take, stopped in her tracks, and stared at me with her mouth wide open. I immediately said, "*Ohayo gozaimasu!*" She broke into a big smile, bowed, and said good morning back to me. I had a feeling then, and it's turned out to be true since, that most people are a little freaked out by this big white guy. Very, very rarely will anyone say hi to me first, except for kids. So I always say hello right away when people stop and stare, and everyone seems to relax and smile.

I soon found the office easy enough. Everyone was surprised to see me. Apparently everyone else had gotten lost their first couple of days there. The coolest thing was the elevator ride up to my floor. The elevator was really huge inside, and it was full of about ten or fifteen office ladies, all dressed in their office uniforms of white blouses, pink vests, and skirts. They were all absolutely beautiful! The button for my floor had already been pressed, which meant they were all going to my office. Cool! I squeezed into the side. When the door opened at our floor, I, being a gentleman, stepped back to let them all go first, but they all stepped back too! I looked at them, and they all motioned to me to go first. Right then, I thought, *Oh yes, this is going to be great!* I would soon realize, though, how much Japanese women appreciated good manners—like letting them go first, opening doors for them, pulling out chairs, and even just commenting on how nice they looked. That just wasn't done by guys here.

From the first day I loved Japan—the food, the people, and the history. There was so much to see and do. America only had a little more than two hundred years of history; Japan had over two thousand years. At six foot one, I was just an average-size guy, maybe a little above average, in America. But here, I was big! *"Okii,"* everyone said when they stared at me. I really didn't mind people staring; I definitely stuck out like a sore thumb. I would meet other foreigners in time, and they would always complain about people staring at them. I would just tell them, "Hey, you are like a movie star here. Enjoy it! Go home, and no one will ever look at you or give you a second thought."

For my first few days I had two or three office girls that spoke English very well with me at all times out of the office, so I didn't have to worry about speaking Japanese. I always carried a small Japanese dictionary with me and was learning a little, but I really wanted to learn more. Each night after work I would head back to Nippori Station by myself. My second night I didn't want to go back to my apartment; I wanted to do something! It had started snowing early my first morning here, not heavy, but everything was snow-covered, beautiful, and quiet. When I came out of the station, the area around looked completely dead, not a person in sight. It was pretty dark and quiet. I had heard about yakitori, grilled chicken on small sticks like shish kebab. It sounded good to me right now. I ran into a really old man walking alone through the snow on the sidewalk. I pulled out my little pocket dictionary, stopped him, and asked, *"Yakitori wa doko desu ka?"* ("Where is a yakitori restaurant?") He pointed to a shop right in front of me that had a red lantern hanging over the door. I said, *"Arigatogozaimas!"* ("Thank you!") and walked in.

When I opened the door and walked in, I was shocked. It looked as if everyone in this town must be in here. It was huge and completely full of people, but I hadn't heard a sound outside. All the tables were full, but there was one seat open at the counter in front of the grill where all the kebabs were cooking. Right as I sat down, the cook placed an order for another customer on the counter. It looked really good, and with my little book already out I asked, *"Kore wa nan desu ka?"* ("What's that?")

"Skoonei!" he said.

"Chicken balls!" said a waitress who had just walked up behind me.

I didn't know chickens had balls! It was actually ground chicken made into golf ball–sized balls on a stick. I ordered the same, and to this day skoonei is still one of my favorites. Before my order even came up, a guy tapped me on the shoulder and asked if I would like to join his group of friends at their table. They wanted to practice their English. I happily joined them and had a really great time. This would happen again and again everyplace I went, and it was wonderful.

After a few days I started going out on my own more often. The company provided bento box lunches, small prepared lunchboxes, but they were small and a little dry for me. So I told them to stop getting one for me and went out for lunch each day on my own. I went to convenience stores and bought sandwiches. I checked out some department stores' box lunches, but they were too expensive. However, during the week at most big department stores, they had lots and lots of food and drink samples where you could try just about anything. A few times I would go into the department stores for lunch and walk out happy and full without spending any money!

Checking around for something better and cheaper, I found an old mom-and-pop store that had some pretty good things to eat but very limited selection. I got a few things plus something to drink and went to the counter and uh-oh! Every place I had been to before had had a cash register, and when they rang me up, I could just read the numbered price and count out the coins or bills. There was no cash register here, though. When the grandma said something to me, I knew she was telling me how much, but I had no idea what she was saying, I pulled out all my bills and coins and held them out to her with both hands. She calmly picked out what it was and said thank you. She could have taken anything; I wouldn't have known. This honesty, kindness, and appreciation for others and others' possessions was something I had seen from the first day I'd come to Tokyo, and I would see it again and again in the future.

I hadn't really thought to learn about the money at all when I came, but it wasn't just the money; it was numbers, especially counting, counting anything, that I needed to learn as soon as possible. That night I went to Nihonbashi and Kinokunia, one of oldest bookstores in Japan, with a huge selection of books written in English. I found exactly what I needed: info on money and numbers! The money wasn't hard. There were only six coins—1\, 5\, 10\, 50\, 100\, and 500\—and only four bills or paper money: \1000, \2000, which is very rare, \5000, and \10,000. The numbers went into the millions, and that wasn't really hard either; however, there were many different words used for counting many different things, different words used for numbering drinks, people, cars, time, animals, books/magazines/newspapers, floors in a building, and so on. These would take me a long time to learn. The numbers written in Japanese kanji weren't that hard either. But for dates, I needed to know the kanji characters for all the emperors to know when a date was. For example, consider the date *Showa niju hachi, ni gatsu, tsui tachi*. *Showa niju hachi* means the twenty-eighth year of the reign of Emperor Showa, or 1953. *Ni gatsu* means February, and *tsui tachi* means the first. February 1, 1953, my birthday. One of my students, in kanji, wrote the emperors' names I would need in the back of my small phone book. After that I simply matched the characters from whatever I was reading to the ones in my book to figure out an exact date.

After that I felt a little more comfortable. I still went out a lot with staff or students who always took care of me, but I really wanted to learn more. I finally got tired of not being able to read signs, menus, and so on. I wanted to learn to read. There are three types of written characters: kanji, hiragana, and katakana. Hiragana and katakana collectively are known as kana. Kanji are old characters taken from Chinese, of which there are thousands and thousands. I know maybe a couple hundred. I don't use them every day, and, of course, if you don't use them, you lose them.

Hiragana underlies the basic structure of the writing system. Most people don't know that hiragana was created by women back in the ninth century because they weren't allowed to write in kanji. It's used now by children before learning kanji. Then there is katakana, which is limited in its usage to words of foreign origin, such as names of people, places, animals, and the like. Kana, both hiragana and katakana, use forty-six basic characters, and each character can be modified for many other sounds.

So back to Kinokunia I went again. I bought two books. The lady at the bookstore recommended that I studied hiragana first, then katakana. That was how the children started also. So I did, and it was a whole new world for me. I could read menus! That was one of the coolest things. But I could read so many different things, from billboards to brochures. Now I could read almost everything, but I couldn't understand it all. However, being able to read it, I could now at least look it up in a dictionary. I couldn't believe I'd wasted so much time before. I could have been reading so much sooner. It was just so nice being cared for and looked after every day. But learning to read wasn't really that hard and only took two weeks for each book. The kanji, forget it. There are just so many characters, and the funny thing is a single character can be used two, three, or four different ways. But, believe it or not, there are lots of adults here who can't read all the kanji either! Isn't it funny, though? I am a very literate, well-educated college graduate, yet I'm very illiterate here. I can't read everything. Newspapers? Won't happen! They're almost all kanji. Talk about the literate illiterate!

Soon I found a meat shop very close to my office that sold all types of wonderful bento lunches. I met the owner, Tamotsu, and his family. He would become my lifelong best friend in Japan. He was a fishing fanatic, and we fished a lot together in some really cool places. There was so much to see and do in Japan. On that first short contract I traveled around a lot. You don't need a car to get around. There are so many cars in Tokyo that before you can even buy one, you have to prove that you have a parking spot for it. But trains and subways go almost everywhere; plus there are lots of buses and taxi cabs. I bought a mountain bike, and that was all I needed to go almost everywhere. I really had a lot of fun everywhere I went, and I met so many cool people. Everyone was just as curious about me as I was about them. And everything I found was so different, fun, and exciting. But the most special thing I found in Japan was my wife.

Though our company had a helicopter at Tokyo Heliport, we didn't use it for training. I flew it about every weekend or so, but the students wouldn't fly here. At that time, in the United States, a small training airplane cost between $50 to about $80 an hour. A small training helicopter was about $100 to $120 an hour. In Japan the same small airplane was about $350 an hour and up, while helicopters were $1000 an hour and up! So students could go live and train in the United States for cheaper than just obtaining a license in Japan would be. After obtaining their license in the United States, they would return to Japan and easily, after lots of paperwork, change their FAA license over to a JA license. The pilot school was a ground school only, and after finishing my course they would go directly to Corona, California, where they would begin their flying. Each thirty-day class consisted of about ten to twenty students, men and women. I taught them all the aeronautical knowledge, regulations, and weather they would need to know, but I was also prepping them for their written tests. When I returned to the pilot school in Corona, I would find out that all the students from all six of my classes had passed their written tests on their first try after getting to the United States. The students hadn't been doing that before! On my sixth and last class of my contract I met my future wife. Most classes were made up of rich kids in their late teens or early twenties with a few older guys and gals thrown in. The bubble had just burst in the Japanese economy a month before I got here, but it would be some time before we would see the effects. For the time being it was business as usual. Most of these rich kids were spoiled brats who had quit or gotten thrown out of various colleges and were actually getting sent away by their parents. Too much of an embarrassment for their parents!

From the very first day when the young guys would get a little rowdy, KN would yell at them and tell them to shut up and settle down. She was in her late twenties, and I liked her from the very beginning. She seemed to be like the *mama-san* and kept everyone in line. She was unassuming, confident, and smart as hell. She was very pretty with beautiful long black hair. As with all the other students, she would come in early in the morning and study English for three hours. After lunch they would begin my class. A few students spoke English pretty well, but the majority spoke very little. She spoke a little but was learning very fast. She was a great student as well as a great class leader.

About two weeks before she was due to go to America, three weeks before I would go back, I stopped in the break room where she was sitting by herself. I asked her if she would like to go out to have a beer with me. She instantly put up her hands, waving them at me, and said, "No, no, no!" My big old ego took a nosedive straight into the ground! I walked back to my office but stopped, turned around, and went back. I went back in and asked her, in my slowest English and the little amount of Japanese I knew, if she understood what I had asked her. She said that she thought I'd asked, "Do you like beer?" I told her no, that I'd been asking her out on a date. She instantly perked right up and said, "Yes, yes, yes!"

We went out on our first date that night and went out one more time before she left. I really liked her from the very first time I met her, even more so after we dated in Tokyo. We didn't really start dating until after I went back to California. I really didn't think I would ever get married. I hadn't found anyone since my high school sweetheart that I'd even thought about spending the rest of my life with. But after some time spending almost every day and night with Kaori, I just knew. Somehow, I saw in her that she would be the best wife and mother I could ever imagine. I asked her, and she said yes. We waited until I went back to Japan on my next contract and got married.

I was absolutely correct! And after twenty-four wonderful years, she has been not only the best wife, beyond my wildest dreams, but also my lover and my best friend for life! She has been an absolutely wonderful mother, tough as can be but loving and caring. Together we raised a wonderful son and daughter, but I give her most of the credit. Yes, we both have made our children the way they are, but I think they're so very special because of her. Our children are both so very special in their own ways and very different. Our son just graduated from college this year, and our daughter will do the same next year. They are two beautiful, bilingual, happy, and outgoing people. Parents always say how great their kids are and that they're the best, but our kids truly are just wonderful human beings, and I am so proud of them and am so much in love with their mom.

My first class of pilot students in Tokyo. Though I would teach both airplane and helicopter students, these were helicopter only.

Japan's *Trendy* magazine with a story about me and the Tokyo pilot school.

Pilot students took me to ski across from Mount Asama,
an active volcano also known as Mini Fuji because
it resembles Mount Fuji's shape so closely.

Me (*back row, fourth from right*) at my first geisha show in Tokyo.

About the Author

Craig Wooton is a real life Walter Mitty! His experiences would satisfy three lifetimes, let alone one. Monkeys and elephants were his friends. Live witness on the set of Twilight Zone: The Movie tragedy, and a Bikini atoll Hydrogen bomb test. He still resides in Japan with his amazing wife, Kaori, and wonderful son and daughter, Cory and Nicole.

Printed in the United States
By Bookmasters